DALLAS SIGHTSEEING

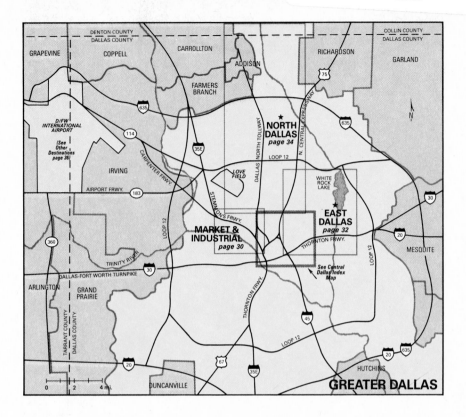

GREATER DALLAS

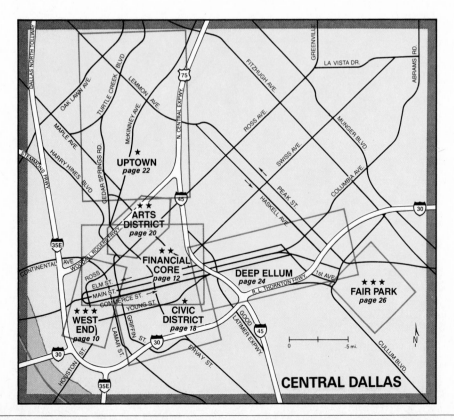

CENTRAL DALLAS

WHERE THE EAST ENDS AND THE WEST BEGINS

Cowboy humorist Will Rogers, an unabashed Fort Worth partisan, fifty years ago popularized that city's reputation as the place "where the West begins." An equally appropriate subtitle for its twin companion on the North Texas prairies might be "where the East ends," for modern Dallas is a cosmopolitan megapolis whose charm and sophistication reflect a century of close interaction with venerable metropolises to the northeast.

Both Dallas and Fort Worth are relative newcomers to the American urban scene. Texas lies just a bit too far west to have had the dependably navigable river systems that provided frontier highways from the Atlantic to the Mississippi. In the days when the only alternatives to water travel were horses, mules, and shoe leather, Texas' principal towns understandably hugged the Gulf Coast. It was not until after the Civil War that a flurry of railroad building finally opened inland Texas to serious settlement. Dallas and Fort Worth, formerly frontier villages surrounded by unusually fertile prairies and sometimes hostile Indians, were among the principal beneficiaries.

In 1873 Dallas became the intersection point of Texas' first intercontinental rail lines linking the state with the already vast rail network of the northeast. The town quickly blossomed as Texas' gateway for receiving the latest fads, fashions, goods, and gadgets from worldly St. Louis, Chicago, and beyond. A decade later Fort Worth, only thirty miles farther west, became the terminus for railroads building to link Texas with California and Colorado. As a result the city was soon flooded by trainloads of cattle, oil, and grain—the newly won bounty of an enormous Western hinterland.

These two Victorian children of the railroads have maintained their separate identities as they matured into their modern destiny as Sunbelt giants, the vibrant commercial and cultural capitals of a region larger than New England and New York combined.

ISBN 0-394-75705-X
L.C. 87-46192

Maps by Jerry Guthrie
Design and composition by The Sarabande Press

Manufactured in the United States of America

DISCOVER Guides are developed and produced by Virginia and Lee McAlester

This volume was made possible, in part, by funding from the Communities Foundation of Texas

DISCOVER

DALLAS

FORT WORTH

Alfred A. Knopf
New York

CONTENTS

DALLAS

DALLAS

Now the nation's seventh largest city, Dallas is a Sunbelt boomtown of towering skyscrapers and sprawling suburbs whose meteoric growth began with the arrival of railroads in the 1870s. Serving a rich farming region, the city became a center for wholesale trade and financial services, which are still its principal activities.

Dallas was founded in 1842 by John Neely Bryan (1810-1872), a Tennessee lawyer turned Indian trader and land speculator, but it remained only one of dozens of obscure frontier villages until railroads first built through North Texas in the 1870s. Dallas then gained an advantage that was to become the foundation for all its future growth and prosperity—it became the critical crossing point for the state's first intercontinental rail lines.

RAILROAD JUNCTION

Texas' first short railroad lines were built in the 1850s and radiated inland from the deepwater ports of Houston and Galveston. These local lines were intended only to solidify those coastal towns' long-held monopoly on the export of raw materials (principally cotton, grain, and timber) and on the import of the vast array of manufactured goods demanded by the state's frontier economy.

After the Civil War the Houston and Texas Central Railroad (H&TC) was slowly extended northward to link the state's vast interior with Houston. It reached Dallas in 1872 and the next year was completed to Denison, near the Oklahoma border. There it connected with the Missouri, Kansas and Texas (MKT or "Katy") line that had just arrived

from St. Louis after building southward through Oklahoma (then the Indian Territory). This gave the fledgling Texas rail system its first direct tie to the remote but extensive rail network of the northeastern states.

WHOLESALE CENTER

The result, unexpected by the H&TC's Houston owners, was that rail transport soon began to challenge the cheaper but much slower oceangoing shipping centered on Houston and Galveston. This was particularly true for the import of high-value manufactured goods. St. Louis was already one of the country's principal wholesale centers; along with Chicago it supplied much of the developing West. Aggressive St. Louis merchants with their vast warehouses of goods could now make deliveries to Texas in only a few days by rail, a great competitive edge over the many weeks required for water transport from New York or Boston wholesalers to Houston or Galveston.

At first Dallas had no more of an advantage as a distribution point for these manufactured goods than did dozens of other small towns along the H&TC main line, but this would soon change. A major east-west railroad, the Texas and Pacific (T&P), was building westward from the Arkansas

border enroute to El Paso and California. This line would also provide connections to St. Louis and the eastern rail network via a line building southwestward across Arkansas.

Some farsighted Dallas citizens realized that the crossing point of these two intercontinental rail lines would likely become the principal trade and transportation hub for much of northern and western Texas. As a result, Dallas' representative to the state legislature managed to add a seemingly trivial amendment to the Texas and Pacific enabling act stating that the line must pass within a mile of "Browder Springs," a virtually unknown location that happened to be the water supply for the small town of Dallas.

The T&P reached Dallas in 1873, only a year after the H&TC. As predicted, the town suddenly became a major trade center as St. Louis and Chicago merchants rushed to establish branch warehouses at this unique transportation node.

MIDWESTERN OUTPOST

Modern Dallas was thus born as a child of the Midwest, the overland gateway through which much of Texas was to receive the latest fashionable products of the nation's factories. Dallas soon gained a reputation as the most sophisticated and "eastern" city in the Southwest, a heritage that paved the way for its modern role as a national wholesaler of home furnishings, clothing, gifts, and computer systems.

While much of Texas' bulk exports of cotton, grain, and timber continued to leave Houston or Galveston by ship, these ports' former importance for the import of manufactured goods plummeted as Dallas prospered. The town's vital role in capturing this railroad-centered import trade is seen in its explosive early growth.

In 1870, just before the first railroad arrived, Dallas had an estimated permanent population of about 1,000. Galveston with 13,000 was the state's largest city and Houston with 9,500 was third, behind San Antonio's 12,000. By 1890, just twenty years later, Dallas had 38,000 inhabitants and was the largest city in the state, whereas Galveston (29,000) had slipped to third behind San Antonio (37,000); Houston (27,000) was now fourth. Since 1910 Dallas has consistently ranked second in population among Texas cities, yielding first place to San Antonio in 1910 and 1920 and to Houston in each census since 1930.

Slowed only briefly by the nationwide economic recession of the 1890s, Dallas continued its dramatic growth through the first three decades of this century. The 43,000 inhabitants of 1900 doubled to 92,000 in 1910, leaped again to 159,000 in 1920, and reached an amazing 260,000 by 1930.

This prosperity was largely a reflection of the steadily multiplying agricultural output, mostly cotton, yielded by the fer-

RAIL JUNCTION, 1910 *This historic photo shows a busy day at Dallas' original Union Terminal, which was located about a mile east of the county courthouse. The train on the left has just arrived from Houston on the H&TC tracks; the T&P tracks are behind the terminal building. The trolley cars in the foreground are on Elm Street.*

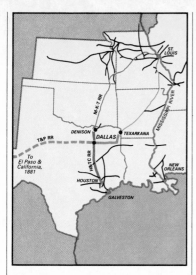

SOUTHWESTERN RAILROADS, 1873 *In that year Dallas became the crucial crossing point of the north-south Houston and Texas Central (H&TC) line and the east-west Texas and Pacific (T&P) line. At Denison and Texarkana these lines connected with other newly constructed railroads that linked Texas with St. Louis and the northeastern rail network.*

tile farm lands of northern Texas, lands for which Dallas served as the principal transportation node, wholesale market, and financial center. By 1925 almost 10 percent of the entire world cotton crop was being grown within a one-hundred-mile radius of the city.

OIL WINDFALL

Although portrayed as being closely associated with oil production in the popular television series of the same name, Dallas has always had less direct ties to petroleum than have other Texas cities, such as Houston, Beaumont, Midland, or even Fort Worth. The great north-south belt of fertile Blackland Prairie upon which Dallas, Waco, and Austin grew up has yielded few oil or gas fields, making it a barren dividing strip between the prolific production of both eastern and western Texas. For this reason, Dallas lacks the many drilling contractors, oil field supply houses, well service companies, and district production offices that dominate typical oil towns.

The city's relation to the oil industry has centered instead on its broader role as a financial center. Several large Dallas banks pioneered in the now routine concept of lending money for field development by using as collateral the underground reserves of oil or gas already discovered. Because of these sophisticated banking services, the city has long attracted the corporate headquarters of energy-related companies, both large and small, a trend that accelerated during the OPEC-inspired oil boom of the 1970s.

Dallas' most direct benefit from an oil discovery came at an opportune time — just as the nation was entering the Great Depression of the 1930s. In the fall of 1930 the discovery well of the supergiant East Texas Oil Field, located about one hundred miles east of the city, was brought in by a small Dallas operator named Columbus M. "Dad" Joiner (1860-1947).

Subsequent exploitation of this enormous find involved many Dallas oilmen and financiers, among them the legendary Haroldson Lafayette Hunt (1889-1974), whose personal holdings are said to have contributed more oil to the Allied powers during World War II than all other world sources combined. Hunt's Dallas-based heirs still rank among the nation's wealthiest individuals. Although Dallas by no means escaped the devastating results of the Depression years (the city's explosive growth, for example, slowed to a crawl during the decade), the trickle-down effect of this new wealth made the economic strain less severe in Dallas than in most American cities.

INDUSTRY ARRIVES

The 1940s opened a new chapter of prosperity for Dallas. With the outbreak of World War II the War Department, as it was then called, adopted a policy of encouraging defense industries to locate throughout the nation's vast interior. There they had not only an untapped labor supply but also less vulnerability from aircraft attack than did the factories concentrated in the old manufacturing centers of the Northeast.

In 1940 the North American Aviation Company constructed a huge aircraft factory in the small town of Grand Prairie, ten miles west of downtown Dallas. Soon this plant was employing an unprecedented thirty thousand workers, who ultimately produced twenty-four thousand bombers, fighters, and training planes for the war effort.

Dozens of smaller war-related industries followed North American's lead and suddenly, for the first time, manufacturing joined wholesale marketing and financial services as a major contributor to Dallas' economy. The wartime industrial boom accelerated in the postwar years, as the area's many plants converted to peacetime production and as new light industry was attracted by the city's mild climate, large labor supply, low tax rates, and sophisticated financial services. In 1948 the Chance Vought Aircraft Division of United Aircraft Corporation moved its entire production facility from Connecticut to the former North American plant in what was then the largest industrial relocation in the nation's history.

SUNBELT BOOM

Dallas not only gained a new postwar role as a manufacturing center, but also expanded its traditional leadership in marketing and finance as hundreds of national corporations established new regional headquarters and distribution centers in the city. Some, among them such giants as American Airlines, American Petrofina, J.C.Penney, Kimberly-Clark, and National Gypsum, chose the Dallas area for their world headquarters. In addition to such relocations, many homegrown Dallas companies, including Texas Instruments (electronics), Southland Corporation (Seven-Eleven stores), Electronic Data Systems (data processing, now a division of General Motors), Mary Kay (cosmetics), Frito-Lay (snack foods), and Dr Pepper (soft drinks) have grown to national importance.

All this hectic industrial and commercial expansion has made Dallas one of the nation's fastest growing cities. In 1940, just before the outbreak of World War II, the population stood at 294,000. Each decade since has seen the addition of more than

RAIL JUNCTION TODAY *Street names provide the only reminders of Dallas' historic rail crossing site, now near the heart of downtown. The original tracks have long been rerouted, but Pacific Avenue (named for the Texas and Pacific line) and Central Expressway (namesake of the Houston and Texas Central) follow the original rail routes.*

100,000 new residents as the total climbed to 434,000 in 1950, jumped almost 250,000 to reach an amazing 680,000 in 1960, then climbed to 844,000 in 1970 and 965,000 in 1980.

Equally important has been the explosive growth of satellite suburbs as formerly sleepy country villages have blossomed into large cities lying beyond the limits of Dallas proper. Chief among these, with their 1950 to 1980 population growth, are Garland (11,000–139,000) and Mesquite (2,000–67,000) on the east, Richardson (1,000–73,000) and Plano (2,000–72,000) on the north, and Irving (3,000–110,000) and Grand Prairie (15,000–71,000) on the west.

DALLAS SIGHTSEEING, AN OVERVIEW

Ten distinctive Sightseeing Districts, which combine to include most of the city's visitor attractions, are summarized on the map inside the front cover and treated in detail on the following pages.

The heart of the modern city is the **Financial Core**, occupying the northern half of the Central Business District (CBD), an area where dozens of tall office towers now rise to define a distinctive urban skyline. Immediately southwest of the Financial Core lies the **West End**, site of the original riverbank town, where many early landmark buildings still survive. Among these is a historic warehouse district recently renovated to become a lively center of restaurants, shops, and nightclubs. In 1963 the West End was also the scene of the tragic assassination of President John F. Kennedy.

Adjacent to the Financial Core on the south lies the **Civic District**. Formerly a declining neighborhood of modest commercial buildings, the area has been revitalized since the early 1970s by a series of municipally-owned improvements clustered around a striking City Hall building. A second important area of civic improvement lies at the northern edge of the CBD, where an eleven-block **Arts District** is rising, anchored by the dramatic new Dallas Museum of Art, completed in 1984.

VICTORIAN LANDMARK *Cumberland Hill School, built in 1888, is among the city's few surviving buildings from the last century. In 1971 it was carefully restored and converted into modern offices as downtown Dallas' first historic preservation project.*

Just beyond the CBD on the north lies the **Uptown** district, a rapidly changing area that includes many of Dallas' near-downtown shops, galleries, restaurants, and high-rise dwellings. Immediately east of the CBD lies funky **Deep Ellum**, once the town's industrial center and heart of its black community. Some of the neighborhood's modest commercial buildings now house avant-garde theaters, galleries, and clubs. Adjoining Deep Ellum on the southeast is **Fair Park**, a 277-acre museum and exhibition center that is of international importance as the unaltered site of the 1936 Texas Centennial Exposition, complete with original Art Moderne buildings, murals, and sculpture.

Beyond these attractions of central Dallas stretch the residential districts, shopping centers, and suburban office towers of **North Dallas** and **East Dallas**, where much of the city's affluent housing has been concentrated since early in the century. To the west of central Dallas lies the **Market and Industrial District**, a vast area of low-rise warehouses anchored by a dramatic wholesale Market Center, all built on land reclaimed from the Trinity River bottoms by an elaborate 1930s flood-control system.

Several additional attractions that are scattered throughout the city's suburbs are treated in a final section called "**Other Destinations**."

THREE-STAR HIGHLIGHTS

Visitors with limited time should not miss the city's eight "three-star" attractions, all of which are in or near the Central Business District:

VICTORIAN TOWN 1872-1900

WEST END	
Old County Courthouse**	1892
FINANCIAL CORE	
Cumberland Hill School*	1888
First Baptist Church*	1890
CIVIC DISTRICT	
Old City Park** (museum village)	1840-1910
ARTS DISTRICT	
Guadalupe Cathedral**	1898
UPTOWN	
State-Thomas Hist.Dist.* (houses)	1880-1910
DEEP ELLUM	
Continental Gin Co.**	1888 & later
EAST DALLAS	
Wilson Block Hist.Dist.** (houses)	1898-1902
OTHER DESTINATIONS	
Heritage Farmstead** (Plano)	1891

EARLY COMMERCIAL CITY 1900-1930

WEST END			**CIVIC DISTRICT**	
County Criminal Courts Bldg.*	1913		Federal Reserve Bank Bldg.*	1914
John Deere Plow Co. Bldg.*	1902		Scottish Rite Cathedral*	1907
Old Oak Cliff Viaduct*	1912		**UPTOWN**	
Sanger Bros. Store*	1910		Sheppard King House*	1925
Southern Rock Island Plow Co.***			**DEEP ELLUM**	
(Schoolbook Depository)	1901		Ford Assembly Plant*	1913
Union Station**	1916		Pythian Temple*	1916
West End Hist. Dist.**			**MARKET & INDUSTRIAL DIST.**	
(warehouses)	1900-1930		Steam Electrical Station*	1917
FINANCIAL CORE			**EAST DALLAS**	
Adolphus Hotel**	1912		Munger Place Hist. Dist.*	
Busch Bldg.**	1913		(houses)	1905-1930
Dallas High School*	1908		Swiss Ave. Hist. Dist.*** (houses)	1905-1930
Magnolia Petroleum Bldg.**	1922		**NORTH DALLAS**	
Majestic Theatre*	1922		Dallas Hall* (SMU)	1915
Municipal Bldg.*	1914		Lakeside Dr.** (houses)	1910-1925
Neiman-Marcus Dept. Store*	1928			
Wilson Bldg.**	1902			

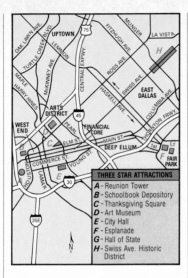

THREE STAR ATTRACTIONS

A - Reunion Tower
B - Schoolbook Depository
C - Thanksgiving Square
D - Art Museum
E - City Hall
F - Esplanade
G - Hall of State
H - Swiss Ave. Historic District

1. In the West End is **Reunion Tower**, a fifty-story revolving observatory that affords a breathtaking panorama of the city.
2. Also in the West End is the **Texas Schoolbook Depository**, now called the Dallas County Administration Building, from which Lee Harvey Oswald is believed to have fired the infamous shots that killed President Kennedy as his motorcade passed below.
3. Located at the heart of the Financial Core is jewel box-like **Thanksgiving Square**, a small triangular park that provides superb views of the towering modern skyscrapers surrounding it on all sides like sheer cliffs.
4. Anchoring the Arts District is the new **Dallas Museum of Art** whose important collections are showcased in an unusually appealing setting of flowing, multilevel galleries.

5. Centerpiece of the Civic District is the new **Dallas City Hall**, a jutting, angular structure overlooking a large ceremonial plaza. This unusual building has been hailed as a masterpiece of modern architecture.
6. & 7. A short drive east of the CBD lies historic Fair Park whose **Esplanade** and adjacent **Hall of State**, built for the 1936 Texas Centennial Exposition, are unique survivors of the grandly ceremonial world's fairs of that era.
8. About two miles northeast of the CBD lies the mile-long landscaped parkway of the **Swiss Avenue Historic District**, a showcase of early-twentieth-century residential planning lined with Eclectic mansions of varying styles.

EXPLORING HISTORIC DALLAS

Important reminders of Dallas' long and colorful history occur in each of the ten geographic districts discussed on the following pages. To aid visitors wishing to get a feel for the city as it appeared in earlier times, the tables below list Dallas' most important landmarks in chronologic order. Each treats a principal era of the city's history:

Victorian Town: Relatively few buildings survive from the period between the arrival of the first railroad in 1872 to the turn of the century, when the town had 40,000 inhabitants, most of whom lived within the boundaries of the modern Central Business District.

Early Commercial City: Many landmarks remain from the important interval between 1900 to 1930, when the city's population exploded from 40,000 to 260,000 as it became the financial and trade center for North Texas' rich agricultural lands.

Depression and World War II Era: As in the rest of the nation, building in Dallas slowed to a crawl during this period. The Era's most important landmarks were built as government-sponsored unemployment relief projects.

Sunbelt Boomtown: Following World War II Dallas resumed its explosive growth as residential suburbs mushroomed to fill most of the county. Since the mid-1970s the once declining downtown core has been revitalized by a host of impressive new office towers, arts facilities, and government buildings.

MODERN LANDMARK *First Interstate Bank Tower, completed in 1986, added a strikingly dramatic shape to the city's skyline.*

DEPRESSION & WORLD WAR II ERA
1930-1945

WEST END	
Dealey Plaza*	1936
FINANCIAL CORE	
Dallas Power & Light Bldg.*	1930
Lone Star Gas Bldg.*	1931
CIVIC DISTRICT	
Farmers Market*	1942
FAIR PARK	
Aquarium*	1936
Esplanade***	1936
Hall of State***	1936
Magnolia Lounge**	1936
Museum of Natural History**	1936
Science Place I**	1936
MARKET & INDUSTRIAL DIST.	
Sylvan Ave.** (flood control)	1932
EAST DALLAS	
DeGolyer House**	1939
Lakewood Blvd.* (houses)	1925-1940
NORTH DALLAS	
Armstrong Pkwy.** (houses)	1925-1940
Highland Park Village**	1931 & later

SUNBELT BOOMTOWN
1945-present

WEST END		**UPTOWN**	
Hyatt Regency Hotel*	1978	Kalita Humphreys Theater*	1959
Kennedy Memorial**	1970	The Crescent**	1986
Reunion Tower***	1978	The Quadrangle*	1965 & later
FINANCIAL CORE		**MARKET & INDUSTRIAL DIST.**	
First Interstate Bank Tower**	1986	Anatole Hotel*	1979
First RepublicBank Plaza*	1985	Dallas Market Center**	1957 & later
Momentum Place**	1987	Infomart*	1985
Plaza of the Americas*	1980	Stouffer Hotel*	1982
RepublicBank Bldg.*	1954	World Trade Center*	1974
Texas Commerce Tower**	1987	**NORTH DALLAS**	
Thanksgiving Square***	1976	Dallas Galleria*	1982
CIVIC DISTRICT		Meadows Museum** (SMU)	1965
City Hall***	1978	NorthPark Center*	1965 & later
Eric Jonsson Library*	1982	**OTHER DESTINATIONS**	
ARTS DISTRICT		Southfork Ranch** (Plano)	1978
Dallas Museum of Art***	1984	Las Colinas* (Irving)	1977 & later
Trammell Crow Center**	1984	DFW Airport* (Irving)	1973

West End ★★★

Site of the original 1842 settlement, this area retains many early-twentieth-century landmark buildings, among them a revitalized warehouse district with lively restaurants, shops, and nightclubs. In 1963 the West End was the scene of the tragic assassination of President John F. Kennedy.

OLD COUNTY COURTHOUSE AND KENNEDY MEMORIAL *The city's most venerable landmark stands adjacent to Philip Johnson's strikingly modern tribute to the martyred President.*

Early Dallas grew up here next to a low bluff overlooking a hard-bottomed ford of the Trinity River, a crossing long favored by passing Indians. Today the only surviving trace of this earliest settlement is its rectangular street grid, which surrounds a courthouse square that has been the seat of Dallas County government since 1850. Even the river is now gone—moved to a new channel a mile west in a massive 1930s flood control project (see "Market and Industrial Area"). Where the river once flowed, automobiles now converge on the **Triple Underpass**, which became familiar to the entire world when it was approached by President Kennedy's motorcade on that fateful November day.

COURTHOUSE AREA

Symbolic heart of the West End area is the **Old Dallas County Courthouse★★** (Main and Houston sts.; 1892; Orlopp and Kusener, Little Rock, architects), a Richardsonian Romanesque monument built of red sandstone that is one of the city's few landmarks to have survived from the last century. Affectionately known as "Old Red," the present courthouse was the fifth to occupy the site. Its original functions have now spilled into several nearby structures. Earliest and most handsome of these is the Beaux Arts **County Criminal Courts Building★** (Main and Houston sts.; 1913; H.A.Overbeck, Dallas, architect), which boasted the nation's first air-conditioned jail cells. Later came the Gothic Revival **County Records Building** (Elm and Record sts.; 1922; Lang and Witchell, Dallas, architects) and finally a massive **New Dallas County Courthouse** (Associated Architects and Engineers, architects) completed in 1966 on Commerce Street across from Old Red. Adjacent to the Records Building is the **Dallas County Historical Plaza**, which features a pioneer log cabin, a large tile pavement map showing early county villages, and several historical markers describing nearby buildings.

WAREHOUSE DISTRICT

Immediately north of the courthouse area lies the town's early wholesale district whose narrow streets have recently become an attractive and lively center of pedestrian activity. Many early warehouse buildings, dating from 1900 to 1930, have been restored to form the core of the **West End Historic District★★**, created in 1976 to revitalize the then largely abandoned neighborhood. The upper levels of the buildings now house modern offices, and the ground floors boast some of the city's most popular restaurants and nightclubs (see West End Historic District under "SiDE Areas"). Several large structures at the district's north end have been converted into the **West End Marketplace**, a bustling, five-story festival market with dozens of shops and fast-food vendors centered around a tall atrium.

The earliest and most architecturally significant West End warehouses face Elm Street, a principal downtown thoroughfare. These are the **Southern Rock Island Plow Company Building★★★**, later the Texas Schoolbook Depository (see below) and now the Dallas County Administration Building (411 Elm St.; 1901; architect unknown); the **John Deere Plow Company Building★**, now 501 Elm Place (1902; Hubbell and Greene, Dallas, architects); and the **Parlin and Orendorff Implement Company**, now the Dallas County Services Building (601 Elm St.; 1905; J.A. Padgitt, Dallas, architect). The original occupants illustrate the fact that by 1891 Dallas had replaced Kansas City as the nation's largest distribution center for farm machinery. This prosperity is also reflected in the handsome facades of the buildings, carefully designed in the latest Chicago-inspired Sullivanesque fashion of the day.

TEXAS SCHOOLBOOK DEPOSITORY; KENNEDY MEMORIAL

In later years the Southern Rock Island Plow Company Building (see above) was destined to play a central role on the blackest day in Dallas' history—November 22, 1963. From a sixth-floor window of the **Texas Schoolbook Depository★★★**, as it was then called, Lee Harvey Oswald is believed to have fired the shots that killed President John F. Kennedy and wounded Texas Governor John Connally as their motorcade passed below on Elm Street approaching the Triple Underpass. A bronze plaque located in adjacent Dealey Plaza (see below) describes that day's tragic events.

The starkly simple **John Fitzgerald Kennedy Memorial★★** (1970) designed by architect Philip Johnson of New York, a

SCHOOLBOOK DEPOSITORY *In earlier days this Chicago-influenced warehouse building, erected in 1901, housed the Southern Rock Island Plow Company, one of the many farm implement distributors attracted to Dallas by the burgeoning regional cotton industry. By 1963 it had become the Texas Schoolbook Depository. Lee Harvey Oswald is believed to have fired the shots that killed President Kennedy from the square sixth-floor window on the right of the building's front facade.*

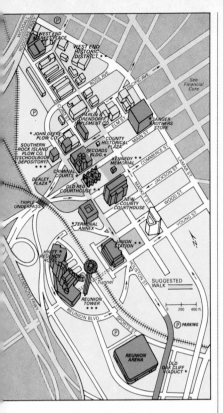

UNION STATION AREA

Two blocks south of the courthouse stands Dallas' original **Union Station★★** (400 South Houston St.; Jarvis Hunt, Chicago, architect), a Beaux Arts monument strikingly faced with glazed white brick. Completed in 1916, it was built to consolidate the five scattered passenger terminals used by the city's nine railroad lines. The arrival of as many as one hundred trains each day made this Dallas' bustling transportation hub for many decades. In 1978 the building, by then mostly deserted and serving only two daily Amtrak trains, was restored to house modern offices and restaurants, the latter in what had been the grand waiting room (located on the second floor to avoid the nearby Trinity's occasional floods!). Union Station now provides a historic gateway to the massive Reunion development across the tracks to the west, with which it connects through an underground tunnel that also provides access to the trains above.

Reunion's mirrored-glass centerpiece is the **Hyatt Regency Hotel★** (300 Reunion Blvd.; 1978; Welton Becket, Los Angeles, architect), whose adjacent sphere-topped **Reunion Tower★★★** affords breathtaking views of the city from both an observation level and a revolving restaurant. These dramatic buildings have become familiar and award-winning symbols on the skyline of Dallas' revitalized downtown. South of Reunion Tower is the city's new nineteen-thousand-seat **Reunion Arena** (777 Sport St.; 1980; Harwood K. Smith, Dallas, architect), scene of numerous concerts, circuses, ice shows, and home of the Dallas Mavericks (basketball) and Dallas Sidekicks (soccer).

North of Union Station is the U.S. Post Office's former **Terminal Annex** (207 South Houston St.; 1937; Lang and Witchell, Dallas, architects), a massive Art Moderne building of white limestone which blends pleasingly with the more elaborate facade of the nearby terminal. Built in the depths of the Great Depression to process the city's train-delivered mail, the long-vacant structure has recently been restored as a handsome Federal office building. The small lobby retains two fine WPA-sponsored **murals★** painted in 1940 by renowned New Mexico artist Peter Hurd (b.1904).

Immediately south of the Union Terminal, Houston Street rises and turns westward onto the **Old Oak Cliff Viaduct★**, now the Houston Street Viaduct (1912; Hedrick and Cochrane, Kansas City, architects), the town's first flood-proof crossing of the wide Trinity floodplain and still its most handsome. Commissioned after a particularly damaging flood in 1908, this mile-long elevated causeway, built with fifty-one reinforced concrete arches, was an engineering marvel of its day.

HOURS AND CHARGES

West End Marketplace: 954-4350. Mon-Thur, 11 am to 10 pm; Fri-Sat, 11 am to midnight; Sun, noon to 8 pm. Admission free. Restaurants and snack bars.

Texas Schoolbook Depository: A permanent exhibit, "The Sixth Floor," is scheduled to open in late 1988.

Union Station - Visitor Information Center: 746-6600. Open 24 hours a day; usually staffed from 8:30 am to 5 pm. Restaurants, 2nd level.

Reunion Tower: 741-3663. Mon-Fri, 10 am to midnight; Sat-Sun, 9 am to midnight. Adults, $1.88; ages 6-12, 75¢. Admission free when visiting revolving cocktail lounge and restaurant levels.

Related Shopping, Dining, and Entertainment (SiDE) Areas: West End Historic District; Downtown Dallas.

Kennedy family friend, is the centerpiece of Memorial Plaza behind the Old Red Courthouse.

DEALEY PLAZA

Dallas' original riverfront settlement is commemorated in this small park located between the courthouse area and the Triple Underpass to the west. Built as a 1936 WPA project, complete with Art Moderne gateways, **Dealey Plaza★** and the adjacent underpass were the symbolic capstones of the massive Trinity flood control project (see "Market and Industrial District"). The Plaza contains a monument to George Bannerman Dealey (1859-1946), early civic leader and founder of the *Dallas Morning News.* A bronze plaque has been added to the Plaza describing the nearby assassination of President John F. Kennedy (see above).

SANGER BROTHERS STORE

One block east of the courthouse square is the former **Sanger Brothers Department Store★**, now adapted for reuse as a part of El Centro Community College (Main and Lamar sts.; 1910; Lang and Witchell, Dallas, architects). An elaborately detailed Sullivanesque landmark, this was long the city's center of style and fashion. The Sanger brothers, Alexander (1853-1925) and Phillip (1841-1902), were among the many "terminus merchants" that arrived with the H&TC railroad in 1872. Soon their sophisticated taste and marketing skill had made them the city's leading retailers, a position they held for more than half a century.

WEST END HISTORIC DISTRICT *Carriage rides are but one of the many attractions of this recently revitalized concentration of early warehouses. Restaurants, nightclubs, sidewalk cafes, the West End Marketplace, and a changing venue of live entertainment combine to create an unusually festive atmosphere.*

Financial Core ★★

From a pre-1945 nucleus centered along Main Street, skyscrapers have radiated northward at an accelerating pace, culminating in a 1980s explosion of new office towers, many of striking design.

When the Houston and Texas Central Railroad reached the Dallas area in 1872, it did not build directly into the small riverbank town but followed a course through vacant land about a mile to the east, along the route now occupied by Central Expressway. The Texas and Pacific Railroad, which arrived only a year later in 1873, was given substantial subsidies to entice it to build closer to the town's original commercial center (now the West End District). Among other incentives, a mostly undeveloped east-west road immediately north of Elm Street was donated for right-of-way. Renamed Pacific Avenue, this route led the busy tracks (removed and rerouted in the 1920s) to a river crossing only two blocks north of the courthouse square.

After the Texas and Pacific had arrived, a bustling passenger terminal, warehouses, and local service industries quickly sprouted around the busy crossing point of the two lines a mile east of town. A mule-drawn streetcar line was built along Main Street to connect the early courthouse area with this thriving new "East Dallas," and soon houses and shops were spreading along Elm, Main, and Commerce streets to fill the gap between the growing town's two centers of activity. By the turn of the century Dallas' commercial center was shifting eastward as new stores, banks, offices, and even the City Hall were built between the old courthouse area and the railroad junction to the east.

MAIN AND AKARD AREA

The intersection of Main and Akard streets, exactly midway between the old courthouse and the new railroad crossing, became the heart of the city in the early

DOWNTOWN LANDMARK *The Flying Red Horse atop the Magnolia Petroleum Building crowned the Dallas skyline for many years.*

1910s when Adolphus Busch, the St. Louis brewery tycoon, located both a grand hotel and a major new office tower in the area. With a flair for self-promotion he named these the Adolphus Hotel and the Busch (now Kirby) Building. The blocks around Main and Akard are still an active node for new downtown construction as well as the site of many of the city's most important pre-1940 landmark buildings.

The **Adolphus Hotel★★** (1321 Commerce St.; 1912; Barnett, Hayes and Barnett, St. Louis, architects) is the sole survivor among a dozen or so grand hostelries that served Dallas in the decades before 1940. Busch spared no expense to create a Beaux Arts architectural masterpiece for his namesake hotel, which is still among

the city's finest. The exuberant ornamentation of its upper floors makes this the most handsomely detailed tall building ever constructed in Dallas. The cylindrical tower on the roof is reputed to be modeled after one of Busch's beer bottles.

The **Busch Building★★**, now the Kirby Building (1509 Main St.; 1913; Barnett, Hayes and Barnett, St. Louis, architects), was a companion structure to the classically inspired Adolphus but has an entirely different architectural legacy. As one of the nation's earliest skyscrapers built with Gothic exterior detailing, it was in the vanguard of a new fashion, for many architects soon came to believe that the soaring, pointed arches that graced Europe's Gothic cathedrals were the most appropriate decoration for soaring modern skyscrapers. A small but beautifully detailed Gothic **elevator lobby★** survives intact.

Across Akard Street from the Adolphus Hotel stands the twenty-nine-story Beaux Arts **Magnolia Petroleum Building★★** (Commerce and Akard sts.; 1922; Alfred C. Bossom, New York, architect). Built as the headquarters of a Texas-based oil company, the structure established a twenty-year record as the city's tallest skyscraper from 1922 until 1942. Several years after completion, a massive, neon-lit sign of Magnolia's familiar Flying Red Horse symbol (now used by Magnolia's successor, Mobil Oil) was hoisted atop the roof and quickly became Dallas' unofficial mascot and beacon. Now mostly obscured by surrounding office towers, the sign burned brightly above the city throughout the Depression and World War II and is today preserved as a beloved local landmark. The building's small **elevator lobby** (enter on Akard St.) has handsome Beaux Arts detailing.

The nearby **Dallas Power and Light Building★** (Jackson St. and Browder Mall with entrance pavilion at 1506 Commerce St.; 1930; Lang and Witchell, Dallas, architects) is one of Dallas' most handsomely detailed Modernistic skyscrapers. The original Art Deco **elevator lobby** survives unaltered. Several blocks east is the Art Deco headquarters of another utility company, the **Lone Star Gas Building★** (301 South Harwood St.; 1931; Lang and Witchell, Dallas, architects), with a **customer service lobby★** that retains its dra-

---

TOP OF THE TOWN

AN ADDRESS IN A CITY'S TALLEST BUILDING LONG HAD A SPECIAL PRESTIGE. IN DALLAS, EACH DECADE SINCE 1900 HAS SEEN AT LEAST ONE NEW HEIGHT CHAMPION EXCEPT FOR THE DEPRESSION YEARS OF THE 1930s.

1902	1909	1913	1922	1942	1954	1958	1964	1965	1975	1985
8 stories	15 stories	17 stories	29 stories	30 stories	36 stories	42 stories	50 stories	52 stories	56 stories	70 stories
WILSON BUILDING	PRAETORIAN BUILDING	BUSCH BUILDING	MAGNOLIA PETROLEUM BUILDING	MERCANTILE BANK BUILDING	REPUBLIC BANK BUILDING	SOUTHLAND LIFE TOWER	REPUBLIC BANK TOWER	FIRST NATIONAL BANK BUILDING	FIRST INTERNATIONAL BUILDING	FIRST REPUBLICBANK PLAZA

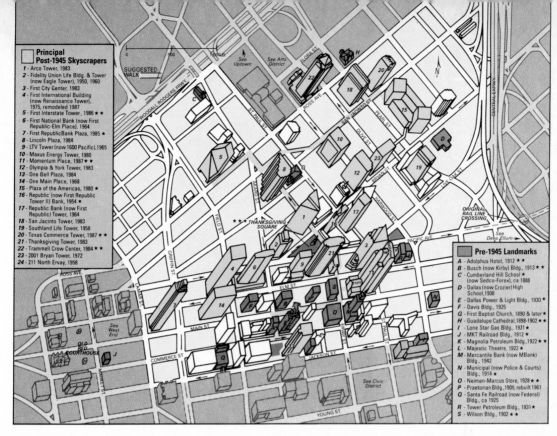

matic original decor marred only by a lowered ceiling.

Two blocks west of the Main and Akard intersection rises the slim, glass-skinned tower of the city's tallest skyscraper. This is the seventy-story **First RepublicBank Plaza**★ (901 Main St.; 1985; JPJ, Dallas, architects), whose step-roofed form is dramatically outlined at night by green argon lighting.

One block east of the intersection is the **Neiman-Marcus Department Store**★★ (1618 Main St.; 1928; Greene, LaRoche and Dahl, Dallas, architects) which by the 1920s had begun to rival the older Sanger Brothers Store (see "West End") as the town's most fashionable retailer. Long guided by the marketing genius of the legendary Stanley Marcus (b. 1905), son of one of the founders, Neiman-Marcus now has multiple branches in Dallas and elsewhere and is still among the nation's fashion leaders. The store's elaborate Christmas catalog pioneered the now popular custom of mail-order shopping for expensive merchandise. Unlike other Dallas retailers, the firm's anchor store remains on its original downtown site, where a smaller 1914 building was enlarged and rebuilt into the present Renaissance-inspired structure in 1928.

The eight-story **Wilson Building**★★ (1621 Main St.; 1902; Sanguinet and Staats, Fort Worth, architects), an early downtown landmark, is of great importance as one of the nation's few surviving skyscrapers of Victorian "banded" design (see next page). Note the superb Beaux Arts-inspired facade detailing.

Facing the Wilson Building across Ervay Street is **Momentum Place**★★ (1717 Main St.; 1987; Philip Johnson and John Burgee, New York, architects), a dramatic Post-International tower whose arched windows and vaulted roofline deftly complement its venerable neighbor. Inside, Momentum Place boasts a vast, two-story banking lobby where visitors can peer downward upon rows of computer operators busily executing financial transactions.

THANKSGIVING SQUARE AREA

Nestled as an oasis among the Financial Core skyscrapers is **Thanksgiving Square**★★★ (between Pacific Ave., Bryan, and Ervay sts.; 1976; Philip Johnson, New York, architect), a tranquil urban park complete with water garden, bell tower, and a striking, snail-shaped chapel. Dedicated to the universal theme of thanksgiving found in all the world's religions, the Square is really a triangle, built above an underground truck terminal that occupies one of the angular street intersections formed by the junction of two early town surveys.

Thanksgiving Square provides a superb vantage point to view the many variations on the International Style theme shown by the surrounding post-1945 skyscrapers.

GOTHIC SPLENDOR *The elaborate elevator lobby of the Busch (now Kirby) Building has survived since 1913.*

THE SKYSCRAPERS OF DALLAS: EVOLUTION OF THE OFFICE TOWER

Dallas' role as a financial and banking center has long given the city more than its share of tall office buildings. By 1940 it could boast of twenty-two skyscrapers, all concentrated in the downtown core. About half are still standing and all but one of these (the Praetorian Building of 1909) have escaped drastic remodeling.

Dallas' explosive growth since 1940 has seen a tenfold increase in office towers, which now number in the hundreds. Many are scattered in suburban clusters that began springing up in the 1960s, but since the late 1970s a burst of dramatic new downtown skyscrapers has reestablished the primacy of the Financial Core. Coupled with downtown's many earlier survivors, these provide a fascinating capsule history of the five eras of tall office building design: Victorian, Eclectic, Modernistic, International, and Post-International.

VICTORIAN
1880–1910

BANDED FACADES. The first tall office buildings resembled several lower buildings stacked on top of each other. Strips of windows one to five stories high were treated as separate decorative units, giving the buildings a characteristic "banded" appearance. Dallas' remarkable Wilson Building is one of the nation's rare survivors of this type.

WILSON BUILDING, 1902

MERCANTILE BANK
(NOW MBANK) BUILDING, 1942

TOWER PETROLEUM BUILDING, 1931

MODERNISTIC
1925–1945

STEPPED WALLS. As skyscrapers became taller and more massive they tended to create dark canyons in the streets below. To relieve this oppressive bulk, new shapes evolved in which the buildings were stepped back in order to become progressively smaller with height. Required in New York City by a 1916 zoning ordinance, these stepped-wall skyscrapers became fashionable throughout the country in the 1920s. Facade detailing was usually simplified into Art Deco adaptations of the Gothic, as in Dallas' Tower Petroleum Building, or was dropped altogether, as in the Art Moderne Mercantile Bank Building. Other important Dallas examples include the Dallas Power and Light Building and the Lone Star Gas Building.

POST-INTERNATIONAL
1965–present

ARCHES, PEAKS, AND MASONRY WALLS. Beginning in the 1960s, a small group of pioneering architects began to reintroduce traditional brick or stone between the windows of skyscrapers and to add simple, classical ornamentation to their facades. Such buildings remained rare until the 1980s, but have now blossomed into a popular alternative to the more severe International style. Dallas' Financial Core has several outstanding examples of this kind, among them the Trammell Crow Center, Texas Commerce Tower, and Momentum Place. Many smaller-scale versions can be seen in the city's suburban office clusters.

TEXAS COMMERCE TOWER, 1987

TRAMMELL CROW CENTER, 1984

MOMENTUM PLACE, 1987

ECLECTIC
1890-1935

THREE-PART FACADES. During the 1890s a more unified tall building design was being worked out by several inventive Chicago architects, led by the masterful Louis Sullivan. They borrowed the principle of the Greek column: a strong base and a decorative crown (the "capital") were connected by a much longer and more uniform shaft, to give a balanced, three-part composition. Decorative details were typically borrowed from either classical Greece and Rome (columns and rounded arches) or from the Gothic cathedral (delicate spires and tall pointed arches). Also common were intricate floral patterns influenced by the Art Nouveau movement. Rooftop towers sometimes extend upward from the main building to increase the height and dramatic effect. Dallas has several fine examples from this period including the MKT, Busch, Magnolia, and Davis buildings. The Busch Building is particularly noteworthy for being among the first in the country to use Gothic detailing.

MKT Railroad Building, 1912

Busch (now Kirby) Building, 1913

INTERNATIONAL
1945-present

GLASS WALLS AND FLAT TOPS. Following the Second World War, skyscraper fashion shifted from walls of stone or brick with multiple small windows to glass-walled buildings dominated by a simple geometric window grid. First introduced by avant-garde European emigrants in the late 1930s, these "International style" skyscrapers are still in fashion and include most of Dallas' tall buildings, both in the Financial Core as well as in the suburban office clusters. International skyscrapers come in many shapes. Earliest were the familiar box-shaped towers which dominated the 1950s and 1960s. More recently, stair-stepped roofs and exotic curving or angular shapes have been introduced to relieve the monotony of the glass box. Dallas has many examples of each type.

One Main Place, 1968 (right); First International Building (now Renaissance Tower), 1975, remodeled 1987 (left)

First City Center, 1983

Most distinctive is the aluminum-clad **Republic National Bank Building★ and Tower**, now First Republic Towers I and II (Pacific Ave. and Ervay St.; 1954; Harrison & Abramowitz, New York, architects; Tower, 1964; Harrell & Hamilton, Dallas, architects). Clockwise from the Republic are **First City Center** (1700 Pacific Ave.; 1983; WZMH Group, Dallas, architects), **211 North Ervay** (1958; Hedrick, Stanley & Morey, Fort Worth, architects), **Thanksgiving Tower** (1601 Elm St.; 1983; Harwood K. Smith, Dallas, architect), **LTV Tower**, now 1600 Pacific (1965; Harwood K. Smith, Dallas, architect), **First National Bank**, now First Republic—Elm Place (1401 Elm St.; 1964; G. H. Dahl and T. E. Stanley, Dallas, architects), **Fidelity Union Life Building and Tower**, now Eagle Tower (1507 Pacific Ave.; 1950; Wyatt C. Hedrick, Fort Worth, architect; Tower, 1960; Hedrick & Stanley, Fort Worth, architects), and **Arco Tower** (1601 Bryan St.; 1983; I. M. Pei, New York, architect).

All of these are International Style skyscrapers, with flattened tops and squared, boxy shapes. Republic Bank and 211 North Ervay show two variations of the exuberant cladding materials favored in the 1950s—aluminum and colored enamel panels. LTV and First National Bank, with their subdued coloring and large expanses of dark glass, are typical 1960s interpretations of the International Style. Thanksgiving Tower has the reflective glass-skin curtain wall perfected in the 1970s, whereas Arco Tower breaks the reflective glass with grey granite. These two also show the 1980s trend toward angular geometric shapes, which culminates in stepped-roof forms such as First City Center.

THE NEW DOWNTOWN AXIS

Beginning with the 1954 Republic Bank Building (see above), post-World War II office towers began to move into the angular street grid above Pacific Avenue, north of the traditional financial center along Elm, Main, and Commerce streets. Today this area is the scene of a new downtown axis growing northeastward along Bryan and San Jacinto streets and Ross Avenue.

International Style office towers tend toward rather austere and utilitarian lobbies and public areas; it was not until 1980 that the Financial Core got a truly innovative interior space, one in the new axis area. This is the mixed-use **Plaza of the Americas★** (703 North Pearl St.; 1980; Harwood K. Smith, Dallas, architect), whose four original buildings (two office towers, hotel, and parking garage) enclose a dramatic **central atrium★**, complete with an ice-skating rink around which are clustered more than three dozen attractive shops and restaurants.

Several of the Financial Core's newest skyscrapers have also made unusual attempts to create appealing public areas. The **First Interstate Bank Tower★★** (1445 Ross Ave.; 1986; I. M. Pei, New York,

THANKSGIVING SQUARE *A tranquil urban oasis amid towering skyscrapers, the park's snail-shaped focal point is a small chapel devoted to the common theme of thanksgiving in world religions.*

architect), a striking, chisel-topped prism of green glass, sits in a landscaped **water garden★★** that serves as a handsome outdoor extension of its marble-trimmed lobby. Two blocks northeast along Ross Avenue is the hip-roofed **Trammell Crow Center★★** (2001 Ross Ave.; 1984; Skidmore, Owings and Merrill, Houston, architects), which continues the public-spirited pattern with an outdoor **sculpture garden★★** and adjacent mini-museum—the **Trammell Crow Pavilion** (see "Arts District"). Across Ross Avenue from the Trammell Crow Center rises the dramatic new **Texas Commerce Tower★★** (2200 Ross Ave.; 1987; Skidmore, Owings and Merrill, Houston, architects), a highboy-roofed Post-International design that is strikingly pierced through the top by glass-walled upper floors served by a dramatic, five-story **sky lobby★**.

Other important post-1945 Financial Core skyscrapers are shown on the map; their changing stylistic fashions are treated on the preceding two pages.

LANDMARK PUBLIC BUILDINGS

The ornate **Majestic Theatre★** (1925 Elm St.; 1922; John Eberson, Chicago, architect) is the only reminder of the many decades when Elm Street was the city's entertainment center, a Great White Way several blocks long, alive with the blazing marquees of more than a dozen large theaters. The Renaissance Revival-style Majestic was the grandest of the lot, built for

vaudeville but converted to movies in the 1930s. The building was donated to the city in 1977 and was renovated to become a spectacular Municipal Performance Hall.

Nearby is the monumental Beaux Arts **Municipal Building★**, now the Police and Municipal Courts Building (2015 Main St.; Mauran, Russell and Crowell, St. Louis, architects), built in 1914 at what was then the extreme eastern end of downtown. This remained the seat of city government until the current City Hall was completed in 1978 (see "Civic District").

EARLY SCHOOLS AND CHURCHES

Much of the northern part of the present Financial Core housed only residential districts until well into the twentieth century. Today the principal survivors from this more tranquil era are a few large school or church buildings that once stood surrounded by many blocks of fine houses.

The Italianate **Cumberland Hill School★**, now part of the Sedco-Forex Complex (1901 North Akard St.; ca. 1888; A. B. Bristol, Dallas, architect), was Dallas' second public school building, constructed only shortly after the city established public education in 1884. Rescued from demolition in 1971, it was privately restored for corporate offices in the city's first major historic preservation project.

A second historic school building in the area is regrettably scheduled not for restoration but for probable demolition. This is the original **Dallas High School★** (2214

Bryan St.; 1908; Lang and Witchell, Dallas, architects), now part of the N. R. Crozier High School Complex. A fine vernacular Beaux Arts structure, the building, under various names, has served many generations of the city's teenagers.

The **First Baptist Church★** (1707 San Jacinto St.; 1890 and later; Albert Ulbreck, Dallas, architect) has stubbornly maintained its downtown location while growing to become the nation's largest Baptist congregation with 20,000 members. The original church building, still intact but now surrounded by massive satellite structures, is an architectural gem combining a polychromed Victorian Gothic basic form with more avant-garde Richardsonian Romanesque arches.

MAJESTIC THEATRE *Once the elaborate centerpiece of Elm Street's Theater Row and now a major center for the performing arts, this grand survivor's earlier neighbors have been replaced by striking office towers.*

Civic District ★

Downtown's south side, centered around a dramatic new City Hall, is being transformed by an expansion of city-owned facilities including a huge Convention Center, a lively Farmers Market, and a fascinating museum village in Old City Park.

OLD CITY PARK *Dallas' first park is today the home of a fascinating museum of architectural and cultural history.*

The area to the south of the Financial Core, located well away from the early T&P and H&TC tracks that surrounded the city on the north and east, contained the town's first exclusive residential area, a long-demolished enclave of Victorian houses called "The Cedars."

In 1884 the Santa Fe railroad arrived in Dallas, building its main line diagonally through the city's south side just beyond The Cedars. With the railroad came the usual switching yards, warehouses, service industries, and laborers' shacks. By 1890 the affluent residents of The Cedars were leaving for more distant and tranquil suburbs, and the neighborhood began a long decline into a railroad-dominated warehouse and industrial district.

OLD CITY PARK

The Victorian houses of The Cedars surrounded **Old City Park★★** (1717 Gano St.; 1876 and later), the town's first public recreation area, which survives today as a fascinating museum village of older North Texas buildings moved in from elsewhere and lovingly restored. Thirty-seven structures, many with period furnishings and craft demonstrations, interpret the life of North Texas settlers from about 1840 to 1910. Included are houses ranging in style from simple log dwellings to elaborate Queen Anne landmarks, as well as an early train depot, hotel, church, school, and small commercial complex. The Park's **Brent Place Restaurant**, housed in a

charming Gothic farmhouse, serves tasty lunches based on authentic period recipes.

FARMERS MARKET

Across the Thornton Freeway from Old City Park is the lively **Farmers Market★** (South Pearl Expressway and Taylor St.; ca. 1942), four city-owned blocks of sheds lined from early spring to late fall with fresh produce from North Texas farms and busy at all times with cold-storage fruits and vegetables purchased from wholesalers for resale by small vendors, sometimes at bargain prices.

PRESBYTERIANS AND MASONS

Faint echoes of the south side's residential past survive in three important landmarks located near the intersection of Harwood and Young streets. Most dramatic is the green-domed, Neoclassical **First Presbyterian Church** (401 South Harwood; 1912; C. D. Hill, Dallas, architect), handsomely sited as the focal point of a crucial jog in Harwood Street.

Immediately to the south is the **Scottish Rite Cathedral★** (500 South Harwood; 1907; Hubbell and Greene, Dallas, architects), another Neoclassical landmark whose elaborate facade, inspired by ancient Rome, stands in striking contrast to the starkly simple Art Moderne mass of its younger cousin across the street—the **Masonic Temple** (507 South Harwood; 1941; Flint and Broad, Dallas, architects).

CITY HALL AND LIBRARY

In the 1970s a massive revitalization of downtown's south side began as the city replaced many blocks of railroad tracks and modest commercial buildings with a vast new civic complex. Centerpiece of the district is the jutting, angular mass of the **Dallas City Hall★★★** (1500 Marilla St.; 1978; I. M. Pei, New York, architect), a widely acclaimed masterpiece of modern architecture set behind an enormous ceremonial plaza facing Young Street. Here are held frequent festivals and holiday events. On the opposite side of the plaza stands the city's new **Eric Jonsson Research Library★** (1515 Young St.; 1982; Fisher and Spillman, Dallas, architects), a spacious and highly functional building whose receding facade complements the thrust of its larger and more aggressive neighbor across the plaza.

CONVENTION CENTER

The largest component of the civic complex lies immediately to the southwest of

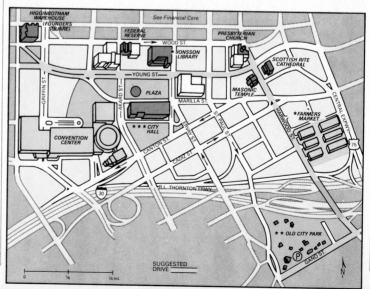

City Hall Plaza. The **Dallas Convention Center** (650 South Griffin St.) grew to its present enormous size in three phases. The original Dallas Auditorium and Colosseum (717 South Akard St.; 1957; George Dahl, Dallas, architect) was expanded with two later showroom additions in 1973 and 1984 (Omniplan, Dallas, architects) In addition to conventions, the facility hosts many public concerts, antique shows, and other special events.

FEDERAL RESERVE BANK

In 1914 the newly organized Federal Reserve System chose booming Dallas over several larger competing cities as its southwestern regional headquarters. In 1920 the system built a small but imposing new home, the Neoclassical **Federal Reserve** Bank Building★ (400 South Akard; Graham, Anderson, Probst and White, Chicago, architects), which was located on a site somewhat south of the principal financial district.

FOUNDERS SQUARE

A refreshing counterpoint to the starkly modern buildings of the civic complex, the **Higginbotham-Bailey-Logan Building**, now Founders Square (914 Jackson St.; 1914 and later; Lang and Witchell, Dallas, architects), is one of the largest and finest of the south side's early warehouses. Long the home of one of Dallas' pioneer clothing manufacturers and jobbers, the historic structure has recently been carefully restored and adapted for use as modern offices.

| HOURS AND CHARGES |

Old City Park: 421-5141. Grounds open daily from dawn to dusk; admission to grounds is free. Historic building interiors are open Tues-Sat, 10 am to 4 pm; Sun, 1:30 pm to 4:30 pm. Last tickets are sold one hour before closing. Wed, Fri, Sat guided tours only at 10:15, 11:15, 12:15, 1:15, 2:15; tour duration 1½ to 2 hours; tour at your own pace on other days. Adults, $3; ages 6-12, $2. Brent Place restaurant lunch sittings at 11:15 am, 12:15 pm, and 1:15 pm, reservations required.

Farmers Market: 748-2082. Daily, 6 am to 6 pm (winter); 5 am to 7 pm (summer).

Dallas City Hall: 670-3957. Mon-Fri, 8 am to 5:15 pm. Information desk on first floor. Cafeteria and snack bar on 7th floor.

Related Shopping, Dining, and Entertainment (SiDE) Areas: Downtown Dallas; West End Historic District; Deep Ellum.

DALLAS CITY HALL *The distinguished New York architect I. M. Pei designed this dramatic angular structure facing a large ceremonial plaza.*

Arts District **

The highlight of this developing sixty-acre site on downtown's north side is the handsome Dallas Museum of Art, which has particularly strong collections of American Colonial furniture and African, Pre-Columbian, and Modern Art.

A principal catalyst in the recent rejuvenation of downtown Dallas was the 1978 decision by the City Council to concentrate new facilities for the arts in an under-utilized eleven-block site in the CBD's northeastern quadrant. The centerpiece of this "Arts District" is the dramatic new home of the Dallas Museum of Art, which opened in 1984 to rave reviews (see below). A second major facility, the **Morton H. Meyerson Symphony Center** (Pearl and Flora sts.; I. M. Pei, New York, architect), is scheduled for completion in 1989. The district also houses the city's Arts Magnet High School and, in temporary quarters, the Arts District Theater, featuring performances by the resident company of the Dallas Theater Center.

The city has purchased additional acres for future arts facilities, but about half of the sixty-acre District remains in private ownership. As a result, the long-term use of much of its prime vacant land remains uncertain. Present plans call for a series of tall office towers to flank a ceremonial central boulevard (Flora Street) that will be lined by a narrow band of low-rise restaurants, shops, and mini-museums.

TRAMMELL CROW CENTER AND SCULPTURE GARDEN *Nineteen French bronzes grace the gardens surrounding this beautifully detailed Post-International skyscraper.*

This pattern can be seen in the District's first new building, the handsomely detailed **Trammell Crow Center**★★ (2001 Ross Ave.; 1984; Skidmore, Owings and Merrill, Houston, architects), a fifty-story Post-International office tower with a small annex, the **Trammell Crow Pavilion**, on Flora Street that showcases temporary exhibitions. Surrounded by attractive **sculpture gardens**★★ on the other three sides, the tower also has unusually lavish lobby detailing.

DALLAS MUSEUM OF ART

Designed by New York architect Edward Larrabee Barnes, the new **Dallas Museum of Art**★★★ (Ross Ave. and Harwood St.; 1984) has quickly become one of the region's most appealing attractions. Centered on a prominent barrel vault, the simple low buildings of the museum complex, faced with striking white limestone, occupy most of a large city block. The vaulted central gallery and its surrounding rooms house one of the Museum's major treasures—its collection of modern Abstract Expressionist paintings, many of which are of heroically large size. Stairstepping upward from the central vault are a series of pleasantly scaled galleries exhibiting, in reverse chronologic order, major works from the Museum's permanent collection. Particularly important are its holdings of Pre-Columbian and African Art, handsomely displayed in the uppermost galleries.

In the relatively short time since its new home was completed, the Museum has made two nationally important acquisitions in the decorative arts. First came the

Emory and Wendy Reves Collection★★, an eclectic and very personal melange of mostly French paintings, furniture, and decorative objects housed in rooms faithfully re-created from the donor's Mediterranean villa.

In 1986 the Museum obtained the remarkable ninety-eight-piece **Bybee Collection of Colonial American Furniture**★★★, which was assembled over a period of thirty years by Faith P. and Charles L. Bybee of Houston. This acquisition instantly made the Museum one of the nation's top repositories of rare American furniture of the very highest quality. About one-third of the collection is now on display in the second-floor American galleries.

ROSS AVENUE MANSIONS

The new Arts District and its surrounding blocks on the north side of the CBD were formerly occupied by one of Dallas' finest residential neighborhoods (see also "Financial Core"). Ross Avenue, once lined with stately mansions, was the city's most fashionable turn-of-the-century address. Today the lone survivor of these early landmark dwellings is the Arts District's **Belo House**, now the Dallas Legal Education Center (2101 Ross Ave.; ca. 1890, facade remodeled ca. 1900; Herbert Green, Dallas, architect), the carefully restored Neoclassical home of Alfred H. Belo (1840-1901), founder of the *Dallas Morning News*.

GUADALUPE CATHEDRAL

A second and still more important early Dallas landmark also survives within the boundaries of the modern Arts District. This is the **Cathedral Santuario de Guadalupe**★★, formerly the Cathedral of the Sacred Heart (2215 Ross Ave.; 1898-1902; architect unknown). This large Gothic Revival structure has served since its completion as the seat of Dallas' Roman Catholic bishop. Built of local brick, this and the Old Red Courthouse (see "West End") are the city's most monumental survivors from the last century.

HOURS AND CHARGES

Trammell Crow Center: 979-6492. Sculpture garden and lobby open 24 hours a day. Concierge will provide pamphlet describing sculpture Mon-Fri, 8 am to 5 pm. Restaurants in upper lobby level.

Dallas Museum of Art: 922-0220. Tues, Wed, Fri, Sat, 10 am to 5 pm; Thur, 10 am to 9 pm; Sun, noon to 5 pm. Museum admission free. Reves Collection admission: Adults, $3; under 12, $1. Museum parking, $2 minimum. Restaurant open 11 am to 2:30 pm.

Guadalupe Cathedral: 741-3954. Open only for masses Mon-Fri, 6:30 am to 8 am and 6:30 pm to 7:30 pm; Sat, 3 pm to 8:30 pm; Sun, 6:30 am to 3 pm.

Related Shopping, Dining, and Entertainment (SiDE) Areas: Downtown Dallas; Uptown.

THE DALLAS MUSEUM OF ART, A SAMPLING

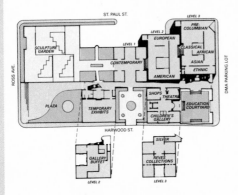

(Left) Seated Man, 800-500 B.C. *Olmec (Mexico, Puebla), serpentine carving, 7" high. This portrait of an Olmec ruler is among the many masterworks in the large Pre-Columbian collection.*

(Right) The Icebergs, 1861 *Frederic Church (American, 1826-1900), oil on canvas, 64 x 112". Church, a master of romantic landscapes, charged admission to view such large and exotic travel scenes in the days before color photography or the National Geographic. This fine example was lost for almost a century when it turned up in 1979. It was purchased at auction for $2.5 million by an anonymous patron who donated it to the museum.*

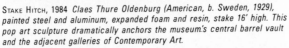

Stake Hitch, 1984 *Claes Thure Oldenburg (American, b. Sweden, 1929), painted steel and aluminum, expanded foam and resin, stake 16' high. This pop art sculpture dramatically anchors the museum's central barrel vault and the adjacent galleries of Contemporary Art.*

Tall Clock, 1720-1740 *Detail (Boston, Massachusetts). A representative masterpiece from the ninety-eight-item Bybee Collection of Colonial American Furniture acquired by the museum in 1986.*

Uptown *

Immediately north of the Central Business District is this rapidly changing area where lively shops and restaurants mingle with striking new office towers as well as with neighborhoods of quaint, turn-of-the-century houses.

The area immediately north of the present Central Business District, today known informally as "Uptown," was originally occupied by turn-of-the-century residential neighborhoods. By the 1950s many of the area's larger houses had been converted into commercial uses—in these were located some of the city's finest specialty shops, art galleries, and restaurants. This tradition continues today but in a more diverse setting. Streets of picturesque early houses are now mingled among strikingly modern commercial buildings, creating a lively urban mixture of offices, shops, and restaurants. Dozens of Dallas' most elegant and fashionable establishments are here, some in quaintly remodeled old dwellings and others in chic new quarters.

UPTOWN RETAIL DISTRICT

Anchoring Uptown on the southwest are the mansard-roofed and New Orleans–grilled towers of **The Crescent★★** (Cedar Springs Rd. and Maple Ave.; 1986; Philip Johnson and John Burgee, New York, architects), a massive, mixed-use project that provides a striking Post-International centerpiece for the area. Beyond the Crescent's nineteen-story office tower lies a matching five-story hotel, the urbane Crescent Court, which steps down to a three-story retail complex built at the apex of the project's triangular site. All these build-

ings are connected by handsome courtyards and gardens that invite leisurely exploration.

Several blocks northeast of the Crescent's retail center is **The Quadrangle★** (2800 Routh St.; 1965; Pratt, Box & Hen-

KALITA HUMPHREYS THEATER *This 1959 classic was among master architect Frank Lloyd Wright's last projects.*

derson, Dallas, architects), a low-rise complex of shops, restaurants, and offices that was one of Dallas' first mixed-use developments. Recently remodeled and expanded, it provides a delightfully human-scaled setting for eating, shopping, or browsing, as does adjacent **PD-9★** centered on Routh and Fairmount streets. This is an area of older houses that have been preserved to become fashionable art galleries, specialty shops, and restaurants.

Bordering the retail district on the south is spirited **McKinney Avenue**, the neighborhood's principal thoroughfare. In 1988 this will be the site of the picturesque McKinney Avenue Trolley, a restoration of a part of Dallas' historic streetcar system that will link Uptown with the nearby Arts District and Financial Core.

STATE-THOMAS

South of McKinney Avenue lies the **State-Thomas Historic District★** (roughly bounded by McKinney Ave. and Fairmount, Boll, and Colby sts.), created in 1984 to preserve the small core of one of Dallas' oldest surviving residential neighborhoods. In this tranquil downtown oasis quaint Victorian cottages from the 1880s and 1890s are being lovingly restored for use as shops, offices, or residences. An adjacent sixty-acre tract, now mostly vacant, has recently been rezoned to encourage an urban residential community of European-style, mid-rise housing.

TURTLE CREEK BOULEVARD

One of the city's most handsome landscaped parkways, **Turtle Creek Boulevard★**, lies just north of the Uptown Area and winds along the southern boundary of Oak Lawn (see below). At the heart of the Turtle Creek parkway system is **Robert E. Lee Park** (Turtle Creek Blvd. and Hall St.), which honors the Confederate commander with both a dramatic **equestrian statue** and with "Arlington Hall," a small replica of his colonnaded Virginia homestead used for public functions. Both were erected for the 1936 Texas Centennial celebrations. Nearby is the grandly Spanish Eclectic **Sheppard King House★** (2821 Turtle Creek Blvd.; 1925; J. Allen Boyle, architect), now restored and expanded to become the restaurant wing of the elegant Mansion Hotel.

Along Turtle Creek Boulevard are concentrated most of Dallas' few high-rise residential buildings. Particularly noteworthy is **3525 Turtle Creek Boulevard** (1957; Howard R. Meyer, Dallas, architect), one of the city's first residential towers and still among its most architecturally distinguished and desirable.

Hidden in the trees across the creek is the **Kalita Humphreys Theater★** (3636 Turtle Creek Blvd.; 1959), home of the Dallas Theater Center and the only theater building designed by Frank Lloyd Wright (1867-1959). This was one of the master architect's last projects. The building's strongly sculptured form and circular core echo his more familiar Guggenheim Museum in New York City, designed at about the same time.

OAK LAWN

Extending northward from the Turtle Creek corridor lies **Oak Lawn**, a large residential district served by slowly upgrading retail strips along Oak Lawn and Lemmon avenues. (The latter was the city's original "Fast-food Row.") Developed as a series of quiet residential neighborhoods between 1900 and 1940, Oak Lawn has been the scene of several waves of apartment and condominium development in the decades since 1950. Still a neighborhood in transition, it is the home of many artists, writers, architects, and others in the creative professions.

SUGGESTED DRIVE

UPTOWN DIVERSITY *The district's many elegant shops, restaurants, and galleries are found in both picturesque old houses (above) and splendid new structures, such as the Crescent (below).*

Deep Ellum

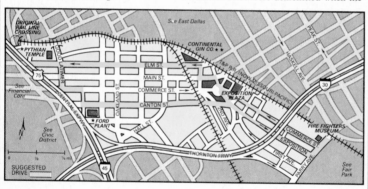

Site of many early industries and once the heart of Dallas' black community, this area contains modest commercial buildings, some of which have recently been renovated for avant-garde theaters, galleries and nightclubs.

PYTHIAN TEMPLE *Now modified as an insurance company headquarters, this landmark structure was once the vibrant focal point of Dallas' black community.*

Dallas' earliest black neighborhoods grew up near the 1873 crossing point of the city's first two railroad lines, about a mile east of the courthouse square (see "Financial Core"). The immediate crossing area was occupied by depots and commercial buildings but farther along the tracks to the north and east spread the homes of Dallas' growing black population, then only recently emancipated from slavery. In Dallas, as elsewhere, the modest dwellings of black laborers and domestic servants became concentrated in narrow bands adjacent to the noisy railroad right-of-way on land that was considered unfit for more affluent housing.

scattered in modest storefront buildings throughout this elongate area lying between the Central Business District on the west and Fair Park to the east.

OLD DEEP ELLUM

The core of the former black commercial district was the several blocks of Elm Street immediately east of the Houston and Texas Central tracks (now the route of Central Expressway). Here were concentrated many small grocery and drug stores, barbershops, walk-up hotels, pawn shops, bargain clothing stores and nightclubs. Some of these were demolished when the

moody genius, Pittman found little demand for his talents. The Renaissance-inspired Pythian Temple, one of his few important commissions, is of great historic importance as Dallas' first major commercial structure built for blacks, by blacks, with black money.

In the 2500 and 2600 blocks of Elm Street, around the former Pythian Temple, stand many modest, two-story commercial buildings, now mostly abandoned, that were once part of Deep Ellum's lively core.

CONTINENTAL GIN COMPANY

The Deep Ellum area is bounded on the north by the Texas and Pacific Railroad right-of-way. Originally isolated from the city's growing financial and commercial districts farther west, and close to the homes of black workers living nearby, this stretch of tracks became the site of many of the city's early industrial plants.

Chief among these was the **Continental Gin Company★★**, now the Otto Coerver Company (3311 Elm St.; ca. 1888 and later; architects unknown), which played a

This black community was served for many decades by a lively commercial district that centered on Elm Street just east of the railroad junction. Known as "Deep Elm" (universally pronounced "Deep Ellum," as it is now affectionately spelled), the area was a miniature Harlem and the home of such legendary folk-blues singers as Huddie "Leadbelly" Ledbetter and Blind Lemon Jefferson.

DALLAS' SOHO

After World War II, Deep Ellum began to lose its retail character as the city expanded and black Dallasites moved to suburban neighborhoods, principally in the southern parts of the city. Through the 1960s and 1970s the district languished as its retail establishments and nearby industries moved elsewhere, leaving behind blocks of vacant buildings. In the early 1980s a Soho-like revitalization began as young artists, theater groups, and owners of art galleries and nightclubs began to renovate some of Deep Ellum's commercial structures. Today much of Dallas' avant-garde artistic activity and nightlife is

H&TC tracks were removed and the right-of-way widened to construct Central Expressway in the late 1940s, and many more have since been razed. Today only a few scattered reminders suggest the long history of these blocks as the vibrant heart of black Dallas.

The most important surviving landmark is the former **Pythian Temple★** (2551 Elm St.; 1916; Sidney Pittman, Dallas, architect), now modified as a part of the Union Bankers Insurance Company Complex. Built as state headquarters for the Black Knights of Pythias, a fraternal organization, the building also housed the offices of many early black professionals—doctors, dentists, and lawyers. A top-floor auditorium and ballroom was the scene of elaborate dances, assemblies, and parties.

The Pythian Temple was designed by black architect Sidney Pittman (c. 1880-1958), son-in-law of the prominent educator Booker T. Washington (1856-1915). In 1913 Pittman closed his successful Washington, D. C. practice and moved his family to Dallas to begin anew, far from the lingering influence of his famous father-in-law. An eccentric and

little-known but pivotal role in the nation's expanding cotton industry. Prior to the 1870s cotton gins had seen few fundamental improvements since the invention of the rotating ginning mechanism by Eli Whitney, almost a century earlier. Laborers, using large baskets, still transferred the picked cotton from field wagons to the ginning machine and similarly hand carried the cleaned fibers to large presses to be compacted into bales. Following the Civil War, various mechanical devices were introduced in an attempt to streamline this cumbersome process, but not any were efficient enough to be widely accepted.

In 1883 twenty-eight-year-old Robert Sylvester Munger (1854-1923), manager of his father's small gin in Mexia, seventy-five miles south of Dallas, conceived of moving the cotton from wagon to gin by suction, using air moving through large, vacuum cleaner-like metal tubes. By adding a conveyor belt beneath the incoming flow, Munger perceived that the raw cotton could also be evenly distributed to a multiple series of ginning machines, rather than the usual one or two, thus greatly increasing the speed of the entire process. From the multiple gins, the cleaned cotton could again be moved by air directly to two alternating presses that prepared the finished bales. Munger quickly applied for patents on his "Ginning System," and in 1884 he moved to Dallas and opened a small plant in the Deep Ellum area to manufacture his new machinery.

Munger's revolutionary system was so successful that his company quickly became the largest gin supplier west of the Mississippi. In 1890 he established a similar plant in Birmingham, Alabama, to serve the southeastern states while his younger brother, Stephen I. Munger (1855-1921), ran the Dallas plant and ultimately took over the day-to-day management of the entire company. In 1899 the

COTTON GIN GENIUS *Dallas inventor Robert S. Munger's many innovations revolutionized the world's cotton industry. His Deep Ellum factory, shown in a 1914 drawing and still intact today, became the nucleus of the long-flourishing Continental Gin Company.*

two Munger factories, by then the nation's largest, merged with several smaller concerns to form the Continental Gin Company with the Munger Brothers as major stockholders; they remained active principals in the flourishing company until their deaths in the early 1920s (see also Munger Place under "East Dallas").

The Munger's original Dallas factory grew in two phases. Along the T&P tracks were small, windowed brick warehouse buildings of simple design that were first built about 1888 and then were expanded eastward in phases until about 1900. These held incoming raw materials and valuable finished machinery awaiting shipment. The actual manufacturing originally took place in large wooden buildings facing Elm Street. In 1914 these earlier wooden structures were replaced by the present handsome factory buildings made of reinforced concrete. These have large window areas for natural light and ventilation and are trimmed with dark brick separated by decorative concrete pilasters. In the 1960s

the entire complex was sold to its present occupants, the Otto Coerver Company, manufacturers of store fixtures and customized interior woodwork.

OLD FORD ASSEMBLY PLANT

Another important early industry was located at the western end of the Deep Ellum area, adjacent to the H&TC tracks. By 1912 Henry Ford was having difficulty meeting the enormous demand for his cheap, mass-produced Model T automobile, introduced in 1908. To speed up delivery, he opened several regional assembly plants, the first in the industry, to supplement his large Detroit factory. Deep Ellum was chosen as the site of the southwestern **Ford Assembly Plant***, now the vacant Adam Hat Building (Canton and Henry sts.; ca. 1913; John Graham, Seattle, architect). Ford's handsomely detailed original assembly building seems amazingly small by modern standards, and in 1925 the plant was replaced by a much larger one in East Dallas that operated until 1970.

FIREFIGHTERS MUSEUM

At the eastern edge of Deep Ellum, across from Fair Park, is the city's oldest surviving fire station. Today this is the home of the **Dallas Firefighters Museum** (3801 Parry Ave.; 1907; architect unknown), one of the few large collections of firefighting memorabilia in the Southwest. Among its prized possessions are "Old Tige," the city's last horsedrawn steam pumper, purchased in 1884, and a 1936 hook-and-ladder truck. The collections include countless other rare and fascinating objects, most of them awaiting funds for proper display.

ENTERTAINMENT CENTER *Once a miniature Harlem with lively jazz clubs and blues singers, today Deep Ellum's many nightclubs feature avant-garde musical fashions for the under-thirty set.*

HOURS AND CHARGES

Dallas Firefighters Museum: 821-1500. Mon-Fri, 9 am to 4 pm. Admission free. Call first as hours can be erratic.

Related Shopping, Dining, and Entertainment (SiDE) Area: Deep Ellum.

Fair Park ★★★

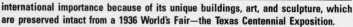

Home of several museums of science, history, and technology, this year-round exhibition and cultural center is of international importance because of its unique buildings, art, and sculpture, which are preserved intact from a 1936 World's Fair—the Texas Centennial Exposition.

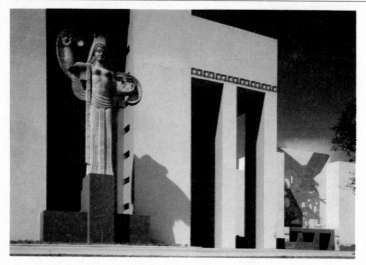

ART MODERNE *Monumental sculpture and murals line the imposing Esplanade. Six statues symbolize the countries that have ruled Texas; this one represents Spain.*

This 277-acre city park and museum center derives its name from the fact that since 1886 it has been the site of the State Fair of Texas, held each October and now the nation's largest annual fair. A community of seven year-round museums of science, history, and technology is also located within the Park.

Most of Fair Park's present buildings were designed for the 1936 Texas Centennial Exposition, a world's fair celebrating the hundredth anniversary of Texas' independence from Mexico. The significance of this assemblage of buildings, recently designated a National Historic Landmark, is two-fold. First, the structures constitute an extraordinary collection of 1930s art, architecture, sculpture, and planning, making the Park important on artistic merit alone. In addition, Fair Park provides the only intact and unaltered pre-1950 world's fair site remaining anywhere in the United States.

ROLE OF WORLD'S FAIRS

Before television, world's fairs were of great economic and cultural importance as a means of introducing new products to the public. They arose with the Industrial Revolution as a supplement to the long tradition of local agricultural fairs, which were places to celebrate the harvest, show off farm animals, and sell minor products. World's fairs, in contrast, stressed the won-

ders of the Machine Age and allowed the public to inspect the latest products from hundreds of manufacturers.

The tradition began in London in 1851 when Prince Albert constructed the enormous Crystal Palace Hall to house the Great Exhibition of London, a fair designed to showcase the burgeoning output of Britain's factories. This exposition also stressed scientific discoveries and international trade.

America's first world's fair was the Philadelphia Centennial celebration in 1876. Numerous others followed, culminating with the great expositions of the 1930s—

Chicago's Century of Progress in 1934, the Texas Centennial in 1936, and the New York World's Fair of 1939. When world's fairs resumed after World War II, their traditional function of introducing new products was rapidly being replaced by television and by more specialized international trade shows.

EXPOSITION SITES

World's fair exposition grounds generally had several types of buildings. Large general exhibit buildings, built by the fair's organizers, featured many smaller exhibitors and their wares. Larger exhibitors often constructed their own buildings, called "pavilions," to show off their products and advertise their names. Both types of exhibit buildings were normally built of nonpermanent materials. One or more substantial museums or other cultural facilities were usually built as permanent contributions to the community. In most world's fair sites, only the latter remain.

Fair Park retains not only a group of permanent museums constructed in 1936, but also all of the larger Centennial exhibition buildings and several original pavilions. Two factors contributed to the survival of this unique assemblage. First, the general planner of the Centennial, Dallas architect George Dahl (1894-1987), working with a small army of collaborating architects, found it cheaper in the depths of the Great Depression to build with stuccoed concrete blocks rather than with the less durable wood and plaster traditionally used for temporary building. Second, the Centennial grounds were also the site of the annual State Fair of Texas, whose directors were in no hurry to tear down buildings that might continue to provide useful exhibition space. The result, a half-century later, is a unique architectural treasure.

FAIR PARK ORIENTATION

The **Magnolia Lounge Information Center★★** (1936) shows continuous brief films on Fair Park and Dallas and is an ideal first stop for a Fair Park visit. The recently

ESPLANADE AND HALL OF STATE *In this recent photograph the park is decked out for the annual October State Fair. The giant Texas Star Ferris wheel gleams in the background.*

MAGNOLIA LOUNGE *Texas' first International style building now houses the official Fair Park Information Center.*

restored building was originally the Centennial pavilion of Magnolia Oil Co. (now a part of Mobil Oil). It was designed by Swiss architect William Lescaze (1896-1969), who helped introduce Europe's new International Style into the United States after emigrating to New York in 1920. The Magnolia Center was the first International building in Texas and contrasts sharply with the Art Moderne theme of other Centennial structures. From 1947 until 1958 the building was the home of an experimental theater-in-the-round whose founder and director, Margo Jones (1911-1955), played a seminal role in the nation's regional theater movement.

ESPLANADE

The heroic **Esplanade★★★** was the focal point of the Centennial Exposition and remains one of the most spectacular public spaces in North America. The statues in front of each of its six open porticos symbolize the six nations that have ruled Texas: Spain, France, Mexico, the Republic of Texas, the Confederacy, and the United States. The center reflecting pool is seven hundred feet long, with dramatic lighting and fountains at each end that are turned on for special events.

At Parry Avenue (the western terminus) are the original **Centennial Entry Gates** (1936), where fleets of streetcars delivered crowds of visitors. On entering the Park these visitors passed the **Spirit of the Centennial Sculpture★** (1936) located on the

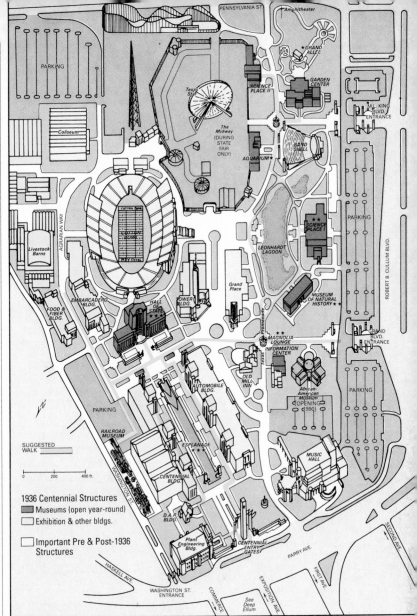

1936 Centennial Structures
- ▪ Museums (open year-round)
- ▫ Exhibition & other bldgs.
- ☐ Important Pre & Post-1936 Structures

south side of the remodeled Plant Engineering Building. The sculpture, a woman perched on a cactus accompanied by a mural and fountain, bears a distant similarity to Botticelli's *Venus Rising from the Sea.* The adjacent **D. A. R. Building** (1936) was originally the Continental Oil Company Pavilion. It is loosely modeled after Mount Vernon, a favorite motif for world's fair pavilions.

The long facade of the **Centennial Building** (1936; originally the Hall of Transportation) marks the northern boundary of the Esplanade; set in its walls are four large bas-relief sculptures symbolic of motion and movement. In addition, the external porticos originally housed eight heroic Art Moderne murals, each depicting a different form of transportation. These were painted over in 1950, but one is now being restored and other restorations are planned.

The current **Automobile Building** (1948) replaced the Hall of Varied Industry that originally made up the southern

boundary of the Esplanade but burned in 1942. The three large porticos were rebuilt in 1986 to restore the Esplanade's 1936 plan and original symmetry (the statues escaped the fire and are the originals).

HALL OF STATE

The spectacular **Hall of State★★★** (1936), now the home of the Dallas Historical Society, marks the eastern terminus of the Esplanade. Designed as a permanent shrine to the State of Texas, this building is among the best of its type left anywhere in the world. The Hall of State is built of native Texas materials and almost every detail is symbolic of the state's flora, fauna, history, or industries. The statue over the entrance is *Tejas Warrior* by Dallas sculptress Allie Tennant (1898-1971); the Tejas Indian tribe gave the state its name. The interior has five ceremonial halls joined by a curved entry foyer called the **Hall of Texas Heroes**, which boasts six statues of Texas Revolutionary patriots as well as a frieze recording the battles leading to independence.

Directly ahead of the main entrance is the building's dramatic centerpiece—the **Great Hall of Texas★★★**. A twenty-five-foot gold seal at the end of the Hall represents the six nations that have ruled Texas. The Hall's towering murals, by Yale art professor Eugene Savage (b. 1883), give a complete history of the state, beginning at the left with discovery in 1519 and continuing clockwise around the room to end with figures representing modern Texas industries—cotton, grain, lumber, oil, and agriculture. The furnishings in this room and throughout the building were specially designed in 1936 and have been carefully preserved.

The remainder of the ground floor is divided into four rooms representing the northern, southern, eastern, and western regions of Texas. In each Regional Hall note the doors, light fixtures, window cornices, wall materials, and floor patterns— all are specifically designed to symbolize the region.

In the right (south) wing of the building, the **North Texas Room★** has carved wooden figures and door details executed by renowned San Antonio craftsman Lynn

Ford (1908-1978). A mural features "Old Man Texas," a popular cartoon character in 1936, presiding over North Texas agriculture as he embraces the skyscrapers of Dallas and Fort Worth. The adjacent **South Texas Room★** features a lush tropical mural with painted side panels that represent important industries of the region.

In the left (north) wing of the building, the **East Texas Room★** features two murals by Dallas artist Olin Travis

TOWER BUILDING *Built as the federal government's contribution to the 1936 Texas Centennial, the striking tower symbolized the Exposition's bold and progressive ideals.*

(1888-1976). One depicts East Texas' rolling hills and peaceful pine forests prior to the discovery of the giant East Texas Oil Field in 1930. The other symbolizes the factories, products, and change that exploded from that discovery. The adjacent **West Texas Room★**, now being converted to a rare-book library, has hand-hewn ceiling beams and walls of mock adobe imprinted with the brands of early ranches. Renowned El Paso artist Tom Lea (b. 1907) executed the murals. One shows a West Texas cowboy, and the other is appropriately called "Three West Texas Folks in a Wagon."

The Hall of State's regional rooms are now used by the Dallas Historical Society for a rotating series of exhibits.

MUSEUM CENTER

In addition to the Dallas Historical Society exhibitions in the Hall of State, Fair Park has six other museums concentrating on differing aspects of science, history, and technology.

The **Dallas Museum of Natural History★★** (1936) emphasizes Texas' wildlife and geology. It contains a magnificent collection of fifty **habitat groups★★★** showing the principal species of Texas mammals and birds recreated in their native settings. Excellent paintings of the state's varied landscapes provide dramatic backgrounds for these exceptionally lifelike and complete displays. Many of the animals shown, including mountain sheep, jaguar, and buffalo, have long since disappeared from their Texas habitats. Other displays include the skeletons of a seventy-five-million-year-old mosasaur (giant sea reptile) and a fifteen-foot-tall ice age mammoth, both found near Dallas.

Science Place I★★ has recently expanded into the handsome building constructed in 1936 for the Dallas Museum of Art (see "Arts District"). This is a hands-on museum that examines the impact of health and medicine, physical and life sciences, machines and technology on our lives. Several new permanent exhibits are in preparation, and the museum also attracts a series of outstanding traveling exhibitions.

The building now housing **Science Place II** was built in 1936 as the Hall of Domestic Science and contains additional science displays plus a thirty-foot planetarium. This was one of the first in North Texas and will soon by replaced by a larger, fifty-foot installation.

The **Dallas Civic Garden Center** began as the Hall of Horticulture in 1936. Its large conservatory has tropical and subtropical plants from South America, Africa, and the Pacific Islands. Outside are a miniature rose garden, a Shakespeare garden, a herb and scent garden for the blind, and the dramatic new **Grand Allee du Meadows★**, a French-style, tree-lined lane with a fountain and floral display as its focal point. Expansion plans call for additional outdoor "theme" gardens.

GREAT HALL OF TEXAS *An awe-inspiring space dominated by heroic murals summarizing the state's history. The six parts of the gold seal, and the six side chairs, symbolize the six nations that have ruled Texas.*

FAIR PARK'S MUSEUMS OF SCIENCE, HISTORY, AND TECHNOLOGY.

AGE OF STEAM *Union Pacific No. 6913, the world's largest diesel-electric locomotive.*

GARDEN CENTER *Grand Allee du Meadows, the first phase of an extensive expansion.*

SCIENCE PLACE *Tooth-Bot, a friendly robot, teaches dental hygiene.*

MUSEUM OF NATURAL HISTORY *Detail of one of the fifty superb habitat groups.*

AQUARIUM *Over 340 species of aquatic life are displayed here.*

The **Dallas Aquarium★**, built in 1936 as the Hall of Aquatic Life, is one of the larger inland aquaria in the United States. More than 340 species of aquatic animals from all parts of the world make their home here, including a large collection of fish native to Texas.

The **Age of Steam Railroad Museum** is located out-of-doors on the tracks where the latest streamlined passenger trains were displayed to Centennial visitors in 1936. The museum owns an important collection of railroad rolling stock, including several fine passenger cars and examples of the largest steam, diesel-electric, and electric locomotives ever built in this country.

OTHER ATTRACTIONS

Band Shell (1936). This outdoor amphitheater has an Art Moderne shell of concrete semi-circles enveloping the stage. It is used for concerts and is the home of the Dallas Shakespeare Festival during the summer.

Leonhardt Lagoon (1936; sculpture 1986). The Lagoon and its surrounding museum buildings were planned in 1936 to provide a romantic, naturalistic counterpoint to the strongly formal Esplanade. In 1986 the large walk-on sculpture was added, allowing visitors to more fully interact with the lagoon and its aquatic life. The sculpture mimics Texas aquatic plants enlarged many times to provide a sort of Alice-in-Wonderland pathway into the Lagoon.

Cotton Bowl Stadium (1930, with later additions). The best external view of this 75,000-seat, partially sunken arena is from the Lagoon area. The stadium hosts, among other events, the annual New Year's Day Cotton Bowl Classic and the Texas-Oklahoma college football rivalry held each October during the State Fair.

Tower Building (1936). Built as the Federal Building, this dramatic Art Moderne structure has a bas-relief on the facade depicting events in Texas history. Enter the left front doors for a peek at the Federal Room with its original 1936 furnishings.

Old Mill Inn (1936). This building, now a restaurant, was an exception to the general Art Moderne theme of the Centennial. It was originally the Flour Milling Pavilion contributed by several flour and feed companies.

Music Hall (1925; Lang and Witchell, Dallas, architects; addn. 1972; Jarvis Putty Jarvis, Dallas, architects). This Spanish Eclectic performance hall seats 3,500 and is the home of the Dallas Summer Musicals and numerous other performances throughout the year.

Embarcadero Building (1936) and **Texas Food and Fiber Building** (1936). These mark the entrance to the "Agrarian Way," the part of the fairgrounds devoted to displays of agricultural products and livestock. The hundreds of pens located in sheds and barns here are filled each October with prize-winning horses, cattle, pigs, sheep, goats, and poultry.

Market and Industrial District

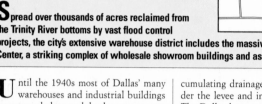

Spread over thousands of acres reclaimed from the Trinity River bottoms by vast flood control projects, the city's extensive warehouse district includes the massive Dallas Market Center, a striking complex of wholesale showroom buildings and associated hotels.

Until the 1940s most of Dallas' many warehouses and industrial buildings were crowded around the downtown core, principally in the historic West End area (see "West End") or in the railroad-dominated south and east sides (see "Civic District" and "Deep Ellum"). Today much of this activity is concentrated in reclaimed land along the Trinity River.

TRINITY RECLAMATION

In 1932 the massive task of rechanneling the flood-prone Trinity River was completed after decades of planning and five years of intensive earth moving, road building and utility rerouting. A new, straight river channel was dug into the center of the flood plain, where it is bounded by high levees two thousand feet apart to contain the river's overflow during floods.

A principal problem with such levee systems lies with tributary streams, which the levees dam off and prevent from flowing into the main river channel. To get around this problem, portions of the old river channel were left, and new depressions dug, outside the levees to act as storage basins or "sumps" for floodwaters from adjacent streams. The sumps, in turn, are connected to powerful pumping stations at the base of the levees that force the ac-

cumulating drainage through tunnels under the levee and into the main channel. The Dallas levee system has several such pump stations that are continually maintained for emergency use when floods threaten.

An instructive look at the old and new river channels, levee system, and pump stations can be seen along **Sylvan Avenue****, the only near-downtown river crossing that remains at ground level rather than being elevated on one of the many "viaducts" constructed between the levees. The meadows of adjacent **Trammell Crow Park*** provide an unusually fine view of the downtown skyline rising behind a small herd of life-sized marble cows sculpted by Dallas artist Harold Clayton (b. 1954).

INDUSTRIAL DISTRICT

Beyond the 1932 levees that confined the river lay thousands of acres of reclaimed bottomland. A principal owner of this land was a visionary real estate developer and civic leader renamed Leslie A. Stemmons (1874-1939), who dreamed of a vast new "Trinity Industrial District" where there would be plenty of space for the city's continued growth as a wholesale market center. The 1930s Depression had left this

dream mostly unrealized when Stemmons died in 1939.

Interrupted by the Second World War, the project was taken over in 1946 by Stemmons' two sons. Determined to carry on, they teamed up with a budding young entrepreneur named Trammell Crow (b. 1914), later to become the nation's largest real estate developer.

Crow suggested they try a new kind of warehouse building on some of the reclaimed land. Instead of traditional warehouses with prominent loading docks on two or more sides and dingy offices buried somewhere within, Crow proposed window-filled facades with large and airy front offices facing carefully landscaped yards. Loading docks and storage areas were

ANATOLE NORTH ATRIUM *One of five huge atria gracing the Market Center's many buildings. This one is in Texas' largest hotel.*

moved to less conspicuous side and rear locations. The new buildings were an immediate success, and the Trinity area quickly became the booming center of Dallas' postwar industrial expansion as well as the foundation of Crow's nationwide real estate empire.

STEMMONS CORRIDOR

In the early 1950s the Stemmons brothers farsightedly donated the right-of-way for what became the first completed segment of the nation's new Interstate Highway System. Opened in 1956 and named the Stemmons Freeway in honor of their father, the ten-lane highway brought much of the traffic between Oklahoma and Central Texas directly through the reclaimed Trinity bottomlands.

Today this "Stemmons Corridor" is lined with a series of industrial parks stretching northward for nearly twenty miles along the Elm Fork of the Trinity. Dominating the freeway frontage are several generations of tall office towers that provide a fascinating survey of modern skyscraper design. Behind these towers spread thousands of acres filled with low-

The Jumping Off Place — Where Dallas Stops

RIVER LAND RECLAMATION *A 1920s advertisement for rerouting the flood-prone Trinity River in order to create thousands of acres of usable land adjacent to downtown. The project was completed in 1932 and is today the site of one of the nation's largest light industrial districts and market centers.*

rise warehouses served by an intricate web of service roads and railroad sidings.

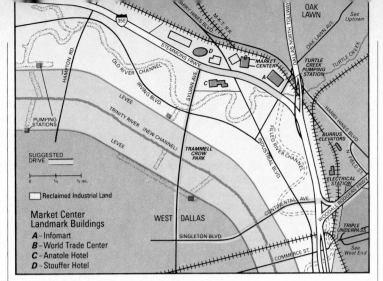

MARKET CENTER

The Stemmons-Crow association led to another unprecedented project that was to play an equally central role in Dallas' postwar growth. In 1955 the team set aside a small part of their vast warehouse district to be occupied exclusively by firms selling interior design items—furniture, fabrics, and related accessories. Known as the Decorative Center, the success of this project quickly led to a large Homefurnishings Mart, built in 1957 on a conspicuous site fronting the newly completed Stemmons Freeway which provides three-minute access to the Central Business District.

Thus began the **Dallas Market Center★★**, now an enormous complex encompassing eight major market buildings and two hotels, which has grown to become the world's largest wholesale mart, attracting half a million retail store buyers every year.

INFOMART

Newest and most spectacular of the Market Center's buildings is the **Infomart★** (1950 Stemmons Freeway; 1985; Martin Growald, Fort Worth, architect) which houses the nation's first computer marketing center with eighty-five company showrooms, library, bookstore, and restaurant, all open to the public. The Infomart building is a dramatic symbol of the new computer-based Information Age, for it is an almost literal copy of London's 1851 Crystal Palace, the first major exhibition hall and central marketplace for the wares of the preceding Industrial Age.

WORLD TRADE CENTER

Two Market Center buildings serve the apparel industry, while less specialized wholesalers are concentrated in the massive, fifteen-story **World Trade Center★** (2100 Stemmons Freeway; 1974, upper floors added 1979; Beran and Shelmire, Dallas, architects). This building's 3.1 mil-

lion square feet of floorspace make it one of the world's largest, in the same league as the 110-story paired towers in New York City that bear the same name (each tower contains approximately 4.5 million square feet) and as Washington's Pentagon Building (3.8 million square feet).

MARKET CENTER HOTELS

The most appealingly human of the Market Center's vast buildings are its two hotels. The handsome 1600-room **Anatole★** (2201 Stemmons Freeway; 1979, north tower added 1984; Beran and Shelmire, Dallas, architects) is Texas' largest hotel and contains one of the region's most dramatic interior spaces in its **North Atrium★★**, a lushly planted oasis hung with banner-like tapestries eight stories high. Developer Crow's fondness for large atria can also be seen in the Anatole's second or South Atrium and in the towering central courts of the World Trade Center and Infomart buildings. The more intimate **Stouffer Hotel★** (2222 Stemmons Freeway; 1982; Dahl Braden PTM, Dallas, architects) across the freeway is the complex's most elegant structure, a delicate, flattened prism of polished granite rising from a flared base and crowned with a lipstick-like truncation at the top.

EARLY INDUSTRIAL LANDMARKS

Along the edge of the reclaimed Trinity bottomlands stand three remarkable industrial buildings that have survived from earlier eras.

In 1917 the city's several competing electrical utilities were consolidated into the Dallas Power and Light Company, which built a large **Steam Electrical Generating Station★** (2600 Flynn Street; architect unknown) on the site of an earlier plant just north of downtown. The plant is an elaborate, arch-windowed structure of red brick towered over by two massive white smokestacks. Still in use as one of several Dallas-area generating stations, the carefully maintained and preserved facility has become a prized city landmark.

Only a few hundred feet north stand the massive grain elevators of the former **Burrus Mill and Elevator Company**, now the Cargill Corp. (2615 Alamo St.; architect unknown), built in the 1920s to convert North Texas grain into livestock feeds. Today used for production of bulgur (partially cooked, cracked wheat), the tall and graceful concrete elevators, standing in the shadow of downtown skyscrapers, serve as a rare visual reminder of Dallas' long ties to North Texas agriculture.

The third and oldest industrial survivor stands about a half-mile farther north along the Katy tracks. This is the **Turtle Creek Pumping Station**, now Turtle Creek Center For The Arts (3630 Harry Hines Blvd.; 1909; C. A. Gill, Dallas, architect). The last of a series of pump stations in this vicinity that for decades supplied most of the city's water, the venerable structure has recently been remodeled to serve as a community arts center.

HOURS AND CHARGES

Infomart: 746-3500. Mon-Fri, 8:30 am to 5 pm. Admission free. Tours daily at 11 am. Restaurant.

World Trade Center: 655-6100. Atrium and first floor open to the public Mon-Fri, 9 am to 5 pm. Admission free. Restaurant.

Related Shopping, Dining, and Entertainment (SiDE) Area: Market District.

INFOMART *The nation's first computer marketing center is housed in a modern copy of London's 1851 Grand Crystal Palace, which ushered in the Industrial Age.*

East Dallas *

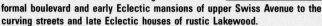

Affluent eastern residential districts show a progression from the Victorian dwellings of the Wilson Block near downtown through the formal boulevard and early Eclectic mansions of upper Swiss Avenue to the curving streets and late Eclectic houses of rustic Lakewood.

Restricted by the periodically flooded Trinity River bottoms to the south and west, much of Dallas' suburban growth has spread north and east from the commercial core. "East Dallas," now a vast wedge-shaped area informally bounded by Central Expressway on the west and the R. L. Thornton Freeway on the south, has long been the site of much of the city's residential expansion (see also "North Dallas"). The heart of early East Dallas centered on affluent Swiss Avenue, whose two and one-half miles today provide a fascinating survey of the city's changing housing fashions from about 1890 to 1930.

WILSON BLOCK HISTORIC DISTRICT

On lower Swiss Avenue near the modern Central Business District is the **Wilson Block Historic District**★★ (2900 block of Swiss Avenue; ca. 1898-1902), the most intact assemblage of houses from the last century in Dallas. This block was purchased as vacant land in the 1890s by newlywed cattleman Frederick P. Wilson (1863-1923), who built a handsome Queen Anne dwelling at 2922 Swiss and then filled out the block with several smaller but carefully detailed houses of similar design "to rent to his friends." Owned by Wilson's only son until 1977, the entire

group of Victorian houses and outbuildings survived virtually unaltered through many decades of neighborhood decline.

In 1980 the Dallas-based Meadows Foundation purchased the entire block and meticulously restored its structures to serve as offices for nonprofit organizations. Later an adjacent vacant block, now called the Beilharz Block (2800 block of Swiss Avenue), was also acquired by the Foundation and filled with additional Victorian houses moved in from scattered locations around the city where they had been threatened by demolition. Today these blocks, and the nearby State-Thomas Historic District (see "Uptown"), provide the best surviving glimpses of pre-1900 Dallas.

DeGolyer House *A 1930s "Mexican hacienda," now surrounded by the gardens of the Dallas Arboretum.*

MUNGER PLACE

About a mile beyond the Wilson Block, Swiss Avenue widens into a handsome divided boulevard at the entrance gates to Munger Place (approximate original boundaries—Fitzhugh, Live Oak, Henderson and Columbia aves.; 1905 and later), one of the most prestigious and successful early suburbs in Dallas.

Because of Dallas' rapid growth in the 1880s and 1890s, homeowners commonly found their brand-new neighborhoods encroached upon by commercial and industrial expansion after only a few short years. Municipal zoning laws were not widely adopted throughout the country until the 1920s; prior to then the principal method of insuring residential stability was by private "deed restrictions" placed on future land use by the developers of new suburbs. Munger Place was one of Dallas' first such restricted suburbs.

Originally opened in 1905 on 120 acres at the then remote edge of East Dallas, the development was the pet project of inventor and cotton gin magnate Robert S. Munger (see "Deep Ellum"). Munger not only permanently restricted the entire area to residential use, but also included subdistricts for housing of differing size and cost. The up-scale side of the neighborhood centered on Swiss Avenue whose one-hundred-foot lots were limited to houses costing $10,000 or more to build. Parallel streets to the southeast scaled down to minimum fifty-foot lots permitting houses costing only $4,000. All were required to be two-story dwellings with ample yards and no front fences or hedges to mar the park-like streetscapes. Because of its careful planning, and permanent guarantee of neighborhood stability through deed restrictions, Munger Place was an immediate success that was soon copied by the developers of Highland Park, north of town (see "North Dallas").

Swiss Avenue Historic District *Dozens of handsome Eclectic Era houses line this landscaped, mile-long boulevard.*

QUEEN ANNE CLASSIC *The Victorian houses of the Wilson Block Historic District have been restored to serve as offices for non-profit organizations.*

SWISS AVENUE HISTORIC DISTRICT

Post-World War II zoning changes allowed apartment construction in much of older East Dallas, and by the 1950s Munger Place was losing many of its fine old houses, particularly along Gaston Avenue, its major thoroughfare. In the early 1970s Dallas' pioneering historic preservation movement got its start when a group of residents banded together to save the landmark dwellings along Swiss Avenue, most of which were still intact. These efforts led to the **Swiss Avenue Historic District★★★**, as well as to zoning changes prohibiting apartment construction in many East Dallas neighborhoods.

Today park-like upper Swiss Avenue, with its deep and unobstructed front yards and landscaped median strip, preserves a fascinating collection of early-twentieth-century housing styles. Avant-garde Prairie-style dwellings inspired by Frank Lloyd Wright are interspersed with numerous other Eclectic Era "Period" styles. Particularly noteworthy are the Prairie style **Higginbotham House★★** (5002 Swiss Ave.; 1913; Lang and Witchell, Dallas, architects), the French Eclectic **Aldredge House★★** (5500 Swiss Ave.; 1917; Hal Thompson, Dallas, architect), and the Italian Renaissance **Saner House★★** (5439 Swiss Ave.; 1916; Hal Thompson, Dallas, architect).

MUNGER PLACE HISTORIC DISTRICT

Post-1950 apartment construction along Gaston Avenue bisected Munger's original development and separated the high-style masonry houses of Swiss Avenue from their less costly, mostly wooden-sided neighbors to the southeast. In 1980 the fifteen-block **Munger Place Historic District★** (rather confusingly named since much of the Swiss Avenue District was also a part of original Munger Place) was created to protect the surviving core of Munger's development. Here can be seen more modest builders' examples of the high-style, mostly architect-designed houses of nearby Swiss Avenue. Particularly favored were simple, four-square shapes with either Prairie or Neoclassical detailing.

LAKEWOOD

Munger Place became fully developed in the mid-1920s as large brick houses filled the remaining vacant lots in the upper blocks of Swiss Avenue. By the late 1920s and 1930s, the affluent heart of East Dallas development was shifting several blocks northeastward to the **Lakewood** neighborhood (approximately bounded by Abrams Rd., Velasco St., White Rock Lake, and Gaston Ave.; ca. 1922 and later), with curving **Lakewood Boulevard★** as its centerpiece. Here can be seen many fine examples of late Eclectic Era housing fashions. Particularly prominent are the Tudor, French Eclectic, and Spanish Eclectic styles, the latter occurring in an unusually fine concentration in Lakewood Boulevard's 7000 block.

WHITE ROCK LAKE

Lakewood Boulevard terminates overlooking **White Rock Lake**, built far beyond the city limits in 1912 to provide a new water supply for rapidly growing Dallas. Today used only as an emergency water source, the lake has become one of the city's premier recreation areas. It is surrounded by waterside parklands traversed by a popular hiking-biking trail and a scenic winding roadway with numerous picnic and recreation sites.

DEGOLYER HOUSE AND DALLAS ARBORETUM

At the southeast corner of White Rock Lake the city is developing the new **Dallas Arboretum and Botanical Garden** that features spectacular spring and fall floral displays. The focal point of the facility is the forty-four-acre former estate of petroleum geologist and oilman Everett Lee DeGolyer (1886-1956), an internationally important pioneer in the use of gravity and seismic techniques in the search for oil. The carefully crafted **DeGolyer House★★** (8525 Garland Road; 1939; Burton Schutt, Los Angeles, architect), patterned after a Mexican hacienda, is being restored as a house museum and memorial to DeGolyer and his accomplishments.

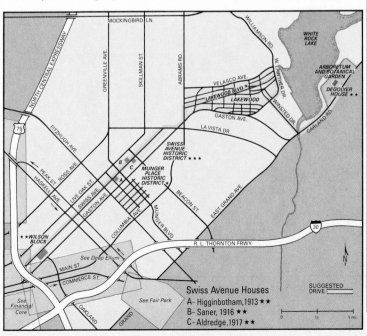

Swiss Avenue Houses
A- Higginbotham, 1913 ★★
B- Saner, 1916 ★★
C- Aldredge, 1917 ★★

North Dallas *

Building on the early successes of the carefully planned island towns of Highland Park and University Park, sprawling North Dallas has become the principal growth axis for affluent post-1950 housing developments, shopping centers, and suburban office parks.

Many of Dallas' finest residential districts have grown up north of the Central Business District in a vast, wedge-shaped tract bounded roughly by Central Expressway on the east and Stemmons Freeway on the west. Known informally as "North Dallas," this area is also the site of dozens of new office parks and shopping centers that have joined the booming suburbs in a northward surge now extending twenty miles from the downtown core.

North Dallas' most affluent neighborhoods center on Preston Road, the early town's principal roadway to the north which led to a crossing point on the distant Red River known as Preston Bend. Today a drive northward on Preston Road provides a thumbnail history of Dallas' twentieth century growth, as the street traverses progressively younger belts of suburban development.

HIGHLAND PARK

Preston Road, the northerly extension of Oak Lawn Avenue (see "Uptown"), begins near the boundary of the small island town of **Highland Park★**. Laid out amid rural cotton fields in 1907, this was one of Dallas' first fully planned residential suburbs and remains today among the city's most desirable (see also the discussion of Munger Place under "East Dallas").

The section east of Preston Road, known as Old Highland Park, was designed by New York landscape architect Wilbur David Cook, who had then just completed

a master plan for the exclusive Beverly Hills development in Los Angeles. Cook designed a series of curving roadways and elegant linear parks focused along Turtle Creek and its smaller eastern tributary known as Hackberry Creek.

The development's largest houses were sited along a small lake created by damming up Turtle Creek. Here along **Lakeside Drive★★** is one of the city's finest residential streetscapes, with handsome Eclectic mansions built from about 1910 to 1925. Eastward from Lakeside Drive, the streets of Old Highland Park were originally lined with less pretentious residences, mostly wood-clad houses built in the vernacular Prairie or Craftsman fashions that dominated the period. All but a very few of these have now been either remodeled beyond recognition or demolished to provide sites for larger houses of varying vintage and design.

On the opposite side of Preston Road stretches the somewhat younger Highland Park West, developed in the late 1920s and 1930s with curving **Armstrong Parkway★★** as its elegant centerpiece. Here the brick-veneered Eclectic fashions of those decades have escaped the remodelings and demolitions that have reconfigured much of Old Highland Park to the east.

MOCKINGBIRD LANE

Mockingbird Lane, the first major east-west crossroad along Preston Road, marks the approximate boundary between High-

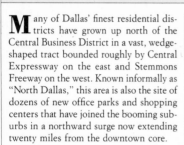

land Park and University Park, its larger and slightly younger companion city that shares a common school system; the two towns are informally known simply as the "Park Cities." Mockingbird Lane links several of North Dallas' most important landmarks. Two miles west of Preston Road it provides the principal gateway to **Love Field**, the city's original 1927 municipal airport that served, with periodic expansions, until the giant Dallas-Fort Worth Airport was completed in 1973 (see "Other Destinations"). After only a brief decline, Love Field is today as busy as ever serving private aircraft and the numerous flights of Southwest Airlines and other regional carriers.

SOUTHERN METHODIST UNIVERSITY

About a mile east of Preston Road, Mockingbird Lane passes the attractive seven-hundred-acre campus of **Southern Methodist University ("SMU")**, Dallas' oldest and most prestigious center of higher education which now serves an enrollment of about nine thousand students. At the center of the campus' unified red-brick architecture is **Dallas Hall★**, now part of Dedman College (rear entrance, 3225 University Blvd.; 1915; Shepley, Rutan and Coolidge, Chicago, architects), a Neoclassical landmark that originally stood alone among acres of cotton fields as the fledgling University's first building.

The campus houses one of Dallas' little-known art treasures, the **Meadows Museum★★**, part of the Owens Art Center Complex of the Meadows School of the Arts (6100 Bishop Blvd; 1965; George Dahl, Dallas, architect), a small jewel box containing one of the finest collections of Spanish paintings in the world outside of Madrid. The collection was donated by Algur H. Meadows (1889-1978), Dallas oilman and philanthropist.

LANDMARK SHOPPING CENTERS

At the intersection of Preston Road and Mockingbird Lane stands the landmark **Highland Park Shopping Village★★** (1931 and later; Fooshee & Cheek, Dallas, architects), a carefully planned Spanish Eclectic

SOUTHERN METHODIST UNIVERSITY *Dallas Hall, built in 1915 as the University's first building, is the focal point of the seven-hundred-acre campus.*

LAKESIDE DRIVE *Some of Highland Park's grandest houses surround this graceful lake, whose shores are lined with colorful azalea blossoms during the spring.*

complex that was one of the nation's earliest suburban shopping centers and the first to include its own off-street parking. Now carefully refurbished, the "Village" is home to about fifty elegant shops.

The carefully detailed and unified Highland Park Village stands in sharp contrast to the more haphazard suburban shopping centers that blossomed throughout the country in the late 1940s and 1950s. Typical of these is **Preston Center** (1948 and later) located two miles farther north at the intersection of Preston Road and Northwest Highway (Loop 12), which was the city's first suburban ring road, begun in the 1930s. Preston Center's multiple owners created an uncoordinated mixture of small shops and large stores centered on a rather dreary, two-level parking structure west of Preston Road. Modern renovation of several original buildings and the addition of tall office structures to the south and west have today softened the effects of the project's original lack of planning.

Two miles east of Preston Center stands Dallas' earliest example of the next phase of suburban retailing, the enclosed shopping mall. This is **NorthPark Center★** (Northwest Highway and Central Expressway; 1965 and later; Omniplan, Harrell & Hamilton, architects), whose single developer spared no expense to create a handsomely landscaped and meticulously designed indoor village with four department stores and one hundred thirty individual shops. Despite many later imitators, NorthPark still ranks among the city's most popular and profitable retail centers.

POST-1950 SUBURBS

Between Dallas' two principal loop highways—Northwest Highway (Loop 12) and the Lyndon Johnson or "LBJ" Freeway (Interstate 635)—Preston Road traverses a series of carefully maintained middle-class suburbs dominated by builders' versions of the Ranch and Contemporary style houses that were popular during the 1950s and 1960s. Along this stretch the most affluent core of development shifted about a

mile westward to **Inwood Road** and **Strait Lane**, around which are clustered numerous **multi-acre estates★**

The region's northward growth since about 1970 has moved beyond the LBJ Freeway to "Far North Dallas," where only a narrow peninsula of land on either side of Preston Road has been annexed into the City of Dallas proper. This is surrounded, in clockwise order, by the booming suburban towns of Farmer's Branch, Addison, Carrollton, Plano, and Richardson. An upscale sample of the Neoeclectic houses that dominate the area's recent growth can be seen in the affluent **Preston Trail** (Preston Trail Dr.; 1967 and later) and **Bent Tree** (Westgrove Dr.; 1972 and later) developments, whose houses surround the landscaped golf course fairways.

Far North Dallas is also the site of much of the city's outlying office development. Low-, mid-, and high-rise office buildings now line much of the LBJ Freeway as well as Dallas Parkway, a major new commercial thoroughfare that extends northward from LBJ parallel to, but about a mile west of, Preston Road (see "Other Destinations"). At the crowded intersection of LBJ and Dallas Parkway is North Dallas' most ambitious mixed-use project, the **Dallas Galleria★** (Dallas Parkway and LBJ Freeway; 1982; HOK, St.Louis, architects), whose buildings include a hotel, two office towers, and four major department stores, all centered on a handsome three-story atrium lined with more than one hundred fifty attractive shops and restaurants.

HIGHLAND PARK VILLAGE *Graceful Spanish Eclectic architecture unifies one of the nation's first suburban shopping centers.*

HOURS AND CHARGES

Meadows Museum: 692-2516. Mon-Sat, 10 am to 5 pm; Sun, 1 pm to 5 pm. Admission free. Call for parking information.

NorthPark Center: 363-7441. Mall open daily, 6 am to 9:30 pm. Shops open Mon-Sat, 10 am to 9 pm; Sun, noon to 6 pm. Restaurants and snack bars.

Dallas Galleria: 702-7100. Mall open daily, 6 am to 9:30 pm. Shops open Mon-Fri, 10 am to 9 pm; Sat, 10 am to 7 pm; Sun, noon to 6 pm. Restaurants and snack bars.

Related Shopping, Dining, and Entertainment (SiDE) Areas: Knox-Henderson; Highland Park Village; Lovers Lane; Snider Plaza; NorthPark; Galleria.

[Map of Dallas/North Dallas area showing: PLANO, COLLIN CO., DALLAS CO., BENT TREE, PRESTON TRAIL, WEST GROVE DR., PRESTON TRAIL DR., RICHARDSON, ADDISON, BELT LINE RD., COIT RD., FARMERS BRANCH, DALLAS GALLERIA, LYNDON B. JOHNSON FRWY., 635, 75, FOREST LN., MIDWAY RD., INWOOD RD., HILLCREST RD., PRESTON RD., ROYAL LN., CENTRAL EXPRESSWAY, WALNUT HILL LN., STRAIT LN., ESTATE AREA, PARK LN., NORTHPARK CENTER, LOOP 12, DOUGLAS AVE., NORTHWEST HWY., PRESTON CENTER, LOVERS LN., UNIVERSITY PARK, DALLAS NORTH TOLLWAY, SOUTHERN METHODIST UNIVERSITY, DALLAS HALL, MEADOWS MUSEUM, HIGHLAND PARK VILLAGE, HIGHLAND PARK, MOCKINGBIRD LN., LEMMON AVE., LAKESIDE DR., WYCLIFF AVE., OAK LAWN AVE., TURTLE CREEK BLVD., HARRY HINES BLVD., TOLL FWY., FITZHUGH AVE., SUGGESTED DRIVE, See Uptown, 0 ½ 1 mi.]

Other Destinations

Among the important attractions dispersed in Dallas' suburbs are an outstanding zoo, a Victorian farming museum, the popular Six Flags amusement park, and Southfork Ranch, home of the fictional television villain J. R. Ewing.

SUBURBAN SKYSCRAPERS *Lincoln Center is typical of several "mini-downtowns" scattered along the city's northern freeway network.*

This final section treats several important attractions that are widely scattered throughout suburban Dallas, rather than being concentrated in one of the ten principal Sightseeing Districts discussed on the preceding pages.

OAK CLIFF

Founded in 1887 as Dallas' sister city on the opposite bank of the wide Trinity River floodplain, Oak Cliff had the advantage of rugged, forested topography where wooded hillsides could be developed into scenic homesites. By 1903, when it was annexed to become a part of Dallas, Oak Cliff had become a thriving residential community of about four thousand inhabitants. Today the district is still a quiet residential enclave separated from the rest of the city by a series of long Trinity River bridges or "viaducts."

Oak Cliff's principal visitor attraction is the fifty-acre **Dallas Zoo★★** (621 East Clarendon Drive), established in 1912 on a heavily wooded creekside tract. Today the Zoo boasts one of the region's outstanding animal collections with over two thousand varieties of birds, reptiles, and mammals. Included are many extremely rare species, among them black rhinos, okapis, bongo antelopes, pygmy geese, and Congo peacocks. A special treat is the **Bird and Reptile House★★**, which features free-flying birds in an exotic tropical rain forest, and "The Other Side," a behind-the-scenes look at reptile care. Long a leader in the difficult art of breeding exotic animals in captivity, the Zoo has recently embarked on an ambitious fifty-five-acre expansion plan that will ultimately replace most of its well-tended cages with open-air habitat displays. The first phase, "The Wilds of Africa," is scheduled to open in 1989.

FREEWAY SKYSCRAPERS

As in other booming Sunbelt cities, Dallas' expansion since the 1960s has been accompanied by scattered clusters of outlying office towers. Most of these are concentrated along the city's northern freeway network, where several "mini-downtowns" provide a fascinating survey of recent fashions in the design of tall buildings.

The most ambitious of these skyscraper clusters are mixed-use developments that include not only office buildings, but also hotels and shopping centers. **NorthPark Center** (Central Expressway and Northwest Highway; 1965 and later), for example, now includes several striking office towers that have been added across the freeway from the highly successful North-Park Shopping Center, the city's first enclosed mall which opened in 1965 (see "North Dallas" and "NorthPark SiDE Area"). Further north, near the intersection of Central Expressway and the LBJ Freeway, is **ParkCentral** (LBJ Freeway and Coit Road; 1972 and later), a carefully planned, six-hundred-acre, development with two large hotels, a medical center, and multiple office towers.

Westward on the LBJ Freeway, at the northwest quadrant of the Dallas North Tollway intersection, stand the cylinder-crowned pink towers of the **Dallas Galleria★** (1982; HOK, St. Louis, architects), whose high-rise hotel and office buildings surround one of the city's largest and most elaborate shopping malls (see "North Dallas" and "Galleria SiDE Area"). The Galleria, and the striking, mirrored glass buildings of **Lincoln Center** (1983; HKS, Dallas, architects) across the freeway, are the gateways to an exotic collection of new office towers and shopping centers that stretch for several miles northward along **Dallas North Tollway**. Still farther west, in the satellite town of Irving, is the region's largest "new downtown," built as a part of the massive Las Colinas development (see below).

PLANO

Located about fifteen miles from downtown as Dallas' most northerly suburb, Plano has blossomed from a small country town into a city of more than 110,000 inhabitants in the short period since 1960. Today it is the home of two important visitor attractions. One of these, Heritage Farmstead, is little known even to area residents. The other, Southfork Ranch, is familiar to millions of television viewers as the seat of oilman-villain J. R. Ewing and his intriguing family.

Heritage Farmstead★★ (15th and Pitman sts., about one-half mi. west of U.S. Hwy 75 Exit 29) provides a fascinating glimpse of early farm life on the fertile Blackland Prairies of North Texas, lands whose enormous cotton production was the original source of Dallas' wealth. Centered on a large and carefully restored 1891 farmhouse, complete with original

BABY GOLIATH HERONS *These exotic African birds are among the many rare species successfully bred at the Dallas Zoo.*

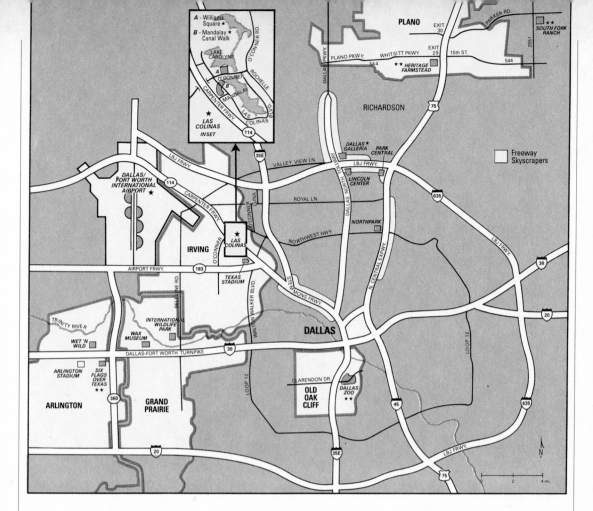

furnishings and fixtures, the museum complex also includes a smokehouse, rootcellar, blacksmith shop, chicken houses, and other typical farm outbuildings.

Just beyond the eastern city limits of Plano is **Southfork Ranch★★** (take Parker Road 6 mi. east from U.S. Hwy. 75 Exit 30, then south one-half mile on FM 2551), formerly a family-run stock farm and today an entertainment complex and monument to the long popularity of the television series *Dallas*, which premiered in 1978. The principal attractions at Southfork are the familiar Neoclassical **ranchhouse**, built in 1970 and today used by the show's producers mostly for outdoor sequences, and a fascinating real-life **oil drilling rig★★**, which is one of the world's largest.

IRVING

Like Plano to the north, the suburban town of Irving, which begins about eight miles northwest of downtown Dallas, has exploded from 2,600 inhabitants in 1950 to a present population of more than 110,000. Along the young city's eastern boundary are two important attractions—Texas Stadium, home of the Dallas Cowboys football team, and Las Colinas, the area's most ambitious and successful "new town." Occupying much of westernmost Irving is the Dallas/Fort Worth International Airport, which was the nation's largest and most up-to-the-minute air terminal when it opened in 1973.

The **Las Colinas Urban Center★** (State Hwy. 114 and O'Connor Blvd.; 1977 and later) is the heart of a twelve thousand-acre "new town" planned and developed by the Dallas-based Southland Life Insurance Company. The huge complex includes not only several separate office and shopping centers, but also a country club, equestrian center, movie production studios, and residential neighborhoods with houses and apartments of varying size and price. Highlight of the Urban Center is the **Mandalay Canal★** (O'Connor and Las Colinas blvds.; 1978), a shop-lined, Venice-inspired waterway complete with red tile roofs, bell towers, and water-taxi rides. Nearby **Williams Square** (4950 O'Connor Blvd.) is dominated by a magnificent

SOUTHFORK RANCH *This is a familiar sight to millions of fans of the* Dallas *television series.*

MINIATURE VENICE *The shop-lined Mandalay Canal of Las Colinas features Venetian water-taxi rides.*

bronze sculpture★ of nine larger-than-life wild mustangs galloping across a granite-bottomed stream. This is the work of the distinguished Nairobi, Kenya, wildlife sculptor Robert Glen (b. 1940).

West of Las Colinas, astride the Dallas-Tarrant County line, is the enormous **Dallas/Fort Worth (DFW) International Airport★** (entrances on State Highways 114 and 183; HOK, St. Louis, and Brodsky, Hopf & Adler, New York, architects), which opened in 1973 after many years of planning and construction. One of the world's largest and busiest, the airport has become a major air freight center and is also a favorite of pilots because of its parallel, oversized runways each having long and unobstructed approach paths. It receives less enthusiastic reviews from travelers with inter-terminal connecting flights.

Designed with a multiple series of sprawling, half-circular passenger terminals that permit local residents to park near their departure gates, pedestrian connections between the widely separated buildings are provided by "Airtrans", a system of computer-controlled, rubber-tired vehicles traveling on winding trackways. Slow and breakdown prone, this costly but inefficient system has given the airport the nation's longest inter-terminal transfer times. For those with time to spare, however, the wide-windowed vehicles provide a scenic tour of the sprawling airport facility as the cars wander from building to building like miniature roller-coasters.

Massive **Texas Stadium** (2401 E. Airport Frwy.; 1971; A. Warren Morey, Dallas, architect), surrounded by 130 acres of parking lots, occupies a triangular freeway intersection in eastern Irving. This 64,000-seat, partially enclosed facility was built specifically to provide optimum viewing conditions for football games and is the familiar home of the Dallas Cowboys. It is also used for college and high school football and for other sporting and entertainment events.

MID-CITIES

Situated squarely between Dallas and Fort Worth, the suburban towns of Grand Prairie, mostly in Dallas County, and Arlington, in adjacent Tarrant County, have also experienced explosive growth over the past few decades and are today known informally as the "Mid-Cities." Because of their intermediate position, they have long been a favored location for regional entertainment facilities.

In 1961 Arlington was chosen as the site for an elaborate, Disneyland-like amusement park called **Six Flags Over Texas★★** (Interstate Hwy. 30 at Hwy. 360 Exit; Randall Duell, Los Angeles, architect), which quickly became a principal regional attraction. "Six Flags," as it is universally abbreviated, was the first successful clone of Walt Disney's pioneering California venture, that had opened in Anaheim only six years earlier to begin the era of "theme parks." Six Flags' success soon led to a chain of related parks with locations in Houston, St. Louis, Atlanta, and central New Jersey.

Six Flags was originally organized into distinctive subunits, each representing one of Texas' six national identities — Spain, France, Mexico, the Republic of Texas, the Confederacy and the United States. Today this unifying "theme" has become less recognizable as the grounds have expanded and as their emphasis has shifted toward revenue-producing vending machines and video games. The park's most popular attractions are its almost two dozen thrill rides, which include a 200-foot parachute drop, the "Texas Cliff Hanger"; a double-loop roller coaster, the "Shock Wave"; and a miniature steam train. The park also features regular shows and concerts, as well as numerous food outlets of various sorts.

Building on the popularity of Six Flags, several other amusement facilities have located along Interstate Highway 30 as it traverses the Mid-Cities. Across from Six Flags is **Wet 'n Wild** (1800 E. Lamar Blvd. at the Hwy. 360 Exit from I-30), one of a popular chain of summertime water parks. This location features forty-seven acres of elaborate swimming pools, water slides, and rides on rafts or surf boards. Four miles east of Six Flags, in the town of Grand Prairie, are two additional attractions. The **International Wildlife Park** (601 Wildlife Pkwy., 1 mi. north of I-30 off of Beltline Rd.) is a sort of drive-through, three-hundred-acre zoo with an emphasis on herds of African hoofed animals, among them handsome giraffes and fierce-looking rhinos. Many of the animals will come very close to your car, hoping to be fed from the buckets of food available as you enter.

Nearby is the **Wax Museum of the Southwest** (601 E. Safari Pkwy. at the Beltline Rd. Exit from I-30), which features hundreds of life-like figures of famous outlaws, movie stars, war heroes, and world leaders. Also included is an optional "Theatre of Horrors," whose grisly displays are not recommended for children or the faint-of-heart.

HOURS AND CHARGES

Dallas Zoo: 946-5154. Daily, 9 am to 5 pm. Adults, $2; ages 6 to 11, $1.25. Weekday parking free; Sat, Sun, and holiday parking, $2. Snack bar.

Heritage Farmstead: 424-7874. Tours Wed-Fri, 10 am to 4 pm; Sun, 1 pm to 4 pm; closed holiday seasons. Adults, $3; ages 4 to 18, $2. Last tickets sold one hour before closing. Tour duration about one hour.

Southfork Ranch: 442-6536. Daily 9 am to 5 pm. Admission to ranch grounds, adults, $4.95; ages 4 to 12, $2.95. Ranchhouse tour, $2 extra (all ages); duration 15 minutes. Oil rig tour, $2 extra (all ages); duration 15 minutes. Snack bar.

Texas Stadium: 438-7676. Tours Mon-Fri, 10 am and 2 pm; Sat and Sun, 11 am, 12: 30 pm, and 2 pm. Tour duration 30-45 minutes. Adults, $3; ages infant to 12, $1.50.

Six Flags Over Texas: 640-8900 (metro). Open June through August, Sun-Thurs, 10 am to 8 pm; Fri and Sat, 10 am to midnight. From mid-March through May and from September through early November, open weekends and school holidays only, generally 10 am to 8 pm but hours may vary. Admission covers all rides and most shows, over 48" tall, $15.95 (2-day ticket, $18.95); age 2 to 48" tall, $9.95. Parking fee. Snack bars and restaurants.

Wet 'n Wild: 265-3013 (metro). Mid-June through late August, daily, 10 am to 9 pm. May through mid-June and late August through September, weekends only, 10 am to 6 pm. Adults, $12.50; ages 3 to 12, $10.50. Snack bars.

International Wildlife Park: 263-2201 (metro). Open daily, 9: 30 am to 3: 30 pm (weather permitting). Charge for ages 3 to adult varies from $5.95 to $9.95, depending on season and whether or not adjacent entertainment village is open.

Wax Museum of the Southwest: 263-2391 (metro). Mon-Fri, 10 am to 5 pm; Sat-Sun, 10 am to 6 pm. Adults, $5.95; ages 4 to 12, $4.95. Last tickets sold one hour before closing. Snack bar.

THE FLUME *Summer visitors delight in this splashy log ride at Six Flags.*

FORT WORTH

Fort Worth, the city "where the West begins," first flourished as a railroad-based center for processing and shipping raw materials—principally cattle, oil, and grain—produced over a vast area of semiarid western Texas. Since the 1940s, aircraft production and light manufacturing have largely replaced these earlier sources of the city's prosperity.

Although Fort Worth shares an airport and an informal nickname ("the Metroplex") with Dallas, its larger neighbor thirty miles east, the two cities differ in background, character, and even physical appearance. Both were obscure frontier villages until the arrival of railroads in the 1870s. Dallas then became the critical crossing point of the state's first intercontinental lines and flourished as the gateway for importing a flood of manufactured goods from the North and East. Fort Worth's fortunes, in contrast, lay to the West. By 1882 the town was the junction point for two railroads (Texas and Pacific; Fort Worth and Denver City) building across hundreds of miles of undeveloped West Texas plains to link the state with California and Colorado. Fort Worth soon became the eastern terminus for raw materials produced by an enormous western hinterland, at first mostly cattle joined after 1910 by oil and grain.

COWTOWN

Founded in 1849 as one of a line of small military outposts defending Texas' Indian frontier, the city began its long history as a livestock center with the great cattle drives that supplied wild Texas beef to the war-starved nation following the Civil War. From 1866 until the late 1870s, when expanding agriculture and fenced pastures forced the drivers to move a hundred miles westward, the town was an important stopover on the principal cattle trail leading northward to railroad-loading points in distant Kansas.

Delayed just beyond Dallas by the financial panic of 1873, Fort Worth's first railroad, the Texas and Pacific, arrived in 1876. The rail line, serving local cotton farmers and stockmen, brought instant prosperity and growth to the frontier village, yet it did not immediately make Fort Worth the livestock capital of the Southwest as local boosters had hoped. Instead, this distinction was to wait another twenty-five years, when new developments would change the nature of the nation's beef marketing.

REFRIGERATED MEAT

Prior to the 1880s artificial refrigeration was a rare luxury, and perishable fresh beef, pork, and mutton were processed by thousands of local slaughterhouses for immediate and nearby consumption. On the other hand, the living raw materials—cattle, hogs, and sheep—could be moved long distances on foot or in cage-like railroad cars.

By the early 1880s refrigerated railroad cars for shipping fresh meat had been perfected, yet their widespread use was delayed for twenty more years by opposition from the nation's network of local slaughterhouses acting in concert with the railroads themselves, which preferred to haul the heavier and bulkier live animals. Only at the turn of the century did vast central packinghouses—concentrated in Chicago, Kansas City, and a handful of other midwestern cities—finally begin to replace local slaughterhouses as the principal source of the nation's fresh meat.

MEAT-PACKING BOOM

In 1901 the two largest Chicago meatpackers, Swift and Armour, began searching for a Texas branch location to take advantage of the state's by then much improved beef herds. Fort Worth, the junction point of the two major rail lines serving the West Texas ranch country, was the logical choice. Their resolve strengthened by a $100,000 local bonus, the two companies in 1902 completed twin packing plants adjacent to Fort Worth's earlier North Side stockyards. Both the plants and the stockyards were soon enlarged, as much of the Southwest's enormous output of livestock converged on Fort Worth for central processing, rather than being shipped directly to countless local slaughterhouses.

In 1902 about 250,000 animals passed through the Fort Worth stockyards; by 1910 the number had increased tenfold, to 2.5 million, as the city became the nation's fourth-largest livestock marketing center, led only by Chicago, Kansas City, and Omaha. This enormous new industry brought Fort Worth a second great population surge, comparable to the railroad boom of the 1880s. The 27,000 inhabitants of 1900 almost tripled to 73,000 by 1910, making the city the state's fourth largest behind San Antonio (97,000), Dallas (92,000), and Houston (79,000), a position it retained until displaced to fifth place by Corpus Christi in 1970.

Meat-packing was to remain a principal Fort Worth industry into the 1960s. By then a post-World War II trend back to smaller and more efficient packing facilities, served by fast truck transport of both livestock and refrigerated meat, had made the giant railroad-based Fort Worth plants obsolete.

OIL TOWN

Fort Worth's historic ties to the oil industry are much more direct than those of nearby Dallas. In 1911 a major new field was discovered at Electra, a small cattle-shipping depot on the Fort Worth and Denver Railroad near Wichita Falls, 120 miles northwest of the city. Soon pipelines were bringing much of this crude oil to newly constructed refineries at Fort Worth, which had the advantage of extensive rail connections for shipping out tank cars filled with kerosene, gasoline, boiler fuel, and other refined products.

Still stronger ties developed from two major discoveries made in 1917 and 1918, when oil prices were particularly high because of the demands of World War I. The

LIVESTOCK CAPITAL *Fort Worth's stockyards were long the bustling nerve center of the Southwestern cattle industry.*

first was a 2,200-barrel-a-day giant drilled at Burkburnett, also near Wichita Falls. This led to a frantic boom that provided major new reserves for the Fort Worth refineries. The following year an entire new oil province was opened when the Texas and Pacific Coal Company, a subsidiary of the T&P Railroad, brought in a 1,700-barrel-a-day gusher at Ranger, a tiny village on the railroad's main line ninety miles west of Fort Worth. As the nearest town of any size, Fort Worth became the focus of the frenzied Ranger activity as oil field supplies poured in and speculators jammed the city's overflowing hotels. Soon pipelines from the Ranger area joined those from the Wichita Falls region to make Fort Worth the booming hub of the North Texas oil industry, a position it retained through the 1920s and 1930s.

GRAIN CAPITAL

Paralleling Fort Worth's rapid rise as an oil center was a lesser-known boom that made the city the principal grain terminal of the southern United States.

A fundamental change in the geography of the nation's enormous wheat crop took place during the decade from 1910 to 1920. Spurred by the demands of World War I, farmers planted new strains of cold- and drought-resistant "Turkey" wheat on thousands of formerly unproductive acres of semiarid plains. These prolific new varieties were particularly adapted to the climate of the belt stretching from western Oklahoma and the Texas Panhandle through western Kansas and Nebraska. By the early 1920s, much of the nation's wheat was being grown in this new agricultural province.

As with the shipping of petroleum products a decade earlier, Fort Worth's excellent rail connections made it a natural terminal for the distribution of much of the newly developed West Texas and Oklahoma grain crop. Soon enormous ele-

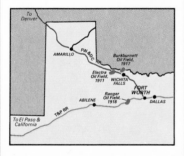

RAILROAD-LINKS TO THE WEST The Texas and Pacific (T&P) and Fort Worth and Denver City (FW&DC) lines began building westward from Fort Worth in the early 1880s to link North Texas with California and Colorado; in the process they opened a vast area of West Texas to settlement and development. Between 1910 and 1920, major oil discoveries near the lines at Wichita Falls and Ranger made Forth Worth an important petroleum refining and distribution center.

WORLD WAR II ASSEMBLY LINE The Consolidated Vultee Plant, now General Dynamics, produced over three thousand of these B-24 "Liberator" bombers between 1941 and 1945.

vators and milling complexes punctuated the skyline as the city became the nation's fourth-largest terminal grain market, a position it still holds today.

AVIATION CENTER

Although Fort Worth remains one of the nation's principal grain terminals, by 1940 the declining production from the old North Texas oil fields and giant new discoveries in far West Texas had combined to greatly reduce the city's importance as a petroleum center. Yet the outbreak of World War II was to replace oil with a new source of prosperity—aircraft manufacturing—that remains of primary importance today.

In 1940 the War Department established a policy of dispersing new industry beyond the traditional manufacturing belt of the Northeast in order to tap new labor supplies and also to make the plants less vulnerable to enemy bombers. Fort Worth became a major beneficiary of this program in 1941 when Consolidated Vultee Aircraft Company (later Convair, now General Dynamics) built an enormous bomber plant on a fifteen-hundred-acre site northwest of town. In 1942 the Fort Worth Army Air Field was established next to the plant, and the two facilities have played a major role in the nation's defense strategies ever since.

In 1947 Convair was awarded the contract to build the B-36 bomber, the nation's first intercontinental nuclear-armed weapon. At the same time the adjacent airfield, renamed Carswell Air Force Base, became one of the principal bases for the Strategic Air Command's nuclear strike force. Today, after numerous changes in aircraft design, Carswell and the General Dynamics plant remain a major component of military defense strategy.

Fort Worth's importance as an aviation center was further enhanced in 1951 when the Bell Helicopter Company relocated

from Buffalo, New York, to the Fort Worth suburban town of Hurst. Now the nation's largest manufacturer of both military and civilian helicopters, Bell's twelve-hundred-acre factory has become a major Fort Worth employer.

SUNBELT ERA

Aircraft production and new light industry were responsible for much of Fort Worth's mid-century growth as the 1940 population of 178,000 jumped to 279,000 in 1950 and to 356,000 by 1960. Since 1960, the city's expansion has slowed, with 385,000 inhabitants recorded in 1980. Some dramatic recent growth has taken place in adjacent suburban towns, particularly Arlington to the east, but Fort Worth has so far missed the explosive Sunbelt expansion seen in such cities as Houston, Dallas, or Phoenix. Though Fort Worth has its share of modern skyscrapers, freeways, and sprawling suburbs, much of the city still retains the look and feel of a less frantic past, a spirit that both residents and visitors regard as a delightful contrast to hectic Dallas only thirty miles away.

FORT WORTH SIGHTSEEING, AN OVERVIEW

Six distinctive Sightseeing Districts, which combine to include most of the city's visitor attractions, are summarized on the map inside the back cover and treated in detail on the following pages.

The original townsite and traditional heart of the city make up much of the modern **Financial Core**, where today sleek glass skyscrapers rub elbows with quaint Victorian storefronts and handsome vintage office towers from the 1910s and 1920s. Adjoining the Financial Core on the southeast is the **Civic District**, a once-decaying industrial area that has been transformed by a series of public improvements that began in the early 1930s and culminated in 1976 with the spectacular Water Gardens Park.

Beyond the Trinity River bluffs that bound the downtown area on the north are the **Stockyards and North Side**, traditional home of Fort Worth industry and site of the Stockyards Historic District, a nationally important collection of early livestock exhibition halls, marketing offices, holding pens, shipping facilities, and packinghouses. Across the Trinity lowlands to the west of downtown is the **Cultural District**, where four important public museums combine with performance halls, exhibition buildings, and public gardens to create one of the region's most impressive attractions.

Much of Fort Worth's early residential growth was concentrated in the **Southside**, where many fine early houses still survive. Since the 1920s the focus of housing development has been the **Westside**, which today also includes much of the city's upscale suburban shopping.

THREE-STAR HIGHLIGHTS

Visitors with limited time should not miss the city's seven "three-star" attractions:

1. In the Financial Core is the imposing **Tarrant County Courthouse**, a late Victorian classic perched near the blufftop site of the military camp for which the city was named.

2. Also in the Financial Core is **Sundance Square**, a charming restoration of several blocks of turn-of-the-century commercial buildings.

3. Centerpiece of the Civic District is **Water Gardens Park**, a multi-acre assemblage of delightful pools, fountains, and landscaping that opened in 1976 to become an instant favorite.

4. About two miles north of downtown is the **Fort Worth Stockyards Historic District**. Its many early structures, centered around the handsome **Livestock Exchange Building**, were long the bustling heart of "Cowtown" and today house a Western-oriented entertainment complex.

THREE STAR ATTRACTIONS
A - Tarrant County Courthouse
B - Sundance Square
C - Water Gardens Park
D - Stockyards Historic District
    & Livestock Exchange Bldg.
    (Stockyards & Northside)
E - Kimbell Art Museum
F - Japanese Garden
G - River Crest

5. Crown jewel of the Cultural District is the internationally important **Kimbell Art Museum**, whose collections are showcased in a much-acclaimed masterpiece of modern architecture.

6. The exotic **Japanese Garden**, located at the opposite end of the Cultural District, provides a rare opportunity to sample the intimate pleasures of oriental landscaping.

7. In the Westside district is the grandest survivor of early Fort Worth residential neighborhoods. This is **River Crest**, where many Eclectic Era mansions cluster around the curving fairways of the River Crest County Club.

EXPLORING HISTORIC FORT WORTH

Important reminders of Fort Worth's long and colorful history occur in each of the six geographic districts discussed on the following pages. To aid visitors wishing to get a feel for the city as it appeared in earlier times, the tables on the right list Fort Worth's most important landmarks in chronologic order. Each treats a principal era of the city's history:

Victorian Town: Relatively few structures survive from the period between the arrival of the first railroad in 1876 to the turn of the century, an interval when the town grew from a few hundred to over 26,000 inhabitants.

Early Industrial City: Many landmarks remain from the important period between 1900 and 1930, when the new meatpacking industries and the North Texas oil boom multiplied the city's population sixfold to 163,000.

Depression and World War II Era: As in the rest of the nation, building and expansion in Fort Worth slowed to a crawl during this period. Many important landmarks were built as government-sponsored unemployment relief projects.

Modern Era: Fort Worth's most distinguished recent landmarks are its extraordinary group of public museums and gardens added to the Cultural District since 1954.

VICTORIAN TOWN 1876–1900

FINANCIAL CORE	
County Courthouse***	1895
Land Title Block**	1889
Sundance Square***	1890's & later
CIVIC DISTRICT	
St. Ignatius Academy**	1889
St. Patrick's Cathedral*	1892
SOUTHSIDE	
Eddleman-McFarland House**	1898
Log Cabin Village* (museum village)	1850–1900
Pollock-Capps House*	1898
WESTSIDE	
Bryce House**	1893

EARLY INDUSTRIAL CITY 1900–1930

FINANCIAL CORE			
Blackstone Hotel*	1929	Marine Creek Bridge*	1910
Burk Burnett Bldg.**	1914	North Side Coliseum**	1908
Criminal Justice Bldg.*	1917	Stockyards Hist. Dist.***	1902 & later
Fire Station No. 1*	1907	Swift & Co. Offices**	1902
First Christian Church*	1914	Texas Electric Plant*	1922 & later
Neil Anderson Bldg.*	1921	Thannisch Block**	1907 & later
Sinclair Bldg.*	1929	Transcontinental Oil Refinery**	1919 & later
Texas Hotel*	1921	**SOUTHSIDE**	
Waggoner Bldg.**	1919	Elizabeth Ave. Hist. Dist.** (houses)	1911–1920
CIVIC DISTRICT		Forest Park Towers*	1917
Flatiron Bldg.**	1907	Kimbell & Lone Star Elevators**	1924 & later
Santa Fe Depot**	1900	Thistle Hill** (house)	1903
STOCKYARDS & NORTH SIDE		**WESTSIDE**	
Exchange Ave. Stairs*	1902	Arlington Heights* (houses)	1920s
Horse & Mule Barns*	1911	River Crest*** (houses)	1900–1930
Livestock Exchange Bldg.***	1902		

DEPRESSION AND WORLD WAR II ERA 1930–1945

CIVIC DISTRICT	
City Hall*	1938
Main Post Office*	1933
T & P Freight Terminal**	1931
T & P Passenger Terminal**	1931
STOCKYARDS & NORTH SIDE	
Cattle Exhibit Bldg.	1936
CULTURAL DISTRICT	
Botanic Garden**	1934 & later
Will Rogers Center*	1936
WESTSIDE	
General Dynamics Plant*	1941 & later
Westover Hills* (house)	1930s

MODERN ERA 1945–present

FINANCIAL CORE	
Worthington Hotel*	1981
CIVIC DISTRICT	
Convention Center*	1968
Water Gardens Park***	1976
CULTURAL DISTRICT	
Amon Carter Museum**	1961 & later
Casa Manana Theater*	1958
Japanese Garden***	1973
Kimbell Art Museum***	1972
Modern Art Museum*	1954 & later
Museum of Science*	1954 & later
WESTSIDE	
River Crest Country Club**	1985
Westover Hills** (houses)	1950s & later

Financial Core ★★

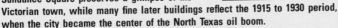

In spite of the modern skyscrapers that punctuate its skyline, downtown Fort Worth retains much of the character of earlier eras. Sundance Square preserves a glimpse of the Victorian town, while many fine later buildings reflect the 1915 to 1930 period, when the city became the center of the North Texas oil boom.

TARRANT COUNTY COURTHOUSE *This Victorian landmark stands near the site of the frontier military camp for which the city was named.*

The small 1849 military camp from which Fort Worth took its name was located here, on the Trinity River bluffs at the site now occupied by several county government buildings. The camp was abandoned only four years after its establishment because the line of frontier settlement, and the need for protection from hostile Comanches, had already shifted seventy miles westward. Settlers soon moved into the post's deserted log buildings, and the former parade ground became a public square and nucleus of the early village.

COURTHOUSE AREA

The present **Tarrant County Courthouse★★★** (100 East Weatherford St.; 1895; Gunn and Curtis, Kansas City, architects) is the third courthouse building to occupy the site. This is an unusually dramatic early Beaux Arts landmark, built of dark pink granite rather than the light limestone typical of the style, which towers majestically over the Trinity lowlands to the north. The building also provides an imposing focal point for brick-paved Main Street, the town's principal downtown axis that today stretches only a half-mile southward before reaching an equally dramatic termination at the circular arena of the city's 1968 Convention Center (see "Civic District").

Across the street from the Courthouse, a bronze plaque set in a large granite boulder on the grounds of the Beaux Arts

Criminal Justice Building★ (200 West Belknap St.; 1917; Sanguinet & Staats, Fort Worth, architects) commemorates the original military camp which occupied the site.

Along the river bluffs north of the Criminal Justice Building lies **Heritage Park**, completed as a 1976 Bicentennial project with walking trails and a small water garden. The park affords dramatic views of the industrial lowlands to the north (see "North Side").

TANDY CENTER; CITY CENTER

Fort Worth's Victorian commercial center stretched several blocks south of the Courthouse along Main Street and adjacent Commerce, Houston, and Throckmorton streets. During the first decades of this century the heart of downtown activity began shifting as new office buildings, stores, and hotels were constructed several blocks farther south. Downtown's early Courthouse district then began a slow slide toward obsolescence, which was abruptly arrested in the 1970s by a single ambitious revitalization project—the massive **Tandy Center** (200 Throckmorton St.; 1977; Growald Architects, Fort Worth).

The project was the brainchild of Fort Worth entrepreneur Charles David Tandy, (1918–1978), whose namesake corporation owns the Radio Shack electronics chain. The Center is a mixed-use complex containing not only two large office towers but also a department store, shops, restau-

rants, and a multistory central atrium complete with ice-skating rink. Connecting at right angles to the principal buildings is the striking **Worthington Hotel★** (200 Main St.; 1981; Paul Rudolph, New York, architect), an elegantly elongated mass of white concrete that extends two blocks eastward by cantilevering above Houston Street. A unique, privately owned subway system connects the entire Tandy complex to a fourteen-acre parking area on the banks of the Trinity a few blocks northwest.

Rising like a slightly irregular giant crystal across Main Street from the Worthington Hotel is the dark, glass-skinned mass of the **First City Bank Tower** (201 Main St.; 1982; Paul Rudolph, New York, architect), with an almost identical twin by the same architect, **City Center Tower II** (301 Commerce St.; 1984), located diagonally southeast on Commerce Street. Collectively called "City Center," these buildings are a project of Fort Worth's billionaire Bass brothers, who tastefully linked the strikingly modern skyscrapers to some of the city's oldest buildings—the quaint Victorian structures preserved in adjacent Sundance Square.

SUNDANCE SQUARE

Massive central-city revitalization projects such as Tandy Center and City Center normally apply the wrecking ball to older commercial buildings, no matter how picturesque. In a rare reversal of this pattern, the Bass brothers, developers of City Center, have chosen to restore several blocks of nineteenth- and early-twentieth-century structures, thus preserving a fascinating glimpse of early Fort Worth.

Called **Sundance Square★★★** in nostalgic reference to the Sundance Kid, a sort of western Robin Hood who once headquartered in the city, the restored complex centers on the 300 block of Main

MODERN LANDMARK *The dramatic Worthington Hotel stretches along two blocks of 2nd Street to link the Tandy Center and City Center projects.*

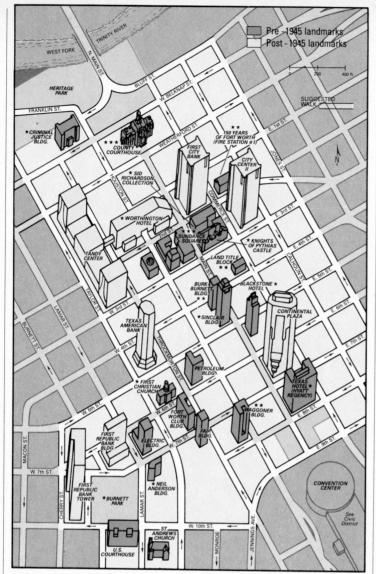

Pre-1945 landmarks
Post-1945 landmarks

SUGGESTED WALK

and adjacent Houston streets. Most of the original buildings in these blocks were modest one- or two-story structures that have been restored, remodeled, or completely rebuilt to create a delightful turn-of-the-century stage set occupied by modern shops, restaurants, nightclubs, and offices. Several buildings have trompe l'oeil facades, painted by distinguished New York muralist Richard Hass (b. 1936), that help to complete the streetscape. A still more dramatic **wall mural** (400 Main St.; 1982) by Hass commemorates the years of the Chisholm Trail cattle drives.

The most architecturally distinguished of the many Sundance Square buildings is the three-story **Knights of Pythias Castle★** (313 Main St.; 1901; Sanguinet & Staats, Fort Worth, architects). Designed to resemble a medieval guild hall, the fraternal order that occupied the building's upper floors also included a symbolic knight-in-armor that stands guard high on the front facade. A more modest building at 309 Main Street has been rebuilt to house the **Sid Richardson Collection of Western**

Art★. Oilman Richardson (1891-1959), great-uncle of the Bass brothers and founder of the family fortune, was an avid collector of works by Frederic Remington (1861-1909) and Charles Russell (1864-1926), pioneer illustrators of cowboys, Indians, and other western themes.

A block east of Sundance Square is historic **Fire Station No. 1★** (Commerce and Second sts.; 1907; Sanguinet & Staats, Fort Worth, architects), which has been renovated to house **150 Years of Fort Worth★★**, a small but fascinating permanent exhibit of objects and photographs summarizing the city's history.

One block south of Sundance Square stands Fort Worth's finest surviving commercial building from the last century, now lonesomely surrounded by parking lots. This is the **Land Title Block★★** (111 E. Fourth St.; 1889; Haggart & Sanguinet, Fort Worth, architects), a two-story Richardsonian Romanesque structure of red sandstone with terra cotta and colored tile trim and elaborate facade detailing of patterned brick.

PETROLEUM ERA LANDMARKS

South of Sundance Square, Main Street and the adjacent area to the west along 6th, 7th, and 8th streets are dominated by numerous fine buildings dating from the period between 1915 and 1930. During this short interval Fort Worth became the thriving center of a major oil boom as giant new fields were discovered along two of the city's principal rail lines—near Wichita Falls to the northwest and around Ranger to the west. Not surprisingly, most of the new buildings were office towers erected to house the numerous accountants, attorneys, engineers, geologists, landmen, and managers that served the burgeoning local petroleum industry.

The first two of these office towers were built at opposite ends of the rising new financial district. Curiously, both were owned by, and named for, Fort Worth cattlemen whose vast Wichita Falls-area ranches were the sites of oil discoveries that multiplied their already substantial fortunes. First came the twelve-story **Burk Burnett Building★★** (500 Main St.; 1914; Sanguinet & Staats, Fort Worth, architects), a handsomely detailed, tripartite structure that housed the offices of Samuel Burk Burnett (1849-1922). Burnett's 6666 ("Four-Sixes") Ranch lands were scattered over several West Texas counties and also covered 400,000 acres of Oklahoma's Comanche Indian Reservation, which Burnett leased from his friend, the famed warrior-chief Quanah Parker.

The Burk Burnett Building's larger but equally carefully detailed counterpart to the south is the twenty-story **W. T. Waggoner Building★★** (810 Houston St.; 1919; Sanguinet & Staats, Fort Worth, architects), built by the legendary cattleman William Thomas Waggoner (1852-1934). Waggoner's million-acre "Three D" Ranch west of Wichita Falls was the 1911 scene of North Texas' first major oil discovery. Both the Burk Burnett and Waggoner buildings were for many years the city's most pres-

ELEGANT BANKING *The lobby of the historic W. T. Waggoner Building has recently been restored to its original 1919 splendor.*

TRIPARTITE CLASSIC *The Burk Burnett Building, completed in 1914 as the city's first oil boom skyscraper, clearly shows the division into base, column, and crown that was the architectural fashion of the era.*

tigious office addresses, and both have recently been restored to their original splendor. The elaborately detailed **banking lobby**★★ of the Waggoner Building is a particularly spectacular example of careful historic restoration.

As the oil boom continued through the 1920s, these early skyscrapers were joined by an expanding group of neighbors, most having the fashionable Gothic-inspired Art Deco detailing of the period. Directly serving the oil industry were the **Petroleum Building** (611 Throckmorton St.; 1929; Wyatt C. Hedrick, Fort Worth, architect), **Fair Building**, now the Commerce Building (307 W. 7th St.; 1930; Wyatt C. Hedrick, Fort Worth, architect), and the **Sinclair Building**★ (106 W. 5th St.; 1929; Wiley G. Clarkson, Fort Worth, architect). The Sinclair Building sports fashionable, New York-inspired stepped walls on its upper floors and served as the southwestern headquarters of a major national oil company.

Along with these office towers, the oil boom also produced two surviving landmark hotels, the Renaissance-inspired **Texas Hotel**★ (815 Main St.; 1921; Sanguinet & Staats, Fort Worth, architects), recently remodeled to become an elegant addition to the Hyatt Regency chain, and the **Blackstone Hotel**★ (601 Main St.; 1929; Mauran, Russell & Crowell, Kansas City, architects), a handsome, stepped-wall Art Deco tower that now stands vacant, awaiting restoration. Nearby is the massive, Renaissance-detailed **Fort Worth**

Club Building (306 W. 7th St.; 1925; Wyatt C. Hedrick, Fort Worth, architect), which not only housed the dining and guest rooms of the city's most exclusive downtown club but also contained commercial offices and ground-floor retail space, the latter now largely obscured by an unsympathetic modern facade.

North of the Fort Worth Club stands the grandest surviving Financial Core church, the Neoclassical **First Christian Church**★ (612 Throckmorton St.; Van Slyke & Woodruff, architects), which was erected in 1914 to house the city's oldest congregation, founded in 1855.

BURNETT PARK

At the southwestern corner of the Financial Core is three-acre **Burnett Park**★, a turn-of-the-century gift to the city by cattleman Samuel Burk Burnett (see above). Recently rebuilt with a grid of concrete walkways separated by small patches of grass and moving water, the park is surrounded by handsome buildings that provide a fascinating panorama of contrasting architectural styles.

Soaring on the west is the forty-story, International style **First RepublicBank Tower** (801 Cherry St.; 1983; Sikes Jennings Kelly, Houston, architects), and to the north is an earlier International style tower, the **First RepublicBank Building** (500 W. 7th St.; 1960; Skidmore, Owings and Merrill, New York, architects). This building's park-side plaza features massive granite sculptures by the Japanese-American master Isamu Noguchi (b. 1904).

Clockwise from the First Republic Building rise the Art Deco **Electric Building**, now the 410 W. 7th Building (1930; Wyatt C. Hedrick, Fort Worth, architect), whose facade ornamentation includes symbolic hands grasping lightning bolts; the Classically inspired **Neil P. Anderson Building**★ (411 W. 7th St.; 1921; Sanguinet & Staats, Fort Worth, architects), which once housed the city's Grain and Cotton Exchanges and whose gracefully curved facade is crowned by four pairs of giant Greek urns; the Gothic Revival **Saint Andrews Episcopal Church** (901 Lamar St.; 1912; Sanguinet & Staats, Fort Worth, architects); and dominating the park's south side, the Art Moderne mass of the United States Courthouse built in 1933 (see "Civic District").

HOURS AND CHARGES

Tarrant County Courthouse: (817) 334-1111. Mon-Fri, 8 am to 4:30 pm. Admission free.

Tandy Center: (817) 390-3720. Mall open daily, 10 am to 10 pm. Shops open Mon-Sat, 10 am to 6 pm. Restaurants and snack bars.

Sid Richardson Collection of Western Art: (817) 332-6554. Tues-Fri, 10 am to 5 pm; Sat, 11 am to 6 pm; Sun, 1 pm to 5 pm. Admission free.

Fire Station No. 1 (150 Years of Fort Worth): (817) 732-1631. Daily, 9 am to 7 pm. Admission free.

W. T. Waggoner Building: (817) 877-3711. Lobby open Mon-Fri, 9 am to 5 pm.

Related Shopping, Dining, and Entertainment (SiDE) Area: Sundance Square.

OLD AND NEW *City Center's twin towers rise behind a part of historic Sundance Square. On the right a knight-in-armor stands guard above the Knights of Pythias Castle.*

Civic District *

Numerous public improvements have revitalized an earlier, railroad-based, industrial area at downtown's south side. These include several large government buildings, a massive Convention Center, and the spectacular Water Gardens Park.

Fort Worth's original townsite, bounded on three sides by steep bluffs above the sinuous Trinity River, was ideal for a military post but created difficulties for early railroads building through the frontier village. When the east-west Texas and Pacific line, the first to arrive, built from Dallas in 1876, it passed about a mile south of the courthouse and town center to avoid the Trinity bluffs. When the first north-south lines arrived in the 1880s, they built about a half-mile east of town to take advantage of the only gently sloping hillside descending into the Trinity valley. Soon railside districts of machine shops, warehouses, and small factories sprang up to border the town on the south and east. This early industrial district had decayed into an urban slum by the 1920s but it was revitalized by a series of dramatic civic improvements that began in the 1930s and continued through the 1970s.

RAILSIDE LANDMARKS

Three historic terminal buildings survive today as reminders of the central role of railroads in Fort Worth's growth. Oldest is the **Santa Fe Depot**★★ (1601 Jones St.; architect unknown), completed in 1900 to serve passengers on one of the principal north-south lines. The building compensates for its modest size with a dramatic Renaissance-inspired exterior of red brick accented by an exuberance of stripes, corner quoins, window surrounds, and other details in contrasting white limestone. The terminal later became the "Union Depot," serving the passenger trains of several of the city's north-south rail lines. Still in use

as Fort Worth's Amtrak passenger terminal, serving only six trains per week, the building's interior is now a shabby ghost of its early grandeur.

The Texas and Pacific line, linking North Texas with West Texas and California, headquartered in Fort Worth and became the town's dominant railroad. This fact is graphically expressed by the T&P's massive Art Deco terminal and office buildings, which define downtown's southern boundary and are among the city's most impressive industrial monuments. These were completed in 1931 as a part of an early renewal project that included several city-financed railroad underpasses to permit Southside residents to drive home without waiting for the endless trains that periodically blocked the roadways.

Standing on the east is the **Texas and Pacific Passenger Terminal**★★ (100 W. Lancaster St.; 1931; Wyatt C. Hedrick, Fort Worth, architect), a twelve-story office tower of buff brick with projecting

corner towers and intricate Art Deco trim in white limestone. On the ground floor are the terminal's now abandoned passenger facilities, including a **waiting room**★★ with heroic Art Deco ceiling decoration, complete with seven-foot chandeliers.

A block further west is the enormous **Texas and Pacific Freight Terminal**★★ (300 W. Lancaster Ave.; 1931; Wyatt C. Hedrick, Fort Worth, architect), an eight-story giant six-hundred-feet-long adorned with an only slightly less elaborate exterior than that of its companion passenger terminal. The building's great size dramatizes the importance of rail-borne freight in the city's pre-1950 economy. Now made obsolete by the expansion of highway trucking, the terminal stands empty, awaiting restoration for some other use.

Between the two huge Texas and Pacific buildings is the equally massive **Main Post Office**★★ (200 W. Lancaster Ave.; 1933; Wyatt C. Hedrick, Fort Worth, architect). This was designed at the same time and by the same architect as its neighbors but in the strikingly different Beaux Arts style. The facade is lined with towering classical columns, each crowned by a capital covered with symbolic cow heads. The original **public lobby**★★ extends the entire length of the building and survives unaltered as one of the region's most lavishly detailed interior spaces. Intricate patterns of colored marble on the floor and walls contrast with bronze grillwork and a gold-leafed ceiling to create an unusually opulent setting.

Regrettably, the Post Office and adjacent Terminal buildings, which are among Fort Worth's most dramatic public landmarks, were visually severed from the rest of downtown by an elevated freeway constructed in the 1960s. In the late 1970s a plan to widen the freeway to within a few feet of the Post Office was successfully blocked by opposition from local preservationists.

HELL'S HALF ACRE AND URBAN RENEWAL

During earlier decades, some of the railroad district's modest commercial buildings housed most of the city's bars, gambling houses, and brothels. Familiarly known as "Hell's Half Acre," these diversions had long given way to general urban decay when the city began a second massive renewal project in the 1960s. This revitalization was dominated by the enormous **Tarrant County Convention Center**★ (bounded by Houston, Commerce, 9th, and 13th sts.; 1968; Preston M. Geren, Fort Worth, architect). An unusually fine example of 1960s Modern design, the Center's wonderful domed arena suggests that a giant flying saucer has just landed in town.

WATER GARDENS PARK

In 1974 the city and county proposed that a dramatic new park featuring artificial

SANTA FE DEPOT *Rounded arches and careful detailing enhance this 1900 railside classic.*

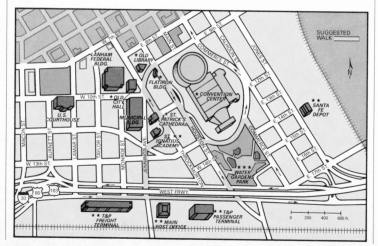

WATER GARDENS PARK *Sure-footed visitors are delighted by a descent into the Active Pool.*

white. This is one of Fort Worth's oldest surviving buildings and is of special importance as a rare Texas example of the mansard-roofed Second Empire style that was popular in the northeastern states a decade earlier.

GOVERNMENT CENTER

In 1893 the growing town's municipal government built a new City Hall many blocks to the south of the County Courthouse on a triangular site formed by the intersecting street grids of two early surveys. This area, along with the Texas and Pacific right-of-way further south, was to become the beneficiary of the first wave of urban renewal undertaken during the Depression years of the 1930s.

In 1933 the federal government completed not only its landmark railside Main Post Office, but also the Art Moderne **United States Courthouse** (500 W. 10th St.; Paul Phillippe Cret, Philadelphia, architect), located near the Old City Hall on a dramatic, block-wide site overlooking Burnett Park (see "Financial Core").

In 1938 the city followed suit by replacing its earlier headquarters building with a new **City Hall★**, now the Public Safety and Courts Building (1000 Throckmorton St.; Elmer G. Withers and Wyatt C. Hedrick, Fort Worth, architects). This is a striking Art Moderne landmark, its white limestone facade accented by stylized columns of contrasting black marble.

The next year the city completed a new **Public Library** across the street (915 Throckmorton St.; 1939; Joseph R. Pelich, Fort Worth, architect). A triangular, two-story structure of Art Moderne design, this fine building has been vacant since the library moved to new underground quarters adjacent to Tandy Center in 1978.

More recent government buildings erected in this area have been larger but less visually appealing. In 1966 the **Fritz G. Lanham Federal Building** (819 Taylor St.; Wyatt C. Hedrick, Fort Worth, architect) went up behind the 1938 City Hall, which was itself soon supplemented across 10th Street by the massive, low-rise **Municipal Building** (200 block of 10th St.; Edward Durrell Stone, New York, architect). Neither of these is among the best work of their distinguished designers.

waterfalls be constructed on a four-block site south of the new Convention Center. Financed by a gift from the Amon G. Carter Foundation (see also "Cultural District") and designed by the distinguished New York architects Philip Johnson and John Burgee, **Water Gardens Park★★★** (bounded by Houston, Commerce, 13th, and 16th sts.; 1976) is a spectacular urban space that has quickly become one of the region's most popular and beloved attractions.

Surrounded by handsomely landscaped concrete terraces, the core of the park consists of three sunken pools of moving water, each with a distinctive character. To the northwest is the tree-lined **Quiet Pool★**, bounded by high walls that are bathed in dramatic sheets of falling water. To the northeast is the **Aerating Pool★** whose spraying jets create an ever-changing atmosphere of sparkling mist. Most imposing of all is the small **Active Pool★★★**, surrounded by stairstepped cliffs down which torrents of water cascade from all sides. A narrow concrete walkway winds downward forty feet through the moving flow. This descent is guaranteed to thrill even the most blasé visitor.

Between these principal water features are landscaped pathways leading to hidden grassy lawns, shaded groves of trees, and even a stairstepped artificial hill-top—the **Concrete Mound**—which offers fine views of the intriguing displays below.

EARLY LANDMARK BUILDINGS

Sandwiched between the massive Convention Center and the new government buildings to the west are three of the city's oldest and most beloved landmark buildings, which have miraculously survived through many decades of neighborhood change.

The city's first skyscraper was the triangular, seven-story **Flatiron Building★★** (1000 Houston St.; Sanguinet & Staats, Fort Worth, architects), erected in 1907 to house doctors' offices. Patterned after larger prototypes in San Francisco and New York, this important landmark is now vacant and awaiting restoration.

One block south of the Flatiron Building is **Saint Patrick's Cathedral★** (1206 Throckmorton St.; 1892; architect unknown), a French-inspired Gothic Revival structure of Texas limestone now painted over in stark white. Originally a parish church, this building became the seat of Fort Worth's Roman Catholic bishop in 1969.

Near St. Patrick's stands the equally impressive **Saint Ignatius Academy★★** (1206 Throckmorton St.; 1889; J. J. Kane, architect), also built of limestone overpainted in

HOURS AND CHARGES

Main Post Office: (817) 885-1564. Lobby open at all times.

Water Gardens Park: (817) 870-7000. Open daily, 7 am to 11:45 pm. Admission free.

Visitor Information Center: (817) 336-8791. 100 East 15th St., Suite 100 in Water Garden Place. Mon-Fri, 8:30 am to 5 pm.

Saint Patrick's Cathedral: (817) 332-4915. Open only for masses Mon-Fri, 7 am and 12 noon; Sat, 8 am and 12 noon; Sun, 8 am to 1:30 pm and at 5 pm.

Related Shopping, Dining, and Entertainment (SiDE) Area: Sundance Square.

Stockyards and North Side **

Early Fort Worth industries were concentrated in the Trinity lowlands north of town; among them was the fascinating Fort Worth Stockyards, a hundred-acre collection of historic structures that today houses a Western-oriented entertainment complex.

LIVESTOCK EXCHANGE *This Mission style landmark once housed the many "Commission Companies" that served buyers and sellers of cattle, hogs, and sheep.*

The bluff-top site upon which early Fort Worth was built looks out over the broad, S-shaped valley of the Trinity River. Both the bluffs and the periodically flooded valley below presented formidable barriers to the town's northward expansion. Until the 1880s the principal occupants of the North Side, as it came to be called, were visiting trail drivers who grazed their cattle herds on the lush river-bottom meadows while seeking supplies and recreation in the hilltop settlement.

As residential districts spread southward, away from the Trinity bluffs (see "Southside"), developers began to eye the empty hillsides that rose beyond the river to the north and west of town. In 1888 a local development company purchased twenty-five hundred North Side acres and hired a renowned New York landscape architect to lay out an elaborate subdivision called "North Fort Worth." Connected to downtown by a long trolley ride, which began with a steep descent down a rickety wooden bridge crossing the Trinity, the development's lots remained mostly unsold until after 1902, when a new industry arrived to create a sudden and explosive expansion on the North Side.

MEAT-PACKING BOOM

Passing cattle herds had long made the North Side's grassy meadows the center of the region's livestock trade. In 1886 the Union Stock Yards Company was organized to construct fenced pens in the area

for holding the animals awaiting sale and rail shipment. In 1890 the stockyards were joined by the Fort Worth Dressed Meat and Packing Company, which planned to slaughter livestock for long-distance shipment as fresh meat. This had then only recently become possible because of newly perfected refrigerated railroad cars. The large plant the company built next to the stockyards was a financial failure, but it did pave the way for the arrival of two giant Chicago-based packinghouses that had pioneered the practice of refrigerated rail shipment.

In 1901 Swift & Company and Armour & Company simultaneously chose the Fort Worth stockyards as the site for enormous new southwestern facilities, and the boom was on. By 1910 Fort Worth's population had tripled and the North Side's hills were rapidly being covered with modest suburbs housing workers attracted by the new meat-packing industry.

STOCKYARDS HISTORIC DISTRICT

To accommodate the frenzied activity generated by the arrival of Swift and Armour, the old stockyards were reorganized and completely rebuilt. Over the years additional structures were added to become what is now the **Fort Worth Stockyards Historic District*** (1902 and later), a large, multibuilding complex centered on Exchange Avenue east of its intersection with North Main Street.

Today weekly rodeos and cattle auctions, the latter attracting only a relative handful of traders, provide a colorful but distant echo of the stockyards' once hectic livestock trade. After many decades of service, the by then obsolete Armour plant shut down most of its operations in 1962, followed by Swift in 1971. The cattle, hogs, and sheep of earlier days are now replaced by tourists and local fun-seekers, drawn to the symbolic heart of Cowtown by the many Western-oriented shops, restaurants, nightclubs, and special events that fill many of its historic buildings.

LIVESTOCK PENS

The core of the active stockyards was the many acres of pens that held animals brought in for sale, after which they were either shipped elsewhere or processed in the nearby packinghouses. On the north side of Exchange Avenue were hundreds of wooden cattle pens connected by an intricate series of narrow, paved walkways. These pens needed no overhead shelter because cattle, when well fed and watered, are little affected by even the hottest direct sunlight. In contrast, pens on the south side of Exchange Avenue were designed for hogs, sheep, horses, and mules, all of which require shelter from continued exposure to sunlight. The hog and sheep areas, nearest the packing plants, had slat-fenced pens for cross-ventilation and elevated, canopy-like wooden or concrete roofs to provide shade.

Only a small portion of the many acres of original cattle, hog, and sheep pens survive today, and most of these are in dilapidated condition. Best preserved are the **cattle pens** immediately north and east of

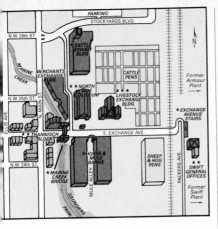

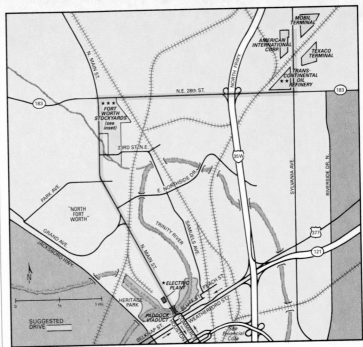

the Livestock Exchange Building that are still used for weekly cattle auctions held in a small arena adjacent to the Exchange.

Most elaborate of the original livestock holding areas are the **Horse and Mule Barns★** (122-124 E. Exchange Ave.; 1911; architect unknown), located at the west end of Exchange Avenue away from the packing plants (these animals were only traded, not slaughtered). The handsome brick buildings originally contained not only animal stalls but also traders' offices and large areas for hay and grain storage. Centered on "Mule Alley," the brick barns are decorated with fashionable Mission style parapets. Along Exchange Avenue their brick facades are covered with stucco and crowned with red-tile roofs to blend with the Exchange Building across the street.

LIVESTOCK EXCHANGE

Nerve center of the bustling stockyards was the **Livestock Exchange Building★★★** (131 E. Exchange Ave.; architect unknown), a dramatic Mission style structure erected in 1902 at the same time as the nearby packing plants. Now carefully re-

stored and occupied by attractive shops and offices, this historic building originally housed numerous "Commission Companies" that functioned much like modern real estate agents. On arriving with stock to sell, the rancher chose a broker or "commission man" to represent him. This agent was then responsible for arranging holding pens, food, and water, as well as for representing the seller in negotiations with potential buyers. When a sale was made the animals were moved to the buyers' pens, and the broker earned a percentage commission plus reimbursement for pen space, food, insurance, loading and other costs that he paid directly to the Stockyards Company on behalf of the seller.

COLISEUM AND EXHIBITION BUILDINGS

Immediately west of the Livestock Exchange is another early building of great historic significance. This is the Mission style **North Side Coliseum★★**, now Cowtown Coliseum (121 E. Exchange Ave.; Berkley Brandt, Chicago, architect), which seats 2,200 spectators and was erected in 1908 with funds contributed jointly by Swift, Armour, and the Stockyards Company.

Several years earlier, North Side stockmen had begun an annual exposition of prize livestock which served to encourage improved breeding herds while simultaneously publicizing the new Stockyards Company complex. Called the National Feeder's and Breeder's Show, it was held at various outdoor sites until the Coliseum was built as a permanent home. Renamed the Southwestern Exposition and Fat

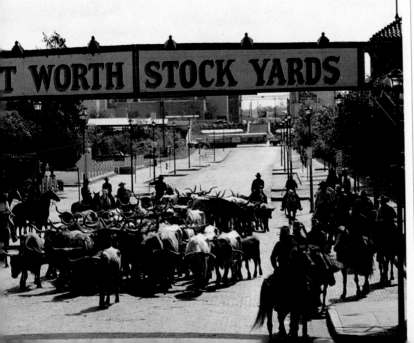

NOSTALGIC CATTLE DRIVE *In this recent photograph a modern herd of Texas Longhorns approaches the historic Stock Yards sign.*

49

FORT WORTH AND
THE CATTLE INDUSTRY

Fort Worth's historic ties to beef cattle have earned the city the playful nickname of "Cowtown." There have, in fact, been three distinct phases to the town's long interactions with cattle.

From 1866 through the late 1870s the small frontier village was an important supply and recreation stop on the fabled Chisholm Trail, along which herds of wild Texas Longhorns were driven to Kansas railhead towns for shipment to the northeast. In 1872 Texas got its own interstate railroad connections and by 1876 Fort Worth had rail service. To the surprise of local boosters, the cattle industry languished. It was not until 1901, when Chicago-based Swift and Armour chose the town as the site of giant new meatpacking plants, that Fort Worth finally became the bustling livestock center of the Southwest.

TRAIL DRIVE ERA
1866–1880

After the Civil War ended, Texas stockmen realized a bonanza by driving herds of the state's plentiful Longhorn cattle to newly constructed railroad loading points in distant Kansas. Demand for beef was very high in the war-deprived northeastern states, and the cattle could be sold at great profit to shippers in Abilene or Ellsworth.

CATTLE TRAILS By 1866, large herds of half-wild Longhorns, descended from the cattle of early Spanish colonists, roamed the South Texas prairies below San Antonio. Other herds, established by prewar Anglo stockmen in the rugged Cross Timbers belt west of Fort Worth, had been abandoned to multiply during the War. Driving large numbers of these cattle over long distances was easiest on the open prairies or plains, for wandering strays and narrow trails made the herds difficult to manage in wooded country. The natural highway for Texas cattle movement thus became the long belt of prairie land that separated the dense woodlands of eastern Texas from the rugged wooded hills of the Edwards Plateau and Cross Timbers farther west. The village of Fort Worth, near the northwestern edge of these central prairies, became a principal supply and recreation stop on this "Eastern" or "Chisholm" Trail. By 1880, settlement and farming of the prairie lands had forced the trail drives to shift a hundred miles, to the "Western Trail" on the plains beyond the Cross Timbers. This newly opened region had been dominated until the mid-1870s by buffalo herds and mounted Comanche warriors.

LONGHORN DRIVE Although photography was a well-developed art by the 1860s, no photographss of the early cattle drives are known to survive. This modern close-up captures some of the spirit of the original drives, which often included a thousand or more animals. The lean but hearty Texas Longhorn is descended from cattle brought to the New World by Spanish explorers in the 1500s. The animals soon multiplied on the vast South Texas grasslands, and local Hispanic stockmen ultimately used only a fraction of the semiwild herds for hides, tallow, or beef. Their meat was stringy and tough—suitable principally for making stews such as "chili con carne." By the early decades of this century, mixing with superior British beef breeds had made the original Longhorn a rare curiosity. The animals survive today only in zoos and exhibition herds.

RAIL TERMINAL ERA
1876-1901

Railroad construction flourished throughout the western states during the 1870s and 1880s. The Texas and Pacific line arrived in Fort Worth in 1876 to give the frontier town direct rail connections to St. Louis and the northeast. In the 1880s, Fort Worth investors built elaborate holding pens, railroad sidings, and a large Hotel and Exchange Building on the North Side's grassy meadows. These improvements were expected to make the town an important cattle-shipping point, similar to the Kansas railheads of the previous decade. Instead, the facilities were used only by local stockmen because the expanding railroad network had created hundreds of similar loading points to serve the vast ranch lands of the West.

FORT WORTH STOCK YARDS HOTEL AND EXCHANGE *This 1890s photo shows prize steers standing lonesomely in front of the original Hotel and Exchange Building, which was razed in 1901 to make room for the new Swift plant.*

RAIL SHIPMENT OF CATTLE IN THE 1870S *No photos survive of nineteenth-century cattle shipments from Fort Worth, but many local scenes must have resembled this 1870s Kansas Pacific cattle train.*

PACKING PLANT ERA
1901-1970

The fortunes of the depressed Fort Worth livestock industry were suddenly reversed in 1901 when both Armour and Company and Swift and Company, giant Chicago-based meatpackers, chose the city as the site for huge new plants. Soon a large fraction of the Southwest's output of cattle, hogs, and sheep was converging on Fort Worth for central processing.

CATTLE PENS, CA. 1940 *Paved walkways connected the many acres of cattle-holding pens. Note the Armour plant in the background.*

ARMOUR AND SWIFT PLANTS, CA. 1940 *Note the elevated walkway over the railroad tracks and parking area. Animals moved along this route from the covered sheep and hog pens in the foreground, and from the open cattle pens out of view on the left, to the Swift plant. Only fragments of these once vast facilities, which are no longer used for meat processing, survive today.*

Stock Show in 1917, the expanding event remained in this North Side location until 1944 when it moved to its larger present home, the Will Rogers Memorial Coliseum (see "Cultural District"). Site of the nation's first indoor rodeo held in 1917, the historic North Side Coliseum still hosts rodeos as well as frequent concerts and other special events.

The "Fat Stock Show," as it came to be called, used many of the stockyards' regular cattle pens and also the enclosed Horse and Mule Barns for temporary livestock display. As the event grew larger and more popular, special livestock exhibition buildings were added around the Coliseum. To the west is the **Merchants Exchange Building** (2445 N. Commerce St.; architect unknown), which occupies a triangular site adjacent to Marine Creek. Originally constructed about 1910, the building has been remodeled several times and today sports stucco-covered walls and Mission style roof parapets that echo the nearby Coliseum and Exchange buildings. The renovated interior now houses retail space for shops and restaurants.

In 1936 the city replaced several earlier exhibition structures north of the Coliseum with the **Cattle Exhibit Building**★, now Billy Bob's Texas (2520 N. Commerce St.; architect unknown). This sprawling structure enclosed three acres of interior space and featured fashionable Art Deco entrance towers. In 1981 the building was renovated and modified to house the "world's largest honky-tonk," which has become one of the stockyards' most celebrated attractions.

SWIFT AND ARMOUR PLANTS

Making up the economic heart of the district were the enormous packing plants of Swift & Company and Armour & Company, each occupying independently owned sites east of the Stockyards Company facilities. Between the plants and the many acres of animal pens ran the multiple tracks of the Fort Worth Belt Railway, built by the Stockyards Company itself to avoid rail congestion and to promote competition among the railroads. This seventeen-mile local line transported cars loaded with cattle, hogs, and sheep directly to and from the marshalling yards of five separate railroad companies.

Today the massive central buildings of both the Swift and Armour plants have been demolished, yet enough satellite structures survive to give a feeling for the original size of the hilltop complex. Streetcar lines joined the adjacent railroad tracks to deliver workers to the **Exchange Avenue Stairs**★ (E. Exchange and Packers aves.; ca. 1902), which are flanked by large, grass-level signs spelling "Armour" and "Swift." Near the top of the steps were the twin plants' headquarters buildings, incongruously designed to resemble southern mansions rather than industrial-age offices. Only one of these, the **Swift & Company General Offices**★★, now the

51

FORMER MEAT-PACKING CENTER *Thousands of workers once climbed these steps every day to their jobs in the giant Armour and Swift plants. The original Swift General Offices building at right now houses a restaurant.*

Spaghetti Warehouse (E. Exchange and Packers aves.; 1902; architect unknown), still survives. Today the structure is occupied by a popular restaurant whose large signs and replaced first-floor windows are the only alterations to the building's handsome exterior. South and east of the General Offices stand scattered accessory buildings of the now demolished Swift central plant. Most are abandoned and in derelict condition.

North of the Swift plant were the mirror-image facilities of Armour & Company, which like its neighbor once included not only a massive central packing plant but also such adjacent facilities as cooling rooms, smokehouses, power plants, garages and wagonyards, salt-pickling areas, ice plants, lard and oleo factories, fertilizer plants, and box and barrel manufacturing buildings. As Gustavus Swift once said, "We use every part of the pig but the squeal." Unlike the Swift complex, several early processing buildings of the Armour Plant are still in use by a cottonseed oil company, which also added some incongruous metal structures to the brick complex in the 1960s.

STOCKYARDS COMMERCIAL DISTRICT

To serve the bustling Stockyards Company complex, an independent commercial district with hotels, restaurants, offices, and shops began to rise to the west, centered on the intersection of Exchange Avenue and North Main Street. This district was separated from the stockyards by the narrow channel of Marine Creek.

In 1910 the Stockyards Company created a dramatic new western entrance by building the **Marine Creek Bridge*** (100 block of E. Exchange Ave.), composed of two tunnel-like arches of concrete that rose above the creek as it crossed Exchange Avenue. On either side of the street the elongate bridge was designed to support large commercial buildings so that both bridge and

creek disappeared behind a continuous line of storefronts. Arching over the street on the west side of the bridge was a large "Fort Worth Stock Yards" sign supported by massive concrete columns. This has survived for three-quarters of a century and is now a beloved area landmark. Today adjacent Marine Creek has been landscaped and given concrete walkways to become **Saunders Park**, which provides picturesque rear views of the large brick buildings unexpectedly perched above the creek.

When the stockyards district first began to promote tourism in the 1950s, many of the nearby commercial buildings were "Westernized" with rustic wooden facades and sidewalk canopies. These additions would have seemed laughably primitive to the buildings' original owners who, in the first decades of the twentieth century, built only in the most "modern" architectural styles. Fortunately, several of the buildings have now been restored to their handsome original appearance. Particularly important is the three-story **Thannisch Block**★★ (101-109 E. Exchange Ave.; 1907 central hotel building, with 1913 additions by Field and Clarkson, Fort Worth, architects), a carefully detailed brick structure that housed shops, offices, and the eighty-six-room **Stock Yards Hotel**★★, all of which are now charmingly preserved.

OIL REFINERIES

The North Side's long association with the cattle industry has all but obscured the fact that it was also the industrial heart of Fort Worth's second major economic boom—the oil bonanza that began only ten years after the packing plants arrived and lasted through the 1950s.

In 1911 important new oil fields were first discovered near Wichita Falls 120

miles northwest of Fort Worth; in 1917-18 additional giant discoveries were made both around Wichita Falls and near Ranger, 90 miles due west of the city. As the nearest important railroad center, Fort Worth became a principal beneficiary of this new North Texas oil province.

When these discoveries were made, the technology had already been perfected for transporting crude oil over long distances by pipeline. Today not only raw crude oil but also refined petroleum products—gasoline, kerosene, fuel oil, etc.—are moved by pipeline, but before about 1950 these final products moved principally in railroad tank cars (or by barge or ship). Served by nine competing railroad companies whose lines fanned out in all directions, Fort Worth made an ideal refinery site. By 1920 a half-dozen eight-inch pipelines were delivering North Texas crude oil to nine large Fort Worth refineries, eight of them located alongside the North Side's extensive railroad network.

As production from the North Texas fields declined during the late 1920s and 1930s several of the refineries closed and were dismantled. By 1940 only four remained, each owned by a major national oil company—Sinclair (now Atlantic Richfield), Marathon (now Sohio), Magnolia (now Mobil), and Gulf. Today only one of these historic industrial landmarks survives intact.

This is the original **Transcontinental Oil Company Refinery**★★, later the Marathon Refinery and now the Amber Refining Company (2500 Premier St.; 1919 and later), whose triangular site remains covered with an amazing forest of vintage machinery and buildings, some dating back to 1919. Purchased in 1930 by the Ohio Oil Company (now Sohio), the refinery operated under that company's Marathon Oil trademark until 1941. Since then it has had a succession of smaller owners, and today only a part of the vast facility is in use. The rest stands like some high-tech modern sculpture in silent tribute to an all-but-forgotten era in Fort Worth's past.

Sylvania Avenue, which bounds the old refinery on the east, provides several less direct reminders of the city's historic ties to petroleum. Because of their multiple pipeline connections, abandoned refinery sites are commonly converted into large tank farms where crude oil is temporarily stored for shipment elsewhere and refined products are received for local distribution by truck. Northwest of the Transcontinental Refinery are the **Texaco Terminal Station** (3100 N. Sylvania Ave.) and the **Mobil Terminal Station**, formerly Magnolia Oil Company (3600 N. Sylvania Ave.), which still occupy the sites of long-demolished refineries. Across the street is the enormous modern factory of the **American International Manufacturing Corporation** (3209 N. Sylvania Ave.), manufacturers, since 1924, of "American" brand pumping

ENDANGERED SPECIES *The former Transcontinental Oil Company Refinery, established in 1919, is the sole survivor of the North Side's many petroleum refineries built during the city's oil boom years.*

units that bob up and down above oil wells throughout the world.

PADDOCK VIADUCT

Access from Fort Worth's commercial center to the North Side was long impeded by the steep Trinity River bluffs. Early trail drivers moved their herds down a long, ramp-like finger of land extending northeast of the courthouse to a hard-bottomed river crossing near the present stockyards. Railroad lines entering the city from the north followed a similar route, as does modern Samuels Avenue, which was the North Side's first wagon road.

When the new subdivision called "North Fort Worth" opened in 1888 (see above), its developers constructed a long- and rickety wooden bridge that ramped downward from the bluff-top directly behind the County Courthouse. This pro-

vided streetcars, wagons, buggies, and pedestrians with a more direct route from downtown along newly extended North Main Street. As North Side traffic burgeoned following the opening of the Swift and Armour plants in 1902, the old wooden bridge became inadequate and was replaced in 1914 by the present **Paddock Viaduct** (N. Main and Bluff sts.; Brenneke and Fay, St. Louis, architects), an engineering marvel of its day that used the nation's first self-supporting arches of reinforced concrete to span the periodically flooded Trinity.

West of the Viaduct are the four towering smokestacks of the handsome **Texas Electric Service Steam Generating Plant★** (west side of 100-300 blocks, N. Main St.; 1922 and later), which occupies the site of an earlier plant built after the 1911 merger of several small and competing electricity companies.

Cultural District ***

The Trinity River valley west of downtown houses an extraordinary concentration of civic gardens, museums, performance halls, and other cultural facilities that today ranks among the finest in the Southwest.

Beginning in 1892, when a large tract was purchased for a public park, the Trinity lowlands bordering downtown Fort Worth's western edge have been the favored site for the city's cultural and recreational facilities. Most of the important improvements to this "Cultural District" date from either the 1930s, when the Botanic Garden and Will Rogers Center were inaugurated, or the decades since 1950, when a series of increasingly spectacular museums has been added.

KIMBELL ART MUSEUM

Crown jewel of the Cultural District is its most recent addition—the internationally important **Kimbell Art Museum***** (3333 Camp Bowie Blvd.; 1972; Louis I. Kahn, Philadelphia, architect). The Museum was given to his adopted city by art collector Kay Kimbell (1886-1964), a grain merchant from Sherman, Texas, who moved his mills and elevators to Fort Worth in 1924. A publicity-shy financial genius, Kimbell slowly amassed a large fortune not only from milling operations but also from timely investments in food processing, petroleum, insurance, and real estate (see also "Southside").

Kimbell and his wife had no children and left their entire fortune to the Kimbell Art Foundation, which they instructed to "build an art museum of the highest rank." Using as a nucleus Kimbell's carefully chosen personal collection of European art, the Museum has steadily added a series of coveted masterpieces using a multi-million-dollar yearly acquisition budget that is the envy of the museum world. Today the Kimbell boasts one of the nation's finest small collections of pre-1920 European painting and sculpture. Of equal importance is the building that contains these treasures.

The Museum's designer, Louis Kahn (1902-1974), is coming to be recognized as one of our country's truly great architects—in the same league as Frank Lloyd Wright or Louis Sullivan. The Kimbell Museum was Kahn's last project and is considered by critics to be among his finest.

Expanding on the classical theme of the vaulted roof, Kahn joined together six elongate vaults of lead-sheathed concrete to create a roof with a minimum of supporting columns to interrupt the interior galleries. Filling the space between the widely spaced concrete columns is an exterior wall of contrasting travertine marble. Three of the six vaults are interrupted in the middle to make a dramatic U-shaped entry court graced with small lagoons and a grove of yaupon trees. The outer of the three entryway vaults is left open and

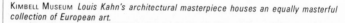

WILL ROGERS CENTER *The Art Moderne coliseum building (left), home of the annual Fat Stock Show, stands next to the decorative Pioneer Tower.*

forms a long porch that reveals the beautiful simplicity of the building's structure. Regrettably, few visitors use this formal entry, which serves mostly pedestrian traffic. Kahn, who never learned to drive, was less concerned about the basement-level entrance on the opposite side, which serves the parking lot for those arriving by car.

Perhaps Kahn's greatest achievement is the quality of the natural light that diffuses through the building "like so much celestial vapor," to use the words of an enthusiastic critic. This effect is achieved by linear three-foot-wide skylights that run down the crest of each roof vault. Beneath these are polished aluminum reflectors that impart a pale blue color as they deflect sunlight onto the vaulted concrete ceilings, from which the light cascades into the galleries below.

AMON CARTER MUSEUM

The Kimbell Museum's collections of European art are nicely complemented by the nearby **Amon Carter Museum**** (3501 Camp Bowie Blvd.; 1961 with additions in 1964 and 1977; Philip Johnson, New York, architect), which specializes in American art. Amon G. Carter (1879-1955), a tirelessly energetic Fort Worth booster and publisher of its major newspaper, the *Star-Telegram*, had less worldly tastes in art than did Kay Kimbell. He and his oilman friend Sid Richardson (see "Financial Core") held a friendly competition to see who could amass the largest collection of works by Frederic Remington (1861-1909) and Charles Russell (1864-1926), pioneer painters of western themes, particularly cowboys and Indians.

KIMBELL MUSEUM *Louis Kahn's architectural masterpiece houses an equally masterful collection of European art.*

DINOSAUR COMBAT *One of the many intriguing displays in the Fort Worth Museum of Science and History.*

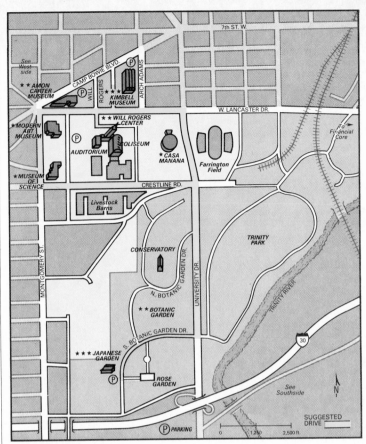

Carter's will provided funds for a small public museum to display his collection, and this building, which makes up the public exhibition galleries of the current museum complex, opened in 1961. Designed in the latest Formalistic fashion of the day, its colonnaded entrance overlooks a hillside courtyard with a dramatic view of the downtown skyline. The Carter Museum's board, with more limited resources than the Kimbell, has focused on building a superb research archive of paintings, drawings, photographs, and documents relating to the western United States. To house these materials, two large but inconspicuous wings, open only to researchers, were later added behind the exhibition galleries. At the same time, the exhibition collection has been slowly expanded to include a broader spectrum of important works by American artists of all regions and periods.

MODERN ART MUSEUM

Further complementing the Kimbell and Carter collections is the nearby **Modern**

Art Museum of Fort Worth★ (1309 Montgomery St.; 1954 with later additions; Herbert Bayer, New York, architect). Originally the city's municipal museum of art, this institution now takes up where its newer neighbors leave off by emphasizing the Abstract art of our own century. The Museum supplements its small but high-quality permanent collection with special exhibitions of works by contemporary artists.

SCIENCE MUSEUM

Rounding out the Cultural District's museum complex is yet a fourth facility, the **Fort Worth Museum of Science and History★** (1501 Montgomery St.; 1954 with later additions; Wilson, Peterson, and associates, Fort Worth, architects). The museum's well-conceived exhibits stress human biology, geology, anthropology, and computer science. All are favorites of local schoolchildren, as are the astronomy and laser shows presented in the **Noble Planetarium**. A popular recent addition is the state-of-the-art **Omni Theater★**, which presents spectacular films on varying science-related subjects. These are projected onto a domed screen, eighty feet in diameter, that envelopes the audience with sight and sound.

COLISEUM COMPLEX

The Cultural District's four museums have been built since the 1950s on land once

occupied by the "Fort Worth Frontier Centennial." This was a 1936 exhibition conceived by publisher Amon Carter as Fort Worth's answer to the official Texas Centennial Celebrations that were held the same year in nearby Dallas. Built on a sloping hillside overlooking Trinity Park, the Fort Worth Centennial emphasized Western themes and centered on a new Coliseum complex which Carter hoped would eventually house the city's annual Fat Stock Show (see "Stockyards and North Side").

To finance this ambitious facility in the depths of the Great Depression, Carter sought federal unemployment relief funds. (Dallas, as the official site, had received massive state appropriations.) Rebuffed by the secretary of the interior, Carter appealed to his friend James Farley, then postmaster general. Farley reported to President Roosevelt that "Amon wants to build a cowshed," which was approved and rushed to completion. The result is the **Will Rogers Center★★** (3301 W. Lancaster Ave.; 1936; Wyatt C. Hedrick, Fort Worth, architect), named for another Carter friend, the popular cowboy-entertainer and folk philosopher whose life was cut short by a 1935 plane crash.

The Center includes not only Amon's cowshed—the large Coliseum building—but also a matching smaller Auditorium. Between them is the tall "Pioneer Tower," which became the Exposition's visual centerpiece. The unified Art Moderne facade of the three adjacent buildings is carefully finished with monumental limestone en-

THE KIMBELL ART MUSEUM, A SAMPLING

(Right) MISS MAY SARTORIS, CA. 1860 *Frederic Leighton (English, 1830-1896), oil on canvas, 68 × 43".* Leighton, one of Victorian England's most acclaimed artists, lovingly portrays an elegant sixteen-year-old dressed in country riding habit. The subject is the daughter of an intimate friend of the artist.

(Above) SAINT JAMES FREEING HERMOGENES, CA. 1430 *Fra Angelico (Italian, 1387-1455), tempera and gold on wood, 10 X 8⅝".* In this jewel-like miniature by a Renaissance master, the repentant sorcerer (in red robe) is forgiven and blessed by the Apostle (at right with halo), while the sorcerer's demons cower in the background.

(Right) MAN IN A BLUE SMOCK, CA. 1896 *Paul Cézanne (French, 1839-1906), oil on canvas, 32 × 25".* This is among the finest of the relatively few portraits by the "father of modern painting," who is best known for his landscapes.

(Left) THE MATADOR PEDRO ROMERO, CA. 1796 *Francisco de Goya (Spanish, 1746-1828), oil on canvas, 33 × 26".* In this superb portrait one of Spain's greatest artists captures the character of one of that country's most renowned bullfighters. Romero's carefully emphasized right hand is said to have killed an incredible six thousand bulls, with never an injury to the matador himself.

(Left) THE CHEAT WITH THE ACE OF CLUBS, CA. 1630 *Georges de la Tour (French, 1593-1652), oil on canvas, 39 × 62".* The innocent young aristocrat on the right is receiving a lesson on the evils of gambling in this satirical study which was inspired by Carravagio's The Cardsharks, painted in Rome thirty years earlier and now hanging nearby in the Kimbell collections.

trance columns and a decorative tile frieze depicting events in Texas history.

During World War II, Carter finally succeeded in moving the Fat Stock Show to the Will Rogers complex, where it has been held every year since 1944. Behind the original buildings is a massive series of livestock barns and exhibition structures that serve not only this annual January extravaganza, but also a year-round series of rodeos, horse shows, circuses, and other special events.

CASA MANANA

To round out his 1936 Frontier Celebration, Amon Carter hired famed New York showman Billy Rose and gave him an enormous budget to create spectacular entertainment for Centennial visitors. Summarizing his instructions, Rose told reporters: "Dallas has all that historical stuff so we don't have to worry about that. We can just show the people a good time." Among ninety-two separate attractions that he staged were Indian battles, cattle drives, circus acts, sideshows, and appearances by Hollywood celebrities. The grand highlight was the long-remembered *Casa Manana Revue*, a sort of Americanized Folies-Bergère featuring five hundred seminude dancers on a giant revolving stage.

All of these events took place in now demolished structures, but their spirit survives on the same site in the **Casa Manana Theater*** (3101 W. Lancaster Ave.; A. George King, architect) built in 1958 as a small forerunner to today's giant "superdomes." Designed primarily to house Fort Worth's popular series of Summer Musicals, the eighteen-hundred-seat theater-in-the-round is covered by one of the nation's first "geodesic domes," a column-free, self-supporting metal shell that had recently been perfected by structural innovator A. Buckminster Fuller (1895-1983). The aluminum-covered dome for the first time permitted spectators to watch the musicals in air-conditioned comfort.

ORIENTAL TRANQUILITY *The delightful Japanese Garden, a part of the Fort Worth Botanic Garden, is a rare gem of landscape art.*

BOTANIC GARDEN

South and east of the Cultural District's museums and exhibition complex is **Trinity Park**, which stretches for almost two miles along the west bank of the Trinity River's Clear Fork. As part of a 1933 unemployment relief program, the city designated a hillside site within the Park for construction of a formal **Rose Garden** (Botanic Garden Drive; 1934; Hare and Hare, Kansas City, architects) featuring a grand axis of terraces, beds, and pools cascading downslope from a hilltop shelter pavilion. This became the nucleus of today's **Fort Worth Botanic Garden**** (University and Botanic Garden drives; 1934 and later), with 115 carefully planned and maintained acres of meadows, forests, streams, paths, and shelters. The Garden's latest addition is a glass-enclosed **Conservatory** (N. Botanic Garden Drive; 1986; Hahnfield and Associates, Fort Worth, architects) which houses a diverse and colorful collection of exotic tropical plants.

The Botanic Garden's most extraordinary attraction is the fascinating **Japanese Garden***** (Botanic Garden Drive; 1973; Kingsley Wu, Denton, Texas, architect), where in a few steps the visitor travels six thousand miles across the Pacific to enter an authentic Oriental wonderland. Built on the six-acre site of an old gravel pit, the Garden's narrow, shaded pathways lead to such visual surprises as a Meditation Garden, Teahouse, Pagoda, waterfalls, pools stocked with colorful Imperial Carp, and even a Moon Viewing Deck.

HOURS AND CHARGES

Kimbell Art Museum: (817) 332-8451. Tues-Sat, 10 am to 5 pm; Sun, 11 am to 5 pm. Admission free. Charge for traveling exhibits. Restaurant.

Amon Carter Museum: (817) 738-1933. Tues-Sat, 10 am to 5 pm; Sun, 1 pm to 5:30 pm. Admission free.

Modern Art Museum: (817) 738-9215. Tues, 10 am to 9 pm; Wed-Sat, 10 am to 5 pm; Sun, 1 pm to 5 pm. Admission free.

Museum of Science and History: (817) 732-1631. Mon-Thur, 9 am to 5 pm; Fri-Sat, 9 am to 8:30 pm; Sun, noon to 5 pm. Admission free.

Noble Planetarium (in Museum of Science): (817) 732-1631. Shows year-round on Saturday and Sunday afternoons. Additional summer shows, Mon-Fri, 2 pm and 3 pm. Ages 4 to adult, $2.50; under age 4 not admitted.

Omni Theater (in Museum of Science): (817) 732-1631. Shows, Tues-Thur, 1 pm, 2 pm, 7 pm, 8 pm. Fri, same plus 9 pm. Sat, 11 am, and hourly 1 to 4 pm, 7 to 9 pm. Sun, hourly 1 to 4 pm, 7 and 8 pm. Adults, $4.75; under 12 years, $3.

Botanic Garden: (817) 870-7686. Daily, 8 am to 11 pm. Admission free. Picnic areas.

Conservatory (in Botanic Garden): (817) 870-7686. Mon-Fri, 10 am to 5 pm; Sat, 10 am to 5 pm; Sun, 1 pm to 5 pm. Last ticket sold one-half hour before closing. Adults, $1; ages 5 to 19, 50¢.

Japanese Garden (in Botanic Garden): (817) 870-7685. Tues-Sun, 10 am to 5 pm. Tues-Fri, adults $1; ages 5 to 19, 50¢. Sat-Sun, adults, $1.50; ages 5 to 19, 50¢. Food for Japanese carp, 25¢.

Related Shopping, Dining, and Entertainment (SiDE) Area: Cultural District.

AMON CARTER MUSEUM *An expanding collection of American art is being built around the founder's gift of Western paintings.*

Southside *

Most of Fort Worth's early residential growth was concentrated to the south of downtown, which was the only direction the city could expand without crossing the flood-prone valleys of the Trinity River.

THISTLE HILL *This 1903 cattle baron's home was rescued from demolition and is now a house museum.*

Fort Worth's residential districts of the 1880s and 1890s spread westward, away from the railroad-dominated east side of town, but their growth was soon limited by high bluffs above the Trinity River's Clear Fork, which confined the town on the west. By the turn of the century, the city's growth was mostly southward, where the only obstructions were the tracks and rail yards of the Texas and Pacific Railroad.

SILK STOCKING ROW

Fort Worth's Victorian residential neighborhoods were concentrated just south and west of the commercial district as the street grid expanded to the edge of the Trinity bluffs. The up-scale heart of this large district centered on Summit Avenue, an area that became the local "Silk Stocking Row." Today only a handful of houses, now scattered among many blocks of commercial buildings and vacant lots, hints at this neighborhood's residential beginning.

Most important of the surviving houses are two splendid bluff-top mansions saved from demolition by the timely intervention of local preservationists. The **Eddleman-McFarland House★★** (1110 Penn St.; 1898; Howard Messer, Fort Worth, archi-

tect) is a superbly detailed Chateauesque landmark of yellow brick trimmed with red sandstone. Elaborate copper roof detailing is a rarely seen Victorian embellishment. Now the home of Fort Worth's Junior League, Sunday afternoon tours feature the original lavishly inlaid and carved woodwork of the downstairs rooms. Adjacent is the Queen Anne style **Pollock-Capps House★** (1120 Penn St.; 1898; attributed to Howard Messer, Fort Worth). This is a larger but less lavishly detailed structure of red brick with white limestone trim that has been recently renovated for private offices.

THISTLE HILL

By the 1890s Fort Worth's residential street grid had begun spilling southward beyond the T&P tracks. There Pennsylvania Avenue began to supplement the older Summit Avenue area as a favored address for the town's affluent gentry. Standing as a dramatic focal point at the intersection of Summit and Pennsylvania avenues is the area's principal surviving landmark, now known as **Thistle Hill★★**, originally the Wharton House (1509 Pennsylvania Ave.; 1903; Sanguinet & Staats, Fort Worth, architects). Of Neoclassical design, the

house was a wedding gift from cattle baron W. T. Waggoner (see "Financial Core") to his daughter Electra and her husband, Philadelphia socialite A. B. Wharton. The Whartons moved to Electra's vast West Texas ranch in 1911 and sold the house to a cattle baron friend, Winfield Scott (1849--1911). Scott employed the original architect to completely redesign the house's interior while only slightly altering the exterior. Scott died while these changes were under way, but his widow made the house a local showplace until her death in 1938. Barely saved from destruction in 1976, the historic structure is now being carefully restored as a house museum open to the public.

RYAN PLACE

As residential development spread farther southward from Fort Worth's growing commercial center, so also did a serious disrupting influence. In 1880 the town's first north-south railroad, the Missouri-Kansas-Texas (MKT or "Katy"), bisected the Southside, and by 1903 four additional rail lines had sliced it into elongate wedges, with narrow residential districts separated from each other by noisy tracks, freight yards, and industrial buildings. More modest housing became concentrated in the strips to the east of the Katy tracks (the approximate route followed today by Interstate Highway 35W), whereas more affluent subdivisions grew between the rail lines to the west.

As new railroads built through the Southside, many homeowners found their neighborhoods suddenly blighted by industrial encroachment. To insure permanent residential stability, developer John

EDDLEMAN-MCFARLAND HOUSE *This elegant Victorian landmark is now a museum and the home of the Fort Worth Junior League.*

C. Ryan in 1911 opened **Ryan Place** (approximate boundaries Jessamine, Hurly, and Berry sts., and the Santa Fe Railroad), the city's first highly restricted residential subdivision located at the then southern limit of Southside growth.

Ryan's restrictions stated that all houses were to be of masonry construction with uniform street setbacks and side yards. Still more important, in those days before city zoning ordinances, the deed to each lot specified that the original purchaser and all future owners could build only dwellings on the land, thus insuring against commercial encroachment.

ELIZABETH AVENUE HISTORIC DISTRICT *From 1911 to about 1920 many of Fort Worth's most fashionable houses were built on this street.*

The restrictions also specified the minimum cost of the houses, with the largest and most expensive concentrated on Elizabeth Boulevard, located at the development's north end and named for Ryan's wife. Soon this street began to replace Pennsylvania Avenue as the site of the city's most elegant new homes. Because of Ryan's careful deed restrictions, these have all survived to become the **Elizabeth Avenue Historic District★★**, a fascinating collection of large dwellings mostly built between 1911 and 1920 in the popular Italian Renaissance and Prairie fashions of the day.

FOREST PARK

During the 1920s and 1930s the affluent heart of Southside development shifted westward toward the wooded bluff-tops that overlooked the Trinity River Valley. Here such still fashionable neighborhoods as **Berkeley** (centered on the intersection of Forest Park Blvd. and Windsor Place) and **Park Hill** (Medford Court and Winton Terrace) provide handsome streetscapes lined with many fine examples of Craftsman, Tudor, Colonial Revival, Spanish Eclectic, and other popular housing styles of the pre-World War II decades.

As development began on the bluffs above the Trinity, the city purchased a

FORT WORTH ZOO *Visitors have close-up views of numerous reptiles in the popular Herpetarium.*

riverside tract below to create **Forest Park**, an extension of the Trinity Park system that occupies the opposite riverbank to the north (see "Cultural District"). The new park was linked to the neighborhoods above by a winding roadway flanked by the **Forest Park Entrance Towers★** (Park Place Ave. and Forest Park Blvd.; 1917; John Pollard, Fort Worth, architect). These are tile-roofed and arched-windowed masses of rubble stone that hark back to an era when cities occasionally built function-less monuments merely to please the eye.

Today Forest Park also houses two of the park system's most important visitor attractions. A short distance downslope from the Entrance Towers is the **Fort Worth Zoo★** (2727 Zoological Park Drive), now in the midst of a long-term modernization program that will replace old-fashioned cages with open habitats surrounded by inconspicuous, moat-like barriers. The Zoo also includes a fascinating **Aquarium** featuring both oceanic and freshwater life.

Still more impressive is the Zoo's **Herpetarium★★**. In separate rooms, one for each continent, are dozens of glass-fronted enclosures affording close-up views of exotic lizards, turtles, frogs, toads, crocodiles, and snakes. Each species has its own carefully created native environment, ranging from sandy deserts to lush tropical rain forests. Most of the collection's reptiles and amphibians are harmless but also included are some of the world's deadliest cobras, vipers, and rattlesnakes, all safely isolated behind thick glass barriers.

Across University Drive from the Zoo is **Log Cabin Village★** (University Drive and Log Cabin Lane; 1966 and later), an authentically furnished group of seven pioneer log houses moved from rural sites and carefully restored. Most of these were originally built during the 1850s in the Cross Timbers belt west of Fort Worth, which was then a remote Indian frontier. A visit to the village, which has demonstrations of candlemaking, corn milling and other early crafts, vividly recalls the rugged lifestyle of pioneer families living on the edge of westward settlement.

TEXAS CHRISTIAN UNIVERSITY

In 1910 the principal building of a small Waco, Texas, college operated by the Christian (Disciples of Christ) Church was destroyed in a disastrous fire. Seeking to rebuild on a larger site, the trustees were enticed to move to Fort Worth by the city's offer of $200,000 in cash, as well as a remote fifty-six-acre Southside hilltop, to which a trolley line and utility service were to be provided without charge. By 1912 **Texas Christian University** (2800 South University Drive; 1912 and later) had completed three new buildings and had begun its long tenure as Fort Worth's most distinguished institution of higher learning. Today the University's sixty-building campus, mostly built of uniform light-buff brick, serves an enrollment of about six thousand.

GRAIN ELEVATOR COMPLEX

The most dramatic industrial monuments along the Southside's many miles of radiating rail lines are a group of huge grain elevators sandwiched together between the Katy and Santa Fe tracks along South Main Street. Begun in the 1920s as a part of the city's rapid rise to become the principal grain terminal of the southern United States, the **Kimbell Milling Company Elevators★★** (east side of 1900-2000 blocks of S. Main St.; 1924 and later) stand just across Main Street from the slightly younger **Lone Star Elevators★★**, now the Producer's Corporation (west side of 2000 block of S. Main St.; 1930 and later). Passing through the center of this complex, with towering walls on all sides, the visitor is suddenly transported into a futuristic canyon of white concrete.

Dwarfed by the towering elevators are the adjacent, one-story brick buildings of the **Kimbell Milling Company Offices** (1929 S. Main St.; 1934; architect unknown). These were formerly the headquarters of the vast grain, food processing, oil, and real estate empire amassed by art collector and philanthropist Kay Kimbell (1886-1964), whose will established Fort Worth's internationally important Kimbell Art Museum (see "Cultural District"). During Kimbell's lifetime many of the museum's treasured masterpieces hung in these unpretentious buildings.

KIMBELL ELEVATORS *One of the largest of many grain elevator and milling complexes scattered around the city.*

Westside *

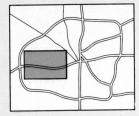

Spurred by improvements made for Camp Bowie, a World War I Army training center that was dismantled in 1919, much of Fort Worth's affluent residential development since the 1920s has been concentrated on the hills beyond the Trinity River to the west of downtown.

The first attempt to expand the city westward beyond the Trinity River barrier took place in 1890 when the Chamberlain Development Company of Denver, Colorado, bought two thousand acres and platted them into small homesites. This new subdivision, called Arlington Heights, occupied a strip of high ground between the two branches of the Trinity River (West Fork and Clear Fork) that converge just beneath downtown's Courthouse bluffs.

To provide access from downtown, the developers extended West 7th Street across a bridge over the Clear Fork, through the wide river bottoms, and up to a hillside junction with the subdivision's new main street—Arlington Heights (now Camp Bowie) Boulevard. Following the custom of the day, the developers also built a trolley line along the route, terminating at a now long-demolished amusement park bordering Lake Como.

Lacking water and sewer service and without city police or fire protection, most of Arlington Heights' lots remained unsold. The largely vacant subdivision passed through several ownerships over a twenty-year period until its fortunes changed for the better in 1917.

As the United States began its whirlwind military buildup to enter World War I, Army officials chose Arlington Heights' two thousand acres of empty lots as a training site after the city agreed to provide sewer, water, and electric service to supplement the long-underused trolley line. Soon the area was filled by the tents and temporary buildings of Camp Bowie, one of Texas' four principal Army Training Centers. Named for Alamo hero Jim Bowie, the camp prepared over 100,000 troops for fighting in the French trenches during its short lifetime.

After the armistice in November 1918, the camp was quickly dismantled, but the area now had the advantage of full utility service and became the focus of new residential growth. By 1920 the long-vacant homesites of **Arlington Heights*** were filling with hundreds of new, one-story "bungalows," most of them brick-veneered versions of the popular Craftsman housing fashion of the period. Today a drive along the tree-lined streets that made up the core of this large district (see map) provides a glimpse of a typical middle-class residential neighborhood of Fort Worth's oil boom years.

CAMP BOWIE BOULEVARD

Arlington Heights' main thoroughfare retained its wartime name to become today's Camp Bowie Boulevard, a three-mile commercial strip that includes many of Fort Worth's upscale stores and shops. The principal reminders of the Boulevard's more tranquil early days are its grassy median strip, originally much wider, along which the streetcars once ran, and its picturesque 1929 brick paving, which survives only because of loud citizen protests each time the city has proposed to cover the venerable bricks with asphalt.

Much of the older Camp Bowie strip is slowly upgrading, as its gas stations, stores, and fast-food shops are being either renovated or replaced by new multitenant retail buildings. About a mile beyond the original end of the brick-paved Boulevard today stands the **Ridglea Shopping Center** (6000-6300 blocks of Camp Bowie Blvd.; 1940 and later), a large retail complex with several multishop components of different vintage. Here are concentrated many of the city's upscale boutiques and services that cater to affluent Westside residents.

RIVER CREST

As the small lots of Arlington Heights and adjacent neighborhoods filled with middle-class bungalows following World War I, so also did the city's elite begin to abandon their previously favored Southside neighborhoods for new river bluff developments along the Westside's northern edge. Most prestigious of these was **River Crest***** (irregular boundaries, see map;

WESTOVER HILLS *This residential suburb was founded in 1930 and is still among the city's most prestigious.*

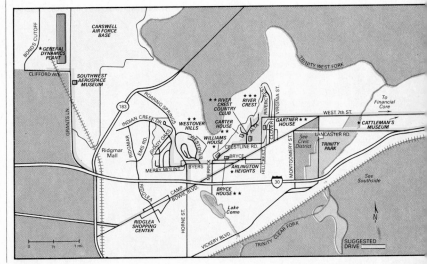

1911 and later), where a relatively small number of large homesites were sandwiched around the golf fairways of the exclusive River Crest Country Club. Opened in 1911, the area was home to only a few wealthy pioneers until the 1920s, when it quickly became the city's favored site for new mansions and estates.

POST-MODERN CLASSIC *The new home of the River Crest Country Club provides an attractive centerpiece for a neighborhood of early-twentieth-century houses.*

Among the River Crest area's most important and unmodified landmarks from the pre-1920 period are the Chateauesque **Bryce House★★** (4900 Bryce Ave.; Sanguinet & Messer, Fort Worth, architects), built in 1893 as one of the few houses of the original Arlington Heights venture, and the exuberantly Neoclassical **Williams House★** (4936 Crestline Rd.; 1909; architect unknown).

Exploration of the neighborhood's many winding, dead-end streets yields views of the far more numerous dwellings built in the Eclectic housing fashions of the 1920s. Two of the most important of these are the rambling, Craftsman style **Carter House★★** (1220 Broad Ave.; ca. 1919 and later; original architect unknown), long the home of civic leader, newspaper publisher, and philanthropist Amon G. Carter (1879-1955; see "Cultural District") and

ECLECTIC ERA CLASSIC *Architect John Staub's Gartner House is a distinctive example of the popular Tudor style of the 1920s and 1930s.*

the **Gartner House★★** (935 Hillcrest St.; 1929), a unique design by the distinguished Houston architect John Staub (b. 1892). In this Eclectic Era masterpiece, Staub took the trademark of the popular Tudor fashion of the day—a dominant, front-facing gable—and transformed it into a fanciful, scallop-edged centerpiece of rare delicacy and charm.

Standing nearby as the focal point of the neighborhood is the new home of the **River Crest Country Club★★** (1500 Western Ave.; 1985; Taft Architects, Houston), a striking, Post-modern mass of pink brick that delightfully captures and magnifies the spirit of the grand Period Houses around it.

WESTOVER HILLS

By 1930 most of the River Crest development's few exclusive homesites had been sold and built upon. In that year two Florida land developers moved to Fort Worth and purchased a bluff-top tract immediately to the west of River Crest, which they incorporated as the small island town of **Westover Hills★★** (irregular boundaries, see map; 1930 and later). A labyrinth of curving streets and large lots was laid out on the wooded hills, and these lots soon became the city's most prestigious homesites, a distinction they still retain today.

Divided into two isolated segments by its only through street (Roaring Springs Road), Westover Hills development during the 1930s centered on dead-end Westover Road in the eastern segment. Here can be seen many fine examples of the late Eclectic housing fashions of that decade.

Following World War II, development shifted to the larger segment west of Roaring Springs Road which contains an upscale, architect-designed progression of post-1950 housing styles. These styles begin with the Ranch, Contemporary, and Mansard dwellings that were popular in the 1950s and 1960s and proceed to the Shed, Neo-Modernistic, Neo-French, and related fashions of the 1970s and 1980s, some of which hark directly back to their Eclectic neighbors of the 1930s.

GENERAL DYNAMICS AND CARSWELL AIR FORCE BASE

With the outbreak of World War II, a decision was made that was to profoundly alter development of the Westside's vacant land beyond Westover Hills. This area was bounded on the north by Lake Worth, built in 1914 as a water-supply reservoir and surrounded by thousands of city-owned acres of undeveloped land. Following the Camp Bowie example set twenty-five years earlier, Fort Worth officials offered fifteen hundred lakeside acres for a new aircraft plant to build bombers for the war effort. Completed in 1941, the Consolidated Aircraft Corporation Plant employed an unprecedented thirty thousand workers and was soon joined by an adjacent Army Air Base. Many of these workers lived in modest tract-house developments that began to spread over the nearby hills.

Unlike earlier Camp Bowie, the bomber plant and airfield were not dismantled at war's end but instead were expanded to play a crucial role in the nation's defense strategies during the Cold War years of the 1950s and beyond. In 1947 the Convair

Plant, as it was then called, was chosen to build the giant, six-engine B-36 bomber. With a flight range of ten thousand miles, these were the Air Force's newly designed vehicles for intercontinental delivery of atomic weapons. Soon the adjacent airfield was expanded; renamed **Carswell Air Force Base**, it became a principal component of the Strategic Air Command's early nuclear strike force.

As the giant B-36 bombers became obsolete, the **General Dynamics Plant★**, as it is now called, continued to expand for production of other military aircraft, including the B-58 bomber and the swept-wing F-111 fighter. Today the huge facility manufactures the F-16 Air Combat fighter used by the U.S. Air Force and several NATO allies. With eighteen thousand workers, it is by far the largest single employer in Fort Worth.

The giant plant and adjacent Air Force Base are best seen by driving north along Spur Highway 341. This roadway descends to the plant entrance from a nearby hilltop that offers a panoramic view of the vast facilities. A short distance south of the plant entrance is the **Southwest Aerospace Museum** (300 N. Grants Lane), an undeveloped but intriguing open-air display of vintage military aircraft including the B-36 and B-58 bombers produced by the plant.

WEST SEVENTH STREET

Much of the traffic between the Westside's residential districts and downtown Fort Worth still flows along West 7th Street, route of the original Arlington Heights trolley line of 1890. In the early decades of the century, several near-downtown blocks of West 7th (between about Macon and Penn streets) became the city's "Automobile Row," where affluent Westside commuters were enticed by windows filled with shiny new models. Several of the early showroom buildings still survive.

Today this area is also the site of the intriguing **Cattleman's Museum★** (1301 W. 7th St.), which displays artifacts, photographs, and short video presentations about the Texas cattle industry, complete with a life-sized Longhorn steer. These carefully designed exhibits were opened in 1980 as a part of the new headquarters building of the venerable Texas and Southwestern Cattle Raisers Association, founded in 1877 and located in Fort Worth since 1893.

HOURS AND CHARGES

Southwest Aerospace Museum: (817) 735-4143. Thur-Sun, 10 am to 3 pm. Admission free.

Cattleman's Museum: (817) 332-7064. Mon-Fri, 8:30 am to 4:30 pm. Admission free.

Related Shopping, Dining, and Entertainment (SiDE) Areas: Cultural District; Camp Bowie Boulevard.

BEYOND SIGHTSEEING

Beyond the pleasures of exploring new sights lie the everyday essentials of travel—eating, sleeping, and getting around—as well as the optional activities of shopping and seeking diversion. This final section is intended to simplify, and increase your enjoyment of, each of these challenging aspects of being in an unfamiliar city.

In Dallas and Fort Worth, as in most large cities, interesting places to shop, dine, or find entertainment are not randomly scattered but rather tend to occur in clusters. Typically each cluster has its own distinctive focus and character; understanding these *before* you arrive can save time, money, and disappointment. On the final pages of this book are described sixteen such clusters which, we believe, include the bulk of Dallas' and Fort Worth's non-sightseeing destinations that are of interest to visitors. We call these *SiDE Areas* (for **S**hopping, **D**ining, **E**ntertainment). They are printed on pages with yellow borders for easy reference and each SiDE Area's location is shown on index maps printed inside the front or back covers of the book.

The descriptions of the sixteen SiDE Areas include individual listings for many of Dallas' and Fort Worth's most popular shops, restaurants, theaters, and nightclubs, as well as detailed maps showing their locations. The introductory discussions presented here provide additional background information about Getting Around, Lodging, Shopping, Dining, and Entertainment in the two cities.

GETTING AROUND

Dallas and Fort Worth are twentieth-century cities that grew up with the automobile. As a result, they sprawl over vast areas with great distances separating many destinations. Although the public bus service is comfortable and dependable, routes are often winding, very slow, and not convenient to many sights. Visitors planning comprehensive sightseeing will thus need access to their own car, or to an expensive taxi or limousine service. Note that the costs of the latter options can very quickly exceed the price of a small rental car. On the other hand, car-less visitors should be cheered to learn that several of both cities' most important Sightseeing Districts (West End, Financial Core, Arts District, and Fair Park in Dallas; Financial Core, Civic District, and the Stockyards in Fort Worth) are best explored on foot. Furthermore, all of these destinations are either within the downtown areas or are only a short taxi or bus ride away.

Airport Access

The busy *Dallas/Fort Worth International Airport*, with about 1800 flights daily, handles most out-of-state and many local airline arrivals. It is situated midway between the two cities, about eighteen miles from either downtown. The one-way cab fare to the downtown area is about $22 for each city, but be sure that the cab serves your destination because the two cities have separate local cab companies (see below). A less expensive alternative is the *Super Shuttle*, 329-2000 (metro), comfortable mini-buses with direct service from the airport to any Dallas or Fort Worth destination. One-way service to downtown Dallas hotels is $8; to downtown offices, $10; to downtown Fort Worth hotels, $15; and to downtown Fort Worth offices, $18. Call for reservations as well as for rates to other destinations. *The T Charter Service*, (817) 334-0092 and (817) 870-6230, provides direct buses to seven central Fort Worth hotels. It runs hourly and is $6 one way, $10 round trip, free for children under 12.

Love Field is Dallas' convenient, in-town airport that serves principally Southwest Airlines. This carrier has frequent and affordable flights to many cities in the region—Houston, San Antonio, Austin, Albuquerque, Midland, New Orleans, etc. Taxi fare from Love Field to downtown Dallas is about $10. Super Shuttle service is also available (see above).

Taxis

Both cities are served by large taxi fleets. These generally do not cruise, but wait in cab stands or respond to radio calls. In Dallas the principal companies are *State Taxicab*, 823-2161; *Terminal Cab*, 350-4445; and *Yellow Cab*, 426-6262. Sample fares: downtown to Galleria, $16-18; downtown to Fair Park, $5-6; downtown to Las Colinas, $20. Fares are all metered at $1.30 for the first 1/10 mile plus 10¢ for each additional 1/10 mile or 3/5 minute traffic delay. There is a flat surcharge of 50¢ (day) or $1 (night) for each passenger beyond the first.

The principal Fort Worth cab companies are *American Cab*, (817) 332-1919, and *Yellow Cab*, (817) 534-5555. Fares are metered at rates similar to those in Dallas. Sample fares: downtown to Stockyards or Cultural District, $6-7; downtown to Ridglea Shopping Center, $10-12.

Buses

DART (Dallas Area Rapid Transit) operates comfortable, modern buses throughout the city and adjacent suburban towns. As its name suggests, the agency is also planning a rapid transit rail system, with the first line scheduled to open in the early 1990s. DART provides an efficient *Telephone Information Center*, 979-1111, which is open from 5 a.m. to 10 p.m. on weekdays and 8 a.m. to 6 p.m. on weekends and holidays, as well as two downtown *Customer Assistance Offices*, one at Main and Akard streets, the other at Elm and Ervay streets. These are open from 7 a.m. to 6 p.m. on weekdays only. All will provide routes, schedules, fares (which start at 75¢ and increase with distance), and other information on reaching specific destinations by bus. The most useful DART services for Dallas visitors are the *Hop-a-Bus* and *DART ABOUT* routes in the downtown area. These cost only 35¢ and run every 5-11 minutes on five convenient loops.

The Fort Worth bus system, called *"The T,"* is a rare transportation bargain. Fares throughout the city are only 75¢, and there is *no charge* for rides in the downtown area (Financial Core and Civic Districts). Just ask for a "free zone" ticket when boarding and return it to the driver as you get off. For information about reaching Fort Worth destinations by bus call (817) 870-6200 between 6 a.m. and 8 p.m. on weekdays, or 8 a.m. and 5 p.m. on weekends.

Drivers Note

Texas law requires that everyone in the front seat wear seat belts. In addition, children under two years old must be in an approved restraining seat and those from ages two to four must wear seat belts when riding in either front or back seats. Streets and parking meters in downtown Dallas have tow-away signs that *really* mean it. Carefully observe the tow-away hour, because tow trucks will begin arriving shortly thereafter.

LODGING

Dallas and Fort Worth have an unusual abundance of good hotels and motels providing comfortable lodging at all price levels. Many belong to the familiar national chains (Hyatt, Loews, Hilton, Sheraton, Marriott, Holiday Inn, Howard Johnson's, etc.), and others are part of large regional chains. Only a few continue to be individually owned; these must normally be either very good or very cheap (and sometimes of marginal quality) in order to survive. You'll find it difficult to go wrong staying in any of the numerous establishments shown in the map and listings on pages 66-67. All offer clean and comfortable rooms with both air-conditioning and television, luxuries that were far from universal only twenty-five years ago.

Today the main difference between expensive and more moderately priced accommodations usually lies not in the rooms themselves, but in outside services—the number and quality of in-house restaurants, and the availability of room service, health clubs, meeting rooms, shops, and newsstands. These amenities are found in most large hotels and multistory "motor hotels" but are less common in low-rise motels, which usually provide the best value for those requiring only basic lodging. Note also that the more elaborate establishments catering to convention and business travelers often have much-reduced room rates on weekends.

Perhaps the most important consideration in choosing a hotel or motel is location. Will it be convenient to the places that you want to visit for sightseeing, shopping, or business? For this reason, all of the establishments listed here are also shown on a map that can be easily compared with the "Sightseeing District" and "SiDE Area" maps printed inside the front and back covers of the book. If you plan to visit without a car, a downtown or close-in location in either city will provide many attractions within a short walk, taxi ride, or bus trip. Even if you arrive by car, a careful choice of base location can save many tiresome hours of driving.

If you are planning a lengthy stay, are concerned with specific services, or want to find the very best lodging values, there are several guidebook series that emphasize hotels and motels as a principal subject. Particularly useful are the excellent *Mobil Travel Guides* (Prentice-Hall Press), available in many libraries, bookstores, and Mobil Service Stations throughout the country. These seven regional

TRAVIS WALK *Typical of the area's newer shop and restaurant settings is this human-scaled, mixed-use complex in Dallas' Knox-Henderson SiDE Area.*

volumes appear in yearly editions and include most of the more expensive hotels and motor hotels, as well as a careful selection of moderately priced accommodations. Entries include a summary of services, number and price ranges of rooms, and an overall rating for quality. Dallas and Fort Worth appear in the volume covering the "Southwest and South Central Area."

A popular lodging alternative is one of the many small "bed and breakfast" establishments that have recently sprung up in Dallas and Fort Worth, as elsewhere around the country, to provide home-like overnight stays. Further information can be obtained from *Bed and Breakfast Texas Style* (4224 West Red Bird Lane in Dallas, 298-8586), which handles reservations for fifteen such establishments in Dallas and two in Fort Worth. All offer private baths and breakfasts for rates ranging from $40 to $60 per night for two persons.

SHOPPING

Dallas has been the Southwest's leading shopping city since shortly after the fateful day in 1873 when it became the crossing point of Texas' first intercontinental railroad lines. Soon it was the principal distribution center for a flood of consumer goods brought into the region by rail. Paralleling this rise as a wholesale market was the establishment of many retail stores that specialized in fashionable and hard-to-find merchandise. As a result, Dallas became the region's favored destination for specialty shopping and for the purchase of luxury goods.

Paradoxically, the city's reputation for fashionable shopping expanded from regional to national scope in the midst of the Great Depression of the 1930s. This was the result of the timely combination of a young merchandising genius named Stanley Marcus and the financial windfalls provided by the supergiant East Texas Oil Field, which was discovered in 1930 by a Dallas operator. Marcus, the son of one of the founders of the city's long-fashionable Neiman-Marcus Department Store, quickly realized the publicity value of customers buying jewels and furs during those dark years. Soon his sophisticated marketing techniques and impeccable taste had focused the national press on Neiman-Marcus as one of the country's fashion trendsetters, a reputation it still enjoys today.

A new component was added to the Dallas merchandising scene in the 1950s when real estate developer Trammell Crow built the first unit of what is now the Dallas Market Center, the largest wholesale marketing complex in the world. In it are held over thirty intensive marketing sessions each year that alternately feature men's clothing, women's clothing, home furnishings, gifts, and even computer wares. Thousands of Dallas women, many with the leisure to shop during the rest of the year, eagerly look forward to working as low-paid assistants during the hectic but exciting sessions. Here they are exposed to the latest in fashion, furnishings, and gifts from all over the world, as well as to many of the nation's top retail store buyers. Thirty years of "working the markets" have trained legions of astute and discerning Dallas shoppers, some of whom have moved on to open their own stores. The overall quality of Dallas retailing thus still benefits from the city's role as a wholesale center.

With the unique shopping opportunities of Dallas close at hand, Fort Worth retailing is understandably focused more on everyday needs than on unusual or luxury items. Two exceptions are Western clothing and art, attracted in the first case by the city's long tradition as a livestock center and in the second by its more recent role as the home of three of the Southwest's most distinguished museums of art.

Women's and Children's Clothing

Women's fashions are a Dallas specialty. Several of the SiDE Areas described on the last pages of the book have shops with every emphasis, from top-of-the-line designer originals to distinctive everyday items. These women's wear shops are mostly concentrated in the Highland Park Village, Lovers Lane, Downtown Dallas (particularly *Neiman-Marcus*), NorthPark, and Galleria SiDE Areas. One of the city's most exclusive women's stores is *not* located in one of the SiDE Areas. This is *Loretta Blum*, 526-8770, at 4268 Oak Lawn Avenue in North Dallas near the southern boundary of Highland Park. Here you can find fashions by Krizia, Ungaro, Valentino, Donna Karan, and Anne Klein. Blum also carries a complete selection of accessories as well as evening wear by Scassi, Oscar de la Renta, Herrera, and Chuck Jones.

For infants' and children's clothes, Lovers Lane, NorthPark, and, particularly, several fine shops in Snider Plaza as well as *Wicker Garden's Children* in the Highland Park Village, are all good bets. *Storkland*, in Knox-Henderson, carries a remarkably large selection of items for the under-two set, from cribs and strollers to suits and toys.

Men's Clothing

Quality menswear is somewhat more scattered around the city. Here's a quick review of the highlights. Downtown, *Neiman-Marcus* has one of the nation's largest selections of top-of-the-line Oxxford suits, as well as several less costly labels, whereas *Brooks Brothers* carries that chain's name-brand specialty—conservative, Ivy League fashions. At NorthPark, *Woolf Brothers* has a full line of Hart, Schaffner & Marx suits as well as other quality names, while *Cuzzens* specializes in superb (and expensive) European imports, as does *Bandiera's* in the Galleria. Another shop with fine European menswear is *Hippolyte*, located in the Uptown SiDE Area. Highland Park Village is the home of the *Hermes* boutique, which has superb men's accessories, and *Polo*, featuring that popular brand of sportswear for both men and women. Across from Southern Methodist University, a few blocks south of the Snider Plaza SiDE Area, is one of the city's most complete selections of clothes for boys and college-age young men at *Culwell and Son*, 522-7000, 6319 Hillcrest Avenue. The store also has large men's and women's departments as well as several branches around the city.

Western Wear

Dallas and Fort Worth provide excellent shopping for Western-style clothing. Hides from the Fort Worth Stockyards, for example, long provided the leather for making *Justin Boots*. This legendary, 109-year-old Texas company has been headquartered in Fort Worth since 1925 and today operates a factory outlet at 717 West Vickery Boulevard in Fort Worth's Southside district, (817) 654-3103 (metro). Here you can purchase boots and belts at 40 to 60 percent discounts. In Dallas, Justin boots are also discounted at *Just Justin*, in the Market District SiDE Area.

BOOTMAKER *Western boots and saddles are still custom made by hand at Fort Worth's* M.L. LEDDY'S BOOT & SADDLERY, *a longtime favorite of area stockmen.*

HOTELS AND MOTELS

The Dallas—Fort Worth area's principal hotels and motels are listed below and their general locations are shown on the map at right, which also includes airports and major roadways. This map can be compared with the index maps inside the books' front cover (Dallas) or back cover (Fort Worth), to relate individual establishments to the two cities' Sightseeing Districts and SiDE Areas.

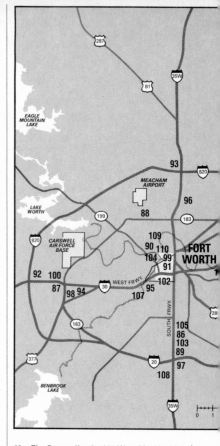

DALLAS

1 ■ **Adolphus Hotel.** 1321 Commerce Street. 742-8200
2 ■ **Ambassador Plaza.** 1312 Ervay Street. 565-9003
3 ■ **Best Western-Dallas North Central.** 8051 LBJ Freeway. 234-2431
4 ■ **Best Western-Garden Inn.** 4103 Belt Line Road, Addison. 991-8888.
5 ■ **Big Town Inn.** 4203 Highway 80, Mesquite. 270-6711.
6 ■ **The Bradford Plaza.** 302 South Houston Street. 761-9090.
7 ■ **Carousel Motel.** 3211 Forest Lane, Garland. 276-8538.
8 ■ **Circle Inn.** 2560 West Northwest Highway. 357-8231.
9 ■ **Colony Parke Hotel.** 6060 North Central Expressway. 750-6060.
10 ■ **Crestpark Hotel.** 4242 Lomo Alto Drive. 526-7421.
11 ■ **Dallas Hilton.** 1914 Commerce Street. 747-7000.
12 ■ **Dallas Hilton Inn.** 5600 North Central Expressway. 827-4100.
13 ■ **Dallas Plaza Hotel.** 1933 Main Street. 741-7700.
14 ■ **Days Inn Motel.** 9386 LBJ Freeway, 690-1220.
15 ■ **D/FW Airport Hilton.** 1800 Highway 26 East, Grapevine. 481-8444.
16 ■ **Doubletree Inn.** 8250 North Central Expressway. 691-8700.
17 ■ **Drury Inn-Dallas North.** 2421 Walnut Hill Lane. 484-3330.
18 ■ **Embassy Suites-Market Center.** 2727 Stemmons Freeway. 630-5332.
19 ■ **Embassy Suites-Dallas Love Field.** 3880 West Northwest Highway. 357-4500.
20 ■ **Executive Inn.** 3232 West Mockingbird Lane. 357-5601.
21 ■ **Exel Inn-Dallas East.** 8510 East R.L. Thornton Freeway. 328-8500.
22 ■ **Fairmont Hotel.** 1717 North Akard Street. 720-2020.
■ **Grand Kempinski Hotel.** See listing for Registry Hotel
23 ■ **Greenleaf Hotel.** 1011 South Akard Street. 421-1083.
24 ■ **Greenwood Inn.** 6950 Stemmons Freeway. 631-6660.
25 ■ **Hampton Inn-Dallas North.** 11069 Composite Drive. 484-6557.
26 ■ **Harvey Hotel-Addison.** 14315 Midway Road. 980-8877.
27 ■ **Harvey Hotel-Dallas.** 7815 LBJ Freeway. 960-7000.
28 ■ **Hawthorne Suites Hotel.** 7900 Brookriver Drive. 688-1010.
29 ■ **The Hilton LBJ.** 4801 LBJ Freeway. 661-3600.
30 ■ **Holiday Inn-Brookhollow.** 7050 North Stemmons Freeway. 630-8500.
31 ■ **Holiday Inn-Crowne Plaza.** 4099 Valley View Lane. 385-9000.
32 ■ **Holiday Inn-Downtown.** 1015 Elm Street. 748-9951.

33 ■ **Holiday Inn-Market Center.** 1955 Market Center Boulevard. 747-9551.
34 ■ **Holiday Inn-Mesquite.** 3601 Highway 80, Mesquite. 279-6561.
35 ■ **Holiday Inn-NorthPark Plaza.** 10650 North Central Expressway. 373-6000.
36 ■ **Holiday Inn-Park Central.** 8102 LBJ Freeway. 239-7211.
37 ■ **Holiday Inn-Regal Row.** 1575 Regal Row. 638-6100.
38 ■ **Hotel Crescent Court.** 400 Crescent Court. 871-3200.
39 ■ **Howard Johnson's-Market Center.** 3111 Stemmons Freeway. 637-0060.
40 ■ **Howard Johnson's-North.** 10333 North Central Expressway. 363-0221.
41 ■ **Hyatt Regency-Dallas.** 300 Reunion Boulevard. 651-1234.
42 ■ **Hyatt Regency-D/FW.** International Parkway, D/FW Airport. 453-8400.
43 ■ **I-20 Duncanville Inn.** 202 Jellison Boulevard, Duncanville. 296-0345.
44 ■ **Inn of Rockwall.** 1130 I-30 and Highway 205, Rockwall. 722-9922.
45 ■ **La Quinta Motor Inn-Central.** 4440 North Central Expressway. 821-4220.
46 ■ **La Quinta Motor Inn-East.** 8303 East R.L. Thornon Expressway. 324-3731.
47 ■ **La Quinta Motor Inn-NorthPark.** 10001 North Central Expressway. 361-8200.
48 ■ **La Quinta Motor Inn-Regal Row.** 1625 Regal Row. 630-5701.
49 ■ **Lincoln Hotel.** 5410 LBJ Freeway. 934-8400.
50 ■ **Loews Anatole Dallas.** 2201 Stemmons Freeway. 748-1200.
51 ■ **Lynn Hotel.** 3401 Gaston Avenue. 824-6331.
52 ■ **Mansion on Turtle Creek Boulevard.** 2821 Turtle Creek. 559-2100.
53 ■ **Market Center Boulevard Inn.** 2026 Market Center Boulevard. 748-2243.
54 ■ **Marriott-Market Center.** 2101 Stemmons Freeway. 748-8551.
55 ■ **Marriott-Park Central.** 7750 LBJ Freeway. 233-4421.
56 ■ **Marriott-Quorum.** 14901 Dallas North Parkway. 661-2800.
57 ■ **Melrose Hotel.** 3015 Oak Lawn Avenue. 521-5151.
58 ■ **Non-Smokers Inn.** 9229 Carpenter Freeway. 631-6633.
59 ■ **Park Cities Inn.** 6101 Hillcrest Avenue. 521-0330.
60 ■ **Park Suite Hotel.** 13131 North Central Expressway. 234-3300.
61 ■ **Plaza of the Americas Hotel.** 650 North Pearl Street. 979-9000.
62 ■ **Quality Inn-Market Center.** 2015 Market Center Boulevard. 741-7481.
63 ■ **Radisson Hotel-Stemmons.** 2330 West Northwest Highway. 351-4477.
64 ■ **Ramada Hotel-Dallas.** 1055 Regal Row. 634-8550.
65 ■ **Ramada Inn-Love Field.** 6900 Cedar Springs Road. 357-8451.
66 ■ **Red Roof Inn-Dallas.** 1550 Empire Central Drive. 638-5151.
67 ■ **Red Roof Inn-East.** 8108 East R.L. Thornton Freeway. 388-8741.
68 ■ **Red Roof Inn-Northwest.** 10334 Gardner Road. 506-8100.

69 ■ **The Regent Hotel.** 1241 West Mockingbird Lane, 630-7000.
70 ■ **Registry Hotel.** 15201 Dallas North Parkway. 386-6000. Name changed to Grand Kempinski Hotel.
71 ■ **The Residence Inn.** 13636 Goldmark Drive. 669-0478.
72 ■ **Rodeway Inn-Central.** 4150 North Central Expressway. 827-4310.
73 ■ **Rodeway Inn-Love Field.** 3104 West Mockingbird Lane. 357-1701.
74 ■ **Sheraton Dallas.** 400 North Olive Street. 922-8000.
75 ■ **Sheraton-Mockingbird.** 1893 West Mockingbird Lane. 634-8850.
76 ■ **Sheraton-Northeast.** 11350 LBJ Freeway. 341-5400.
77 ■ **Sheraton-Park Central.** 12720 Merit Drive. 385-3000.
78 ■ **The Stoneleigh Hotel.** 2927 Maple Avenue. 871-7111.
79 ■ **Stouffer Dallas Hotel.** 2222 North Stemmons Freeway. 631-2222.
80 ■ **The Summit Hotel.** 2645 LBJ Freeway. 243-3363.
81 ■ **Travelers Inn.** 3243 Merrifield Road. 826-3510.
82 ■ **Tropicana Inn.** 3939 North Central Expressway. 526-8881.
83 ■ **Viscount-Market Center.** 4500 Harry Hines Boulevard. 522-6650.
84 ■ **Westin-Hotel Galleria.** 13340 Dallas North Parkway. 934-9494.
85 ■ **Wyndham Garden Hotel.** 110 West Carpenter Freeway. 594-1600.

FORT WORTH

86 ■ **Best Western-Fort Worther.** 4213 South Freeway. (817) 923-1987.

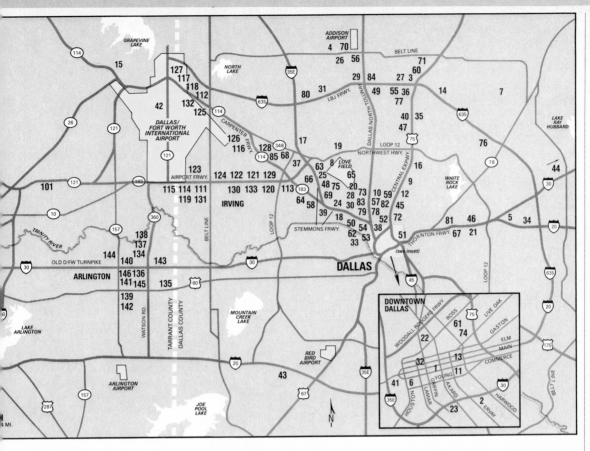

87 ■ Best Western-West Branch Inn. 7301 West Freeway. (817) 244-7444.
88 ■ Best Western-Sandpiper Inn. 4000 North Main Street. (817) 625-5531.
89 ■ Days Inn-Felix Street. 812 East Felix Street. (817) 926-9211.
90 ■ Downtown Motor Inn. 600 North Henderson Street. (817) 332-6187.
91 ■ Fort Worth Hilton. 1701 Commerce Street. (817) 335-7000.
92 ■ Gateway Inn. I-20 and Las Vegas Trail. (817) 246-4961.
93 ■ Great Western Inn. Loop 820 and Highway 156. (817) 625-6211.
94 ■ Green Oaks Inn. 6901 West Freeway. (817) 738-7311.
95 ■ Holiday Inn-Midtown. 1401 South University. (817) 336-9311.
96 ■ Holiday Inn-North. 2540 Meacham Boulevard. (817) 625-9911.
97 ■ Holiday Inn-South. 100 Altamesa Boulevard. (817) 293-3088.
98 ■ Holiday Regent Motor Inn. 3501 West Highway 183. (817) 732-3301.
99 ■ Hyatt Regency-Fort Worth. 815 Main Street. (817) 870-1234.
100 ■ La Quinta Motor Inn. 7888 Highway I-30. (817) 246-5511.
101 ■ La Quinta Motor Inn-Northeast. 7920 Bedford Euless Road. (817) 485-2750.
102 ■ Medical Center Inn. 1010 Southlake Boulevard. (817) 335-4651.
103 ■ Motel 6. 4433 South Freeway. (817) 921-4900.
104 ■ Park Central Hotel. 1010 Houston Street. (817) 336-2011.
105 ■ Quality Inn-South. 4201 South Freeway. (817) 923-8281.
106 ■ Ramada Inn-Central. 2000 Beach Street. (817) 534-4801.
107 ■ Residence Inns. 1701 South University Drive. (817) 870-1011.
108 ■ South Loop Motor Lodge. 6328 South Freeway. (817) 293-5333.

109 ■ Stockyards Hotel. East Exchange Avenue. (817) 625-6427.
110 ■ Worthington Hotel. 200 Main Street. (817) 870-1000.

IRVING

111 ■ AmeriSuites Hotel. 3950 West Airport Freeway. 790-1950.
112 ■ Best Western-Preference Inn. 4325 West Highway 114. 621-8277.
113 ■ Days Inn-Texas Stadium. 2200 East Airport Freeway. 438-6666.
114 ■ Drury Inn. 4210 West Airport Freeway. 986-1200.
115 ■ Embassy Suites-D/FW South. 4650 West Airport Freeway. 790-0093.
116 ■ Four Seasons Hotel. 4150 North MacArthur Boulevard. 717-0700.
117 ■ Harvey Hotel-D/FW Airport. 4545 West John Carpenter Freeway. 929-4500.
118 ■ Holiday Inn-D/FW North. 4441 Highway 114. 929-8181.
119 ■ Holiday Inn-D/FW South. 4440 West Airport Freeway. 399-1010.
120 ■ Holiday Inn-Texas Stadium. 1930 East Airport Freeway. 438-1313.
121 ■ Holiday Motel. 123 West Airport Freeway. 255-1171.
122 ■ Irving Inn. 909 West Airport Freeway. 255-7108.
123 ■ La Quinta Motor Inn. 4105 West Airport Freeway. 252-6546.
124 ■ Lexington Hotel Suites. 1701 West Airport Freeway. 258-6226.
125 ■ Lexington Hotel Suites-D/FW Airport North. 4100 West John Carpenter Freeway. 929-4008.
126 ■ Marriott Courtyard. 1115 West Walnut Hill Lane. 350-8100.
127 ■ Marriott Hotel-D/FW Airport. 8440 Freeport Parkway. 929-8800.

128 ■ Marriott Mandalay. 221 East Las Colinas Boulevard. 556-0800.
129 ■ Quality Inn Hotel-D/FW Airport South. 215 East Airport Freeway. 256-3800.
130 ■ Ramada Inn-D/FW Airport. 120 West Airport Freeway. 579-8911.
131 ■ Rodeway Inn-D/FW Airport. 4110 West Airport Freeway. 399-2005.
132 ■ Sheraton Grand Hotel. Highway 114 and Esters Boulevard. 929-8400.
133 ■ TraveLodge. 110 West Airport Freeway. 438-8500.

ARLINGTON

134 ■ Arlington Hilton. 2401 East Lamar Boulevard. (817) 640-7722.
135 ■ Best Western-Great Southwest Inn. 3501 East Division Street. (817) 640-7722.
136 ■ Best Western-Turnpike Motor Lodge. 2001 East Copeland Road. (817) 461-1122.
137 ■ Days Inn. 1195 North Watson Road. (817) 640-7544.
138 ■ Holiday Inn-Great Southest. Highway 360 North at Brown Boulevard. (817) 640-7712.
139 ■ Holiday Inn-Six Flags. 903 North Collins Street. (817) 261-3621.
140 ■ Lexington Hotel Suites. 1075 East Waldrop Drive. (817) 261-8900.
141 ■ Marriott Courtyard. 1500 Stadium Drive West. 1-800-321-2211.
142 ■ Quality Inn. 1601 East Division Street. (817) 261-2300.
143 ■ Radisson Suite Hotel. 700 Avenue H East. (817) 640-0440.
144 ■ Ramada Inn. 700 East Lamar Boulevard. (817) 265-7711.
145 ■ Rodeway Inn. 833 North Watson Road. (817) 640-7080.
146 ■ Sheraton CentrePark Hotel. 1500 Stadium Drive East. (817) 261-8200.

The world's largest manufacturer of men's hats, *Resistol*, began in a modest downtown Dallas factory in 1927 and moved to a larger plant in suburban Garland in the 1930s. Today the company's brands include "Resistol" Western hats, and "Dobbs" or "Churchill" dress hats. All of these are finished in, and shipped from, the Dallas factory, which has a discount outlet store at 721 Marion Street, Garland, 494-0337. This store also sells other brands of Western wear at regular prices.

Fort Worth's Stockyards SiDE Area has two family owned Western wear stores, *Ryon's* and *M. L. Leddy's*, that have for many decades been favorites of area ranchers and stockmen. A similar longtime establishment is *Luskey's* in the Sundance Square SiDE Area.

Home Furnishings

Dallas' Market District SiDE Area has numerous stores specializing in decorative items for the home. Some of these are wholesale outlets that can be entered only with a professional interior designer. Others will let you browse but will take orders only through a designer; still others are open both to the trade (designers) and to the general public. All welcome serious inquiries about their policies (see also the discussion under "Market District SiDE Area"). Almost every line of custom furniture (both for office and home), wallpaper, decorative fabric, floor covering, and accessory can be viewed in the Market District. Other important groups of strictly retail home furnishing shops are found in the Lovers Lane, Knox-Henderson, Snider Plaza, and Uptown SiDE Areas in Dallas and in the Camp Bowie Boulevard SiDE Area in Fort Worth.

Antiques

Decorative items from the past make up the most complex—and to many enthusiasts the most fascinating—aspect of shopping for home furnishings. Unfortunately, the explosive population growth of the American Southwest long ago outstripped the relatively small supply of fine "local" antiques, many of which now rest permanently in museum collections. Even quality American antiques from the more heavily populated eastern seaboard states have today become relatively scarce and expensive. To meet the enormous antique demand from Market Center buyers and local residents, dealers in Dallas, as elsewhere in the country, have turned to Western Europe,

EXOTIC ART *The* MICHELE HERLING GALLERIES, *in Dallas' Deep Ellum SiDE Area, specializes in pre-Columbian, African, and Oceanic arts.*

particularly England, where many quality items from the late nineteenth and early twentieth centuries are still available at reasonable prices. Most of Dallas' many antique wholesalers and retailers thus feature English or Continental pieces. Of these they have large selections, with "new shipments arriving regularly." A few other dealers specialize in Oriental, Latin American, or Southwestern Indian antiques. Important concentrations of antique shops are found in Dallas' Uptown, Knox-Henderson, Snider Plaza, and Market District SiDE Areas. *Collectors Note*: Don't miss the outstanding Bybee Collection of Early American Furniture in the Dallas Museum of Art.

Art

Both Dallas and Fort Worth have many fine retail art galleries. In Dallas these are mostly found in the Uptown and Deep Ellum SiDE Areas, in Fort Worth in the Cultural District SiDE Area. Most of the galleries feature works by living artists with either local, regional, or national reputations. Prices can be surprisingly low for the former and breathtakingly high for the latter. Styles range from precise realism through impressionistic and "pop" art to pure abstraction. A few dealers specialize in nineteenth- and earlier twentieth-century works, both American and European.

Off the beaten track are Dallas' *D-Art Visual Art Center* at 2917 Swiss Avenue (East Dallas),

821-2522, a nonprofit gallery and training center with regular shows of reasonably priced works, and *Valley House Gallery* at 6616 Spring Valley Road (North Dallas), 239-2441, which features carefully selected works by many fine current and early-twentieth-century American artists.

Books

Book lovers have a special shopping problem since even the largest retail bookstores can stock only a very small fraction of the 200,000

ROOTABAGA BOOKERY *This Dallas shop has one of the region's largest selections of books for children.*

or so books continually available from American publishers (not to mention the millions of older titles that are now out of print and available only in shops specializing in used or rare books). With the exception of the national chains—Waldenbooks, B. Dalton, Doubleday, etc.—whose stock is generally similar everywhere, each independent bookstore or local chain tends to have special strengths. Also unlike the national chains, which can afford high-rent space in malls and large shopping centers, most local bookstores are scattered in out-of-the-way locations with very low rents. Only a few are found in our sixteen SiDE Areas, so we are including here a more complete listing of important Dallas and Fort Worth sellers of both new and used books.

The area's largest selection of new books is found at the five branches of locally owned *Taylors Bookstores*. Most convenient are the North Dallas location at 4001 Northwest Highway, near Preston Road, 363-1500, and the Fort Worth store in the Camp Bowie Boulevard SiDE Area. A second popular local chain is *Bookstop*, which features discount prices and late closings (11 pm seven nights a week). Handiest to downtown of its three Dallas loca-

ANTIQUES *Delightful antique shops, such as* JOHN HENRY STERRY *shown below, are concentrated in Dallas' Uptown, Knox-Henderson, and Market District SiDE Areas.*

tions (none in Fort Worth) is the store at 5400 East Mockingbird Lane, near Southern Methodist University in North Dallas, 828-4210. The *House of Books* at 622 Preston Royal Village (Preston Road at Royal Lane in North Dallas), 363-6569, is treasured by Dallas book lovers for its personal service and carefully selected stock. An unusually large selection of books on architecture and design can be found at the *AIA Dallas Book Shop* in the Uptown SiDE Area. *Rizzoli*, in Dallas' NorthPark SiDE Area, is a handsomely housed branch of the New York publisher-bookseller, which also features many art, architecture, and design titles, as well as general interest books. *Rootabaga*, in Dallas' Snider Plaza SiDE Area, has an extraordinary selection of children's books.

Dallas' best bets for used, out-of-print, and rare books include *Half-Price Books*, 5915 East Northwest Highway in North Dallas, 363-8374 (and with six other smaller Dallas and Fort Worth locations), a local chain with a large selection of used and remaindered books but few rare or valuable titles; *Mary Anne's Books*, in Vikon Village at 2918-F Jupiter Road in the suburban town of Garland, 840-2449, open Thursday through Sunday only, which has a very well selected stock of general used books; *Aldredge Book Store* in Dallas' Uptown SiDE Area, specializing in high-quality used and rare books since 1947; and *Booked Up*, at 4113 Rawlins Street in the Oak Lawn neighborhood, 528-0538, which has many rare literary editions.

For used books in Fort Worth try *Evergreen Books*, at 1500 West Magnolia Avenue in the Southside district, 335-1911, and *Barbers Bookstore*, located downtown at 215 West 8th Street, 335-5972.

Food

Visitors interested in browsing some of the area's best sources for buying fresh and exotic foods should consider the following:
Dallas Farmers' Market, 1010 South Pearl Expressway in the Civic district, 748-2082, is made up of several city-owned sheds that house numerous stalls filled with fresh produce. Many of the stalls are labeled "cold storage" and carry fruits and vegetables that have been refrigerated for shipment and storage. These have items similar to those found in large supermarkets, but perhaps a bit fresher and cheaper.

Of more interest are the "local" stalls, where farmers and truckers sell nonrefrigerated produce brought directly from harvest to market. Between early spring and late fall these stalls (mostly located in the sheds on the east side of Pearl Expressway) have a fascinating variety of local and regional fruits and vegetables. Among these seasonal favorites are peaches, plums, blueberries, blackberries, watermelons, tomatoes, yams, okra, black-eyed peas, and "greens" from East Texas; melons and pecans from West Texas (Pecos County cantaloupes are particularly prized); oranges and grapefruit from South Texas (the delicious "Ruby Red" grapefruit is a favorite gourmet gift); and mangoes, oranges, papayas, and pineapples from Mexico.
Kuby's Sausage House, located in Dallas' Snider Plaza SiDE Area, is a local institution that features superior meats and sausages, as well as a popular German deli-restaurant.
Marty's, 3316 Oak Lawn Avenue near Dallas' Uptown District, 526-4070, is an intriguing specialty shop with excellent wines, full take-out meals, bakery, and carefully selected meats, cheeses, and exotic staples.
Simon David, 7117 Inwood Road in North

Dallas, 352-1781, is a large supermarket with some unusual produce, meats, seafood, and staples.
Whole Foods Market, located in Dallas' Lower Greenville SiDE Area, is a large and complete natural foods grocer with organic produce, bakery, and a small restaurant.

DINING

Dallas, which supports more restaurants per capita than New York City, has emerged as a nationally prominent center of gastronomy during the past decade. Not only have many unusually fine establishments serving traditional fare been opened, but also a group of four local chefs, among them Dean Fearing of the Mansion and Stephan Pyles at the Routh Street Cafe, has pioneered in developing the acclaimed "Southwestern Nouvelle" style of cooking. Their innovative creations subtly combine time-honored regional ingredients with up-to-the-minute "nouvelle" preparation techniques borrowed from France (see below).

Dallas also has an abundance of ethnic restaurants. Most authentic are some of the Mexican and Southeast Asian eateries that cater to the city's large immigrant populations from these areas. Chinese and Italian restaurants are also plentiful, and the city supports several each of Indian, Japanese, Greek, and German, as well as establishments serving such exotic fare as Australian, Czechoslovakian, Ethiopian, Middle Eastern, Rumanian, and Swedish.

Fort Worth, in keeping with its long ties to the Western plains, is more of a beef-and-potatoes town. Nevertheless, some of Dallas' culinary diversity is beginning to spill into its near neighbor with *cordon bleu* results.

Because restaurants change hours, move locations, or even close completely, it's always a good idea to call ahead, or to check in one of the several weekly or monthly restaurant guides listed below, before planning to visit a particular establishment.

Restaurant Guides (Weekly and Monthly)

Dallas and Fort Worth are unusual in having five separate restaurant guides that appear regularly in the local press:

1) By far the most comprehensive is the *Dallas Morning News Guide*, an extremely useful weekly tabloid included with the newspaper every Friday. Over eight hundred Dallas and Fort Worth restaurants are listed. Most listings include a brief review as well as regularly updated ratings for quality.

2) The *Dallas Times Herald Datebook* is a similar weekly publication that appears each Sunday in Dallas' second daily newspaper. About one hundred and fifty Dallas area restaurants are included (none in Fort Worth).

3) Each Friday edition of the *Fort Worth Star-Telegram* includes a comparable entertainment tabloid called *Star Time*. This contains listings and menu summaries, but not reviews or ratings, of about three hundred Fort Worth area restaurants.

4) *D Magazine* is Dallas' popular city monthly that is widely available on local newsstands. It includes in-depth reviews of about one hundred carefully selected area restaurants, including several in Fort Worth.

5) *Texas Monthly*, a magazine treating the entire state, includes a brief but perceptive reviews of about forty Dallas restaurants and another dozen in Fort Worth.

Special Occasion Restaurants

The sixteen geographic SiDE Areas described in the final section of the book include listings of, and brief comments on, dozens of popular Dallas and Fort Worth restaurants of all types and price ranges. For visitors wanting to sample one of the towering peaks of local gastronomy, we are also including here some of the establishments that consistently receive the highest acclaim from both professional critics and knowledgeable patrons. Note that most are formal and costly places where food is taken very seriously and reservations are usually essential. Always outstanding, on a good night these can equal their top-of-the-line counterparts in New York or San Francisco.

DALLAS:

Actuelle. 2800 Routh Street (The Quadrangle, Uptown SiDE Area), 855-0440, lunch and dinner Mon-Fri, dinner only Sat, closed Sun. American Nouvelle menu by distinguished chef amid gazebo-like post-Modern decor. Expensive.
Cafe Pacific. Preston Road & Mockingbird Lane (Highland Park Village SiDE Area), 526-1170, lunch and dinner daily. Acclaimed fresh seafood in casual surroundings with attentive service. Expensive.

ELEGANT DINING *The historic* FRENCH ROOM, *in Dallas' Adolphus Hotel, has recently been restored to its 1912 splendor.*

Cafe Royal. 650 North Pearl Street (Plaza of the Americas, Downtown Dallas SiDE Area), 979-9000, lunch and dinner Mon-Fri, dinner only Sat, closed Sun. Jackets and ties required. Classic French menu with impeccable European-style setting and service. Fixed price, multi-course dinner (currently $34.50).
The French Room. 1321 Commerce Street (Adolphus Hotel, Downtown Dallas SiDE Area), 742-8200, dinner only, closed Sun. Reservations, jackets and ties required. Beautifully restored baroque dining room in historic hotel with carefully prepared French menu. Very expensive.
L'Entrecote. 2201 Stemmons Freeway (Anatole Hotel, Market District SiDE Area), 748-1200, dinner only, closed Tues. Reservations and jackets required. Classical French dining in very sophisticated setting. Expensive to very expensive.

The Mansion. 2821 Turtle Creek Boulevard (a few blocks north of the Uptown SiDE Area), 526-2121, breakfast, lunch, dinner, and late-night suppers daily. Reservations, jackets and ties required. Attentive hotel dining in elegantly restored mansion. Acclaimed chef and creative Southwestern Nouvelle menu. Very expensive.

Plum Blossom. 2201 Stemmons Freeway (Anatole Hotel, Market District SiDE Area), 748-1200, dinner only, closed Sun. Reservations and jackets required. Unusually inventive Chinese dining in striking setting. Expensive.

The Riviera. 7709 Inwood Road (Lovers Lane SiDE Area), 351-0094, dinner only, daily. French-continental fare in carefully appointed surroundings with trendy patrons. Expensive to very expensive.

Routh Street Cafe. 3005 Routh Street (Uptown SiDE Area), 871-7161, dinner only, closed Sun and Mon. Reservations required. Award-winning shrine of Southwestern Nouvelle dining in soft-tech decor. Five-course, fixed-price menu (currently $42).

San Simeon. 2515 McKinney Avenue (Uptown SiDE Area), 871-7373, lunch and dinner daily. Innovative American Nouvelle dining in sleek, post-Modern setting. Expensive to very expensive.

Uncle Tai's Hunan Yuan. 13350 Dallas Parkway (third level, Galleria SiDE Area), 934-9998, lunch and dinner daily. Jackets required at dinner. Upscale Chinese dining with many exotic dishes. Expensive.

FORT WORTH

Cattlemen's Steak House. 2458 North Main Street (Stockyards SiDE Area), (817) 624-3945, lunch and dinner Mon-Fri, dinner only Sat & Sun. Informal mecca for serious beef-eaters. Same location (and decor) since 1947. Moderate to expensive.

Reflections. 200 Main Street (Worthington Hotel, Sundance Square SiDE Area), (817) 870-9894, dinner only, closed Sun. Carefully prepared American Nouvelle menu in sumptuous setting. Expensive.

Saint-Emilion. 3617 West Seventh Street (Cultural District SiDE Area), (817) 737-2781, lunch and dinner Mon-Fri, dinner only Sat, closed Sun. Classic French fare at bargain rates—fixed price, multi-course meal currently $22.

Regional Specialties

Texas straddles the divide separating three great cultural regions—the Old South, the Western Plains, and Latin America—and its culinary traditions are a delightful blend of all three. Dallas and Fort Worth, in turn, sit squarely on the Old South-Western Plains boundary and have long had large and influential Hispanic populations. The cities thus provide many opportunities to sample all three cuisines—Southern "homecooking," the beef-dominated fare of the Plains, and Tex-Mex, the unique Latin cooking that has developed from roots planted when Texas was still a Spanish colony.

SOUTHERN HOMECOOKING. Pork, chicken, cornbread, and biscuits were the staple foods of the Old South. These were supplanted by such vegetable favorites as squash, eggplant, okra, black-eyed peas, yams, and "greens" (the boiled, spinach-like tops of the turnip, mustard, or collard plant). Every local native with a Southern heritage has a favorite home-cooking restaurant—it's always the one most like their grandmother's table. Popular Dallas examples are *Celebration*, at 4503 West Lovers Lane, a few blocks beyond the Lovers Lane SiDE Area, 351-5681, and *Gennie's Bishop Grill*, 308 North Bishop Street in Oak Cliff, lunches only, 946-1752. In the Knox-Henderson SiDE Area, the very popular *Highland Park Cafeteria* serves many traditional Southern specialties, whereas the local *Dixie House* chain, with a branch in the Uptown SiDE Area, has dependable, even though mass-produced, homecooking. Outstanding Fort Worth favorites, both in the Southside district, are the *Paris Coffee Shop*, at 700 West Magnolia Avenue, (817) 335-2041, and *Massey's*, 1805 8th Avenue, (817) 924-8242.

BEEF AND BARBECUE. Frontier beef cattle were usually lean and tough—a far cry from the grain-fed, pen-fattened product that we enjoy today. As a result, steak was traditionally prepared by beating the meat until tender, then coating it with batter and pan frying. This produced a dish known as "chicken-fried steak," whose flavor is improved by a liberal coating of thick cream gravy. Originally a rather uncommon specialty of the pork-dominated South, chicken-fried steak became a staple Western dish as cattle

replaced buffalo throughout the Plains. In Texas, it remains a favorite in local cafes featuring home-style cooking.

Truly tender, moist, and tasty beef could be prepared from lean, grass-fed cattle only by a much more tedious process—very slow roasting in some sort of smoke-filled enclosure, where both the low temperature and the partially trapped steam helped preserve the meat's natural juices. Thus arose the tradition of the Texas "barbecue," originally a festive occasion for which whole quarters of beef were placed in partially covered pits to

BARBECUED BEEF *This succulent Texas specialty is shown in its two principal forms—brisket (left), and ribs (right), with less traditional pork sausages in the middle.*

roast for a half-day, or more, near the fragrant, slow-burning coals of hickory, oak, or mesquite wood.

By the turn of the century the barbecuing process had mostly moved above ground—into large metal or brick enclosures that are still called "pits." There the flow of air to the charcoal fire, and the subsequent escape of smoke and steam, can be carefully regulated to insure properly slow, low-temperature cooking. (Note that a related method of cooking *pork* was traditional in the Old South, even though barbecued *beef* is primarily a Texas innovation. In both regions the process was

later adapted to game, chicken, sausages, and other meats. Further confusion arises because the word *barbecue* is also used today for an entirely unrelated cooking process—fast, high-temperature grilling accomplished directly above hot, flaming coals.)

One of the secrets of good barbecue is the tangy sauce that is occasionally doused on the meat during cooking, both to help preserve its moisture and to impart a subtle flavor. Some of this is usually collected with the drippings and made into a flavorful gravy served over the sliced or chopped meat. Purists sometimes reject the sauce, particularly if it is very thick, sweet, or spicy, preferring instead the delicate flavor of the meat itself. Every barbecue enthusiast and restaurant has a favorite recipe for sauce, which can be prepared with endless combinations of flavors and spices added to the basic ingredients of vinegar, fat, and salt.

By about 1900 barbecued beef, seductively succulent but very slow and tedious to prepare, was being offered for sale by a few Texas butchers and at more numerous roadside "barbecue pits." These were the forerunners of the countless informal barbecue restaurants found today throughout the state—Dallas and Fort Worth have more than their share. Local barbecue eaters tend to be knowledgeable and selective, so that these establishments must normally serve an above-average product in order to survive.

Beef, either brisket or ribs, is the principal offering, but this may be supplemented by pork, sausages, and chicken. The meat is served either on "plates" (rib plate, sliced beef plate, sausage plate, etc.), which include a selection of vegetables on the side, or in sandwiches (either sliced or chopped beef on a hamburger bun). Favored accompaniments include fried okra, raw or fried onions, potato salad, French fries, cole slaw, and ranch beans. Banana pudding, fruit cobbler, or fried fruit pies are the usual desserts.

Two local barbecue eateries have become renowned shrines that attract a large following of serious enthusiasts. In Dallas, *Sonny Bryan's Smokehouse*, at 2202 Inwood Road near the Market District SiDE Area, 357-7120, is a small hole-in-the-wall left over from the roadside barbecue pit era. Sonny begins serving every morning at 10 a.m. (11 a.m. on Sunday) and continues until the day's meat runs out, usually about mid-afternoon. In Fort Worth, *Angelo's*, at 2533 White Settlement Road, several blocks north of the Cultural District SiDE Area, (817) 332-0357, has a similar reputation but a more comfortable setting. Other favorites are the *Colter's* chain, with suburban outlets in both cities, and Dallas' *Dickey's* chain, with a branch in the Knox-Henderson SiDE Area. *Peggy's Beef Bar*, in the Snider Plaza SiDE Area, is also popular.

CHILI. This thick and pungent beef stew is probably Texas' most familiar culinary invention—its roots lie in the cattle-rich grasslands of Hispanic South Texas. Many chili-lovers are surprised to learn that the dish did not originate in Mexico. Even though related stews, flavored with hot chile peppers, have been a staple food of that country since pre-Columbian times, even today these are seldom made with beef and are typically much thinner than true Texas chili (note that *chile*, spelled with an *e*, usually means the spicy pepper whereas *chili*, with an *i*, denotes a chile pepper stew). Food experts believe that today's familiar "chili con carne" (chile pepper stew with meat) was first developed by nineteenth-century street vendors working in San An-

CHILE PEPPERS *Many varieties of these pungent New World spices were developed by pre-Columbian Indians and remain a staple of Latin American and Southwestern cooking.*

tonio, long the capital of Hispanic Texas and a major cattle marketing center. From there, the dish became a favorite with cowboys making the long post-Civil War cattle drives from Texas to Kansas. By the turn of the century it was a staple food throughout much of the Western Plains.

The late Dallas journalist Frank X. Tolbert turned chili cooking into a regional cult when he sponsored the first "chili cookoff," held in the remote West Texas ghost town of Terlingua in 1973. This has led to hundreds of similar events—festive yet dead-serious affairs where teams of chili fans attempt to outdo each other's recipes as judged by an impartial panel of tasters. As with barbecue sauce, the combinations of flavors and spices added to the basic ingredients of chopped beef, onions, and chile peppers is almost without limit. Needless to say, prize-winning recipes are usually closely guarded secrets.

In earlier days small "chili parlors," serving little else but the popular stew, were a common sight in towns throughout the Southwest. Today these are all but extinct because every local cafe, as well as many chain restaurants, serves its version of the familiar favorite. Most of these are scorned by purists who prefer their own special recipes prepared at home.

TEX-MEX. Surprisingly, traditional bowls of Western "chili con carne" are seldom served in the region's numerous Mexican restaurants. Instead, these feature other dishes that evolved in Texas' remote outposts of Latin culture. Cooks in the San Antonio area often added the plentiful local beef, as well as cheese and other Anglo ingredients, to the more traditional Mexican staples of beans, rice, and *tortillas*, flat disks of griddle-cooked cornmeal that are the principal bread of Mexico. These protein-enhanced San Antonio specialties have evolved over the years into a distinctive Latin cuisine that is today known by the very appropriate name of "Tex-Mex."

Like the traditional fare of the Mexican peasant, modern Tex-Mex meals are still built around a base of beans and corn, the latter in the form of the ubiquitous tortilla. The tortillas usually arrive first—as a basket of *tostados*, triangular morsels deep fried and lightly salted, which are served with a bowl of spicy tomato and chile sauce, called *salsa piquante*, which is for dipping and also for adding extra zing to the dishes that follow (tostados were the inspiration for "Fritos," the popular corn chip snack food that was first produced in

Dallas). The beans are included with the main course and may be served in several ways. Most typically they are boiled, mashed into a paste, and then heated with lard to make a dish called "refried beans."

Main course entrees are mostly tortilla-based, and are served with an additional side basket of *soft* tortillas, hot off the griddle. Among the favorite main dishes are *tacos*—crisp tortilla shell sandwiches filled with such ingredients as shredded lettuce, tomatoes, cheese, onions, and ground beef; *enchiladas*—chicken, chopped beef, or cheese tightly rolled in a soft tortilla and covered with sauce, either chile-based or a milder, sour cream-based version; and *tamales*—spicy ground beef wrapped in a covering of corn meal and steamed, then served with a chile sauce. In addition to refried beans, these entrees are usually accompanied by fried rice, a Spanish introduction to the Indian foods of the New World.

Typical Tex-Mex side dishes include *guacamole salad*—mashed avocado variously flavored with onions and chiles; *nachos*—tostados topped with refried beans, beef, or chicken and coated with melted cheese and sliced green chiles called "jalapeños" (the latter, particularly the small white seeds, can sometimes be *very* hot, but are easily removed); and *pralines*—pecan-filled candies with a base of crisp melted sugar, which are the traditional Tex-Mex dessert. (Purists deplore the chewy, caramel-like versions now served at many "Mexican" restaurants.)

Tex-Mex cooking continues to evolve even today. An entree that has gained wide popularity in only the past few years is *fajitas*—marinated slivers of chicken or skirt steak, grilled and served with side dishes of tortillas made from wheat flour (originally an Arizona specialty), onions, sour cream, guacamole, and chile sauce. You put your own selection of these fillings into one of the tortillas, roll it up, and eat it like a finger sandwich.

Dallas has played an important, but little-known, role in popularizing Tex-Mex foods. Originally, Tex-Mex dishes were served mostly in small, family-run cafes called *fonditas*, which had spread from San Antonio to become scattered over much of the state by the early decades of this century. Among these were two Dallas area establishments that later expanded to become the first large chains of Tex-Mex restaurants.

In 1929 the Cuellar family opened a small cafe in the nearby town of Kaufman, and in

SOUTHWESTERN NOUVELLE *Chef Stephan Pyles, one of the originators of this cuisine, with some of the regional raw materials used in his renowned* ROUTH STREET CAFE.

1940 added a second location in Dallas. In the post–World War II boom of the late 1940s and 1950s, additional locations were added and today their popular *El Chico* restaurants have over a hundred branches in Texas and throughout the Gulf South. Still earlier, in 1918, Mike Martinez and his family founded a popular Dallas cafe, *El Fenix*, which they began expanding in the 1950s. Today there are seventeen El Fenix branches in Dallas, Fort Worth, Houston, and Oklahoma City. These two chains, in turn, became the prototypes for the wide popularity of "fast-food Tex-Mex," a watered-down version of the Texas original that is now served at thousands of Taco Bell and similar outlets throughout much of the nation.

El Chico and El Fenix are still popular local eateries, but their mass-produced Tex-Mex favorites are today joined by local restaurants that feature still more authentic, made-from-scratch, dishes. One long-time Fort Worth institution, for example, is said to grind its own corn for tortillas with the primitive stone implements used in pre-Columbian times! This is the legendary *Joe T. Garcia's*, at 2201 North Commerce Street, near the Stockyards SiDE Area, (817) 626-4356. Among the many Dallas Mexican restaurants with enthusiastic devotees are *Mia's*, at 4322 Lemmon Avenue in the Oak Lawn neighborhood, 526-1020, and the *Martinez Cafe*, in the Uptown SiDE Area, run by a descendant of the founders of the El Fenix chain.

SOUTHWESTERN NOUVELLE. With the venerable traditions of Southern, Western, and Mexican cooking to provide inspiration, it was probably inevitable that some creative genius would eventually translate the region's everyday fare into a new form of *haute cuisine*. Fortunately this has already happened, for in the early 1980s four Dallas-based chefs, and a fifth in Houston, were jointly inspired to create the "Southwestern Nouvelle," or "New Southwest," style of cooking. Its principal characteristic is the use of traditional ingredients—for example chile peppers, wild game (venison, quail, duck, turkey), catfish, ham, yams, tortillas, collards, avocados, pecans, and Texas-grown fruits (peaches, grapefruit, berries)—which are lovingly transformed into such sophisticated treats as "a salad of

smoked duck with a peppered mango sauce" or "a perfectly cooked quail with a sweet potato pancake." These final products also draw heavily on the calorie-conscious preparation and presentation techniques of French "cuisine nouvelle."

Today such dishes have become favorites at many top-of-the-line Dallas and Fort Worth restaurants, but the revered shrines of Southwestern Nouvelle cooking remain two Dallas institutions, *The Mansion* and *Routh Street Cafe* (see above under "Special Occasion Dining"), whose distinguished chefs were among the innovative "gang-of-five" that created the new cuisine.

TEXAS WINES. Texas *what*? Francophiles and Californians may scoff, but the state has recently become a major producer of table wines, including some of award-winning quality. Starting from a modest output of only twenty-five hundred cases in 1975, by 1985 the state's production had increased almost a hundred-fold and is still climbing. Much of this comes from large, irrigated vineyards in far West Texas, but some of the best is made at three small wineries—*Cheateau Montgolfier*, *La Buena Vida*, and *Sanchez Creek*—located in Parker County, only about fifteen miles west of Fort Worth. These produce both red and white wines from such classic French grapes as Bordeaux's Cabernet Sauvignon and the Loire Valley's Chenin Blanc, as well as from several fine European-American hybrid varieties. Their relatively small yearly output, totaling about ten thousand cases in 1985, is marketed principally in Texas and can be found at many wine merchants in Dallas and Fort Worth.

FAVORITE LOCAL PRODUCTS. As in most large cities, Dallas and Fort Worth produce a number of specialty foods that are highly prized by local residents but seldom seen elsewhere.

Fletcher's Corny Dogs are frankfurters coated with a thick cornmeal batter and then deep-fried. These "meals-on-a-stick" were introduced at the State Fair of Texas during the 1940s and became local favorites that are now sold year round in many snack bars and at several franchised locations (one is in the NorthPark SiDE Area). Competing Woody's

Corny Dogs are served by many local Dairy Queen shops. Any other brand of corny dog is suspect.

Fruit cakes, popular mail-order Christmas gifts featuring native Texas pecans, are made in three small area towns—the *Collin Street Bakery* in Corsicana, *Mary of Puddin Hill* in Greenville, and the *Eilenburger Butternut Baking Co.* in Palestine.

Collin County Beer, made in the Dallas suburb of Plano, is brewed in the traditional German fashion.

New York, Texas Cheese Cake is an award-winning treat made in the village of New York, Texas, located near Athens about seventy miles east of Dallas. It is sold at Neiman-Marcus-to-Go in the Downtown Dallas SiDE Area.

Fresh cheeses are the specialty of *The Mozzarella Company* in Dallas' Deep Ellum SiDE Area. Several delicious varieties of soft cheese are handmade in the traditional Italian fashion and are used by knowledgeable chefs throughout the country.

Dr Pepper, a popular and distinctively flovored regional soft drink, was developed in nearby Waco in 1885 and has been manufactured in Dallas since 1922.

Chocolate candies can be bought in Fort Worth's *Sweet Shop*, at 2104 West Seventh near downtown, (817) 332-6709. In this outlet store serving a large adjacent factory, you can watch workers carefully preparing such coveted treats as "Fudge Loves" or "Chocolate Truffles."

ENTERTAINMENT

The more than three million inhabitants of the combined Dallas and Fort Worth areas make up the second largest metropolitan center in the southern half of the United States, exceeded in population and physical size only by Los Angeles. Such a vast urban complex supports an enormous variety of recreational activities—everything from rustic saloons to ultra-sophisticated cocktail lounges, avant-garde theater to grand opera, country music to symphony orchestras, and amateur rodeo to the Dallas Cowboys. Much of the two cities traditional nighttime activity— pubs, lounges, theaters, nightclubs, etc.—is located in, and described with, the sixteen SiDE Areas treated on the last pages of the book. This section supplements the SiDE Area descriptions by providing some more general information about entertainment in Dallas and Fort Worth.

Entertainment Guides (Daily, Weekly, Monthly)

The local press provides several useful guides to the Dallas-Fort Worth entertainment scene. The "Today" section appearing daily in the *Dallas Morning News* has a page called "The Arts," which features a listing of each day's "Best Bets" for live entertainment. In addition, the *Morning News* each Friday includes an excellent, magazine-like insert called "The Guide," which has comprehensive listings of every type of entertainment, including special events for the coming week, in both Dallas and Fort Worth. Similar but somewhat less complete guides are included with the Sunday edition of the *Dallas Times Herald* and the Friday edition of the *Fort Worth Star Telegram*. Additional listings can be found in two local magazines that are published each month and are widely available on area newsstands. These are *Texas Monthly*, which covers the entire state, and *D Magazine*, treating Dallas and Fort Worth only. Another convenient source of information is provided by telephone services. *Artsline*, 522-2659, is a 24-hour recording that summarizes the highlights of each day's arts-related events in Dallas. The *Jazz Hotline*, 744-BBOP, provides a similar summary of jazz groups playing at local nightclubs in both cities.

Theater Companies

Most of the theater companies in Dallas and Fort Worth are located in one of the sixteen SiDE Areas and are described on pages 76 to 92. In Dallas these include: *Dallas Repertory Theatre* (NorthPark); *Dallas Theater Center* (Downtown Dallas); *Deep Ellum Theatre Garage*, *Pegasus Theatre*, and *Undermain Theatre* (Deep Ellum); *Greenville Avenue Pocket Sandwich Theatre* (Lower Greenville); *Theatre Three* (Uptown); and the *West End Cabaret* (West End Historic District). In Fort Worth, three companies—*Casa Manana*, *Casa Playhouse*, and the *Fort Worth Theatre*—perform in the Cultural District SiDE Area. Several important theater companies are found in other locations. These include:

Circle Theatre. 1227 West Magnolia (in Fort Worth's Southside district). (817) 921-3040. Presents challenging contemporary plays and musical works, as well as an old-fashioned melodrama during the Christmas season.

Dallas Summer Musicals. Music Hall (in Dallas' Fair Park). 565-1116. June-Aug and in October during the State Fair. Offers exuberant professional musicals and shows under its outstanding director, Tom Hughes.

Hip Pocket Theatre. 1620 Las Vegas Trail North (near Carswell Air Force Base in Fort Worth's Westside district). (817) 927-2833. Summer only. Dinner available. A favorite for its informal outdoor setting. A winter series is performed at Upstairs at the White Elephant in the Stockyards SiDE Area. This company presents original works and adaptations created primarily by artistic director Johnny Simons and composer Doug Balentine.

Shakespeare Festival. Band Shell (in Dallas' Fair Park). Summer only. Starlight productions of Shakespeare in an old-fashioned outdoor band shell.

Music and Dance

CLASSICAL. Both Dallas and Fort Worth support their own professional opera companies and symphony orchestras, as well as numerous ballet troups, chamber music groups,

choral societies, and concert series with touring performers. A sampling of these is listed below.

Dallas Opera. 1925 Elm, Majestic Theatre (Financial Core district). 871-0090. Nov-Dec; Feb-May.

Dallas Symphony Orchestra. Music Hall (in Dallas' Fair Park). 692-0203. Classical Series, Sept-May; Super Pops, Jan-May; Starfest, June-Aug.

Fort Worth Ballet Association. Tarrant County Convention Center Theater (Civic district). (817) 429-1181 (metro). Oct-Apr.

Fort Worth Opera Association. Uses various performance halls. (817) 737-0775. Nov-Mar.

Fort Worth Symphony. (817) 926-8831. Tarrant County Convention Center Theater (Civic district). Sept-May.

Some Other Popular Dallas Groups: Dallas Bach Society, Dallas Black Dance Theater, Dallas Chamber Orchestra, Dallas Lyric Opera, Dallas Wind Symphony, Dallas Classic Guitar Society, Dancers Unlimited, Greater Dallas Youth Orchestra, Voices of Change.

Some Other Popular Fort Worth Groups: Fort Worth Chamber Orchestra, Fort Worth Civic Orchestra, Texas Boys Choir, Texas Girls Choir.

BALLET *More than sixty different dance groups perform in Dallas and Fort Worth.*

JAZZ. Dallas has a strong jazz tradition which dates back to the many creative black musicians that performed in early Deep Ellum. Today the Dallas jazz scene is exploding with local talent, much of it nurtured by Allison C. Tucker, jazz expert and former band director at Lincoln High School, and by North Texas State University in the nearby town of Denton, which has a distinguished program in modern instrumental music and a renowned Lab

JEANNETTE BRANTLEY *This very popular Dallas singer performs with her own jazz combo called Skyward Bound.*

Band. Call 744-BBOP for timely recorded information on local performances, a service provided by the Dallas Jazz Society. Among the popular local performers are *Clockwork* and *Jeannette Brantley's Skyward Bound*, both featuring the jazz-pop fusion sound; *Bob Stewart*, *Marchel Ivery*, and *Claude Johnson* for more traditional jazz; *Shirley McFatter* and *Nancy Paris* for female vocals; and the *Dallas Jazz Orchestra* for jazz with the Big Band sound.

Popular Dallas jazz clubs include *Terilli's* in the Lower Greenville SiDE Area; *D'Jazz* in North Dallas' Caruth Plaza Shopping Area, Suite 208 (Park Lane at Central Expressway), 361- 4338; and *Jazba*, in the Uptown SiDE Area. The *Adolphus Hotel Lobby Bar* in the Downtown Dallas SiDE Area, and *Les Saisons*, 165 Turtle Creek Village in North Dallas, 528-1102, offer a restful, lounge-like atmosphere with live jazz in the background, whereas *Dick's Last Resort*, in the West End Historic District SiDE Area, features rousing Dixieland performers. In Fort Worth the *Caravan of Dreams*, in the Sundance Square SiDE Area, is *the* place for jazz.

COUNTRY-AND-WESTERN. Fort Worth has been famous for music and dancing since the days of the great Texas cattle drives, when the small village became a favorite R&R stop for passing trail drivers and cowboys. The roots of Country-and-Western (C&W) music go back much farther—to the ballads of medieval England, which were stories sung to a simple melody. This tradition of story-telling-in-song was brought to the rural South by early English colonists, and subsequently moved westward. On the open plains, singing, often accompanied by a Spanish guitar or harmonica, became a campfire ritual. Most of the songs were traditional ballads handed down from generation to generation, but creative singers sometimes added verses, tunes, or even made up their own songs. From these humble beginnings has grown modern Country-and-Western music, today an enormous industry that supports countless recording companies, radio stations, songwriters, and performers.

The most popular modern dance performed to C&W music is the Western Two-Step, which resembles couples doing round-the-floor

THEATRE THREE *Founded in 1961, this Dallas favorite is typical of the area's many fine theater companies.*

WESTERN SALOON *Saddles replace bar stools at* BOOGER RED'S, *in Fort Worth's Stock Yards Hotel.*

skating without skates. The Two-Step is supplemented by a number of popular folk and line dances that are descendants of the polkas and schottishes introduced by European immigrants. Two of the most popular of these are the Heel-and-Toe Polka and the Cotton-Eyed Joe.

Fort Worth boasts one of the longest-running C&W variety shows in the country. This is *Johnnie High's Country Music Revue*, performed each Saturday night in the Will Rogers Auditorium (see Cultural District SiDE Area). Equally popular are the city's many C&W clubs, or "honky-tonks," that offer live music and dancing. Several are listed under the Stockyards SiDE Area, which is a great place to sample C&W music. Another Fort Worth favorite, not in the Stockyards area, is *The Stagecoach Ballroom* at 2516 East Belknap Avenue, (817) 831-2261, a "big ol' honky tonk" with a huge dance floor.

Popular Dallas C&W dancing spots are the *Top Rail*, at 2110 West Northwest Highway near Love Field, 556-9099, and the *Longhorn Ballroom*, at 216 Corinth Street near downtown, 428-3128. *Belle Starr*, at 7724 North Central Expressway in North Dallas, 750-4787, has live music nightly and a devoted following of mostly under-thirty C&W fans. Note that pressed jeans, boots, and Western hats are the usual attire at C&W clubs. Some women wear full prairie skirts, rather than jeans, and nearly everyone dances with their hats on!

Spectator Sports

The area has the usual broad range of sporting events. Some of the highlights are listed below and in the table of "Annual Events" on a subsequent page. For detailed and up-to-the-minute listings, see one of the daily, weekly, or monthly guides discussed earlier.

FOOTBALL: The NFL *Dallas Cowboys* play in Texas Stadium located in the suburban town of Irving (see "Other Destinations"). Call 556-2500 for ticket information. Stadium tours available, 438-7676.

BASEBALL: The American League West's *Texas Rangers* play in Arlington Stadium (near the Six Flags amusement park, see "Other Destinations") from April through September. Call (817) 273-5100 for ticket information.

BASKETBALL: The National Basketball Association's *Dallas Mavericks* play in Reunion Arena (see "West End") from early autumn until spring. Call 748-1808 or 658-7068 for ticket information.

SOCCER: The *Dallas Sidekicks* play in Reunion Arena (see "West End") from November to April. Call 760-7330 or 658-7068 for ticket information.

RODEO: Rodeo is a long Western tradition that is great fun to watch. Many of the events were

inspired by the everyday work of the cowboy—roping a steer, breaking in a new horse, or throwing a calf down to be branded. Other events, like the bull riding and barrel racing, were added simply to let cowboys (and, nowadays, cowgirls) show off their prowess. Rodeos traditionally begin with a dramatic Grand Entry Parade and end with the dangerous bull riding. The rodeo clown is not just for fun; his job is to distract the animals to allow a downed rider to escape from dangerous situations. Among the area's most popular rodeo series are:

Mesquite Championship Rodeo. I-635 at the Military Parkway exit in the suburban town of Mesquite, which is east of Dallas, 285-8777. Top rodeo stars strut their stuff every Friday and Saturday night, April through Sept.

Kowbell Indoor Rodeo. Highway 167 in Mansfield, Texas (15 miles south of downtown Fort Worth on Business branch of U.S. Highway 287). (817) 477-3092. Indoor events are held every week all year long. Bullriding on Monday and Friday evenings; rodeo on Saturday and Sunday evenings.

RODEO *The clown can play a crucial role in getting the cowboy safely away from the bucking bull.*

Participant Sports

BIKING AND JOGGING: The four lake or greenbelt trails listed below are local favorites, as is Dallas' tree-shaded Swiss Avenue Historic District (see "East Dallas").

Bachman Lake (just north of Love Field in North Dallas). 3.08 miles. For paddleboat rentals call 351-3990.

Trinity Trail (in Fort Worth's Trinity Park; see "Cultural District"). 8.2 miles. For paddleboat and bike rental information call (817) 335-7472.

Turtle Creek Trail (in Dallas' Uptown district). 1.5 miles. Enter at the footbridge across from the Kalita Humphreys Theater.

White Rock Lake (see "East Dallas"). 9.8 miles. Entrance near Arboretum and at various points around the lake. For paddleboat and bike rental location and information call 823-6933.

GOLF: Dallas has six municipal golf courses and Fort Worth has four. The principal Dallas center is at Tennison Park, 821-3811. This is located off of East Grand Avenue just south of White Rock Lake in East Dallas and has two courses. In Fort Worth, Pecan Valley Park on Lake Benbrook in southwest Fort Worth also has two courses. Call (817) 249-1845 for information. If these courses are full, either can refer you to the other city-owned courses. In

HOME TEAM *The region's best known Cowboys don't ride horses.*

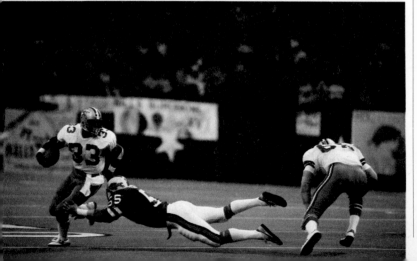

SOUTHWESTERN EXPOSITION *Champion and owner take a well-earned rest.*

addition, the two clubs below are operated by hotels and are open to the public on a daily fee basis.

Hyatt Bear Creek. West Airfield Drive at the DFW Airport in Irving (see "Other Destinations"). 453-8400. Thirty-six holes of top-rated golf. Also racquetball and tennis.

Marriott's Golf Club at Fossil Creek. 3401 Club Gate (near I-35W at Loop 820 on Fort Worth's North Side). (817) 847-1900.

ICE SKATING: Two North Dallas malls, and downtown shopping atria in both Fort Worth and Dallas, have popular ice-skating rinks. These are great places to leave older children for a couple of hours while you shop or sightsee:

Galleria Ice Capades Chalet is in North Dallas' Galleria SiDE Area, 387-5533.

Ice Capades Chalet is located in the Plaza of the Americas atrium in the Downtown Dallas SiDE Area, 922-9800.

Prestonwood Ice Capades Chalet is in North Dallas' Prestonwood Mall on Belt Line Road just east of the Dallas North Tollway, 980-8988.

Tandy Center Rink is in the atrium of Tandy Center in Fort Worth's Sundance Square SiDE Area, (817) 390-3712.

TENNIS: Dallas has five municipal tennis centers, and Fort Worth has two. For information in Dallas call 670-8520, or the large Samuell-Grand Center at 821-3811. It's located at 6200 East Grand Avenue just south of White Rock Lake in East Dallas. In Fort Worth call the Mary Potishman Lard Tennis Center at (817) 921-7960. It's located on the TCU campus in the Southside district. In addition the Hyatt Bear Creek Club, listed under Golf, has excellent tennis facilities.

Some Annual Events

JAN ▪ Cotton Bowl Classic Football Game. Fair Park, Dallas. 634-7525. New Year's Day with parade preceding.

JAN ▪ Southwestern Exposition ("Fat Stock Show"). Will Rogers Center, Fort Worth (817) 244-6188. Late January through early February. Horseshow, rodeo, exhibition, and parade.

FEB ▪ Virginia Slims Women's Tennis. Moody Coliseum at Southern Methodist University, Dallas. 352-7978. February or March.

MAR ▪ Dallas Blooms. Dallas Arboretum. 327-2990. Mid-March through early April. Flowering shrubs enhanced by 200,000 bulbs.

MAR ▪ World Championship Tennis Finals. Reunion Arena, Dallas. 969-5556.

MAY ▪ Art Fest. Fair Park, Dallas. 361-2011. Memorial Day weekend. Works by several hundred jury-selected artists and craftsmen.

MAY ▪ Byron Nelson Golf Classic. Las Colinas, Dallas. 742-3896. Early May.

MAY ▪ Swiss Avenue Tour of Homes. Swiss Avenue, Dallas. 826-7402 or 824-6603. Mother's Day weekend.

JUN ▪ Chisholm Trail Round-Up. Stockyards, Fort Worth. (817) 625-7005. Second weekend in June. Western-theme festival.

JUL ▪ Old Fashioned July Fourth. Old City Park, Dallas. 421-5141. July fourth.

AUG ▪ Fair Park Jazz Festival. Fair Park, Dallas. 426-3400.

SEP ▪ Montage. Arts District, Dallas. 361-2011. Late September. Weekend performing arts festival.

SEP ▪ Pioneer Days. Stockyards, Fort Worth. (817) 626-7921. Weekend trail rides, cookoffs, parades, etc.

SEP ▪ Taste of Texas. City Hall Plaza, Dallas. 748-5200. Labor Day weekend. Food festival.

OCT ▪ State Fair of Texas. Fair Park, Dallas. 565-9931. Middle two weeks of October. Largest annual fair in the United States; features livestock, rides, edibles, entertainment.

NOV ▪ National Cutting Horse Futurity. Will Rogers Center, Fort Worth. (817) 244-6188. The end of November through the first part of December. The world championship competition.

DEC ▪ Candlelight Tours. Old City Park, Dallas. 421-7800. First full weekend in December.

DEC ▪ Christmas at DeGolyer. Dallas Arboretum. 327-8263. Early to mid-December.

DEC ▪ Home for the Holidays. Sundance Square, Fort Worth. (817) 338-2031. Happenings throughout the month.

DEC ▪ Thistle Hill Heritage Christmas. Thistle Hill, Fort Worth. (817) 336-1212.

ODDS AND ENDS

Day Trips

Because of their enormous modern population growth, both Dallas and Fort Worth retain only scattered fragments of their Victorian beginnings. In contrast, only a half-hour's drive away are several delightful small towns that still preserve much of their turn-of-the-century charm. Among these are Granbury,

McKinney, and Waxahachie, whose quaint courthouse squares and grand Queen Anne houses give a much better feeling than do their larger neighbors for North Texas as it appeared in the 1880s and 1890s.

Granbury is thirty-five miles southwest of Fort Worth on U.S. Highway 377, population 3500. A handsome 1891 stone courthouse dominates an old-fashioned town square with several gift and antique shops. Don't miss the restored Opera House which features weekend performances of plays and musicals.

McKinney is thirty miles north of Dallas on U.S. Highway 75 (Central Expressway), population 16,500. The courthouse and square here mostly date from the 1920s. More than a dozen discount outlets have moved into its old stores, making it a fun destination for bargain shopping. Nearby streets north and west of the square, including Virginia, College, Tucker, and Bradley, retain many fine old Queen Anne houses.

Waxahachie is thirty miles south of Dallas, just off of Interstate Highway 35E, population 15,000. A dramatic 1895 courthouse dominating a stage-set square with many early buildings has made this town a favorite place for shooting period movies. Don't miss the many fine Victorian houses strung out along West Main Street and Marvin Avenue.

Further Reading

These selected titles provide a good starting point for visitors wanting to dig more deeply into the culture, history, and architecture of Dallas and Fort Worth. Several have extensive bibliographies.

Greene, A.C. *A Place Called Dallas* (Dallas County Heritage Society; 1975); *Dallas: The Deciding Years* (Austin, Encino Press, 1973). Two engaging and irreverant books by a well-known Dallas historian and literary critic.

Historic Preservation League. *A Guide to the Older Neighborhoods of Dallas* (Dallas, 1986). Overview of revitalized residential areas. Good source for those interested in buying an old house.

Jackson, Joan F., and Glenna Whitley. *Places to Go with Children in Dallas and Fort Worth* (San Francisco, Chronicle Books, 1987).

STATE FAIR OF TEXAS *Big Tex surveys the nation's largest annual fair, held in Dallas each October.*

VICTORIANA   *Large Queen Anne houses have mostly disappeared from Dallas and Fort Worth, but many fine examples survive in small nearby towns. This one is in Waxahachie.*

Outstanding survey of activities that will appeal to children and grown-ups alike; includes many lesser-known destinations.

Kimbell Art Museum. *In Pursuit of Quality* (New York, Harry N. Abrams, 1987). A beautifully illustrated history of this superb Fort Worth museum and its collections.

McDonald, William L. *Dallas Rediscovered* (Dallas Historical Society, 1978). Fascinating photo-history of the city's growth from 1870 to 1925.

Payne, Darwin. *Dallas, An Illustrated History* (Woodland Hills, California, Windsor Publications, 1982). The best overall history of Dallas, from founding to the present day.

Schmelzer, Janet L. *Where the West Begins* (Northridge, California, Windsor Publications, 1985). The best general history of Fort Worth, with excellent illustrations.

Sanders, Leonard. *How Fort Worth Became the Texasmost City* (Fort Worth, Amon Carter Museum, 1973). Carefully annotated catalogue of a comprehensive exhibition of historic Fort Worth photographs.

Tomlinson, Doug, and David Dillon. *Dallas Architecture 1936-1986* (Austin, Texas Monthly Press, 1985). Perceptive text by Dillon, award-winning architecture critic of the *Dallas Morning News*, and splendid black-and-white photographs by photographer Tomlinson.

Trim, Laura. *Short Trips In and Around Dallas* (Dallas, LDT Press, 1984). An excellent guide for North Texas excursions. Includes history, maps, events, special shops, and restaurants for many small towns. Good coverage of Dallas and Fort Worth as well.

Safety

Crime is an ever-present reality in modern America. It can occur in new malls and older shopping centers, in inner-city historic districts and in quiet residential suburbs, in small towns and in giant cities, during the day or at night. We encourage you to observe the following basic precautions recommended nationwide by public safety officers. Once these simple rules are followed, relax and enjoy yourself; you'll be as safe as at home.

1. Don't take walking tours at night.
2. Avoid walking in deserted areas when alone; other people nearby are a great deterrent to crime.
3. Don't wear flashy jewelry, or expose large amounts of cash when making purchases.
4. Use the valet parking services provided at night by many restaurants (the custom is to tip $1-2 when the car is returned to you).
5. When returning to a parked car at night, walk purposefully and have your key out and ready.
6. Keep the doors of your car locked while driving, as well as when parked.
7. Don't leave valuables or suitcases exposed to view in an empty car. Place them in the trunk, out of sight.
8. Don't leave valuables in your hotel room; use the extra bolts and safety chains provided on the door.

WORLD CHAMPIONSHIP TENNIS   *This competition is one of dozens of special events held in Dallas' Reunion Arena.*

Telephones

The area code for Dallas is 214 and for Fort Worth it is 817. Throughout this book, telephone numbers given *without* an area code prefix are 214 numbers; all 817 numbers are listed *with* this area code. Calls between Dallas and Fort Worth normally involve modest long-distance charges. Many businesses have toll-free "metro" numbers, particularly those located in the suburban areas of Arlington and Grand Prairie located directly between the larger cities. *Note*: You cannot normally dial a metro number using the area code. For example, if you are in Dallas and try to dial a Fort Worth metro number preceded by the 817 area code, you will be told the call cannot be completed as dialed. You must dial it as if it were a local call, *without* the area code. Always try this first should you get a "cannot be completed" message. Conversely, should you unsuccessfully dial a number as a local call, try it with the other city's area code before you give up.

Time and Temperature

Continuous time and temperature recordings are available in Dallas and Fort Worth by calling 844-6611 (metro). Both cities are on Central Standard Time.

Wearables

Dallas tends to be somewhat more dressy than Fort Worth. People in sportswear are the norm throughout much of both cities, but men in jackets and ties and women in heels and dresses are in the majority in some Dallas locations. These include the more upscale shops in the Galleria, NorthPark, Highland Park Village, and Uptown areas, as well as many office buildings of the Financial Core during weekday business hours. Upscale restaurants in both cities also tend to be dressy, as do performances of the symphony, opera, and some theater companies. Adults wearing pressed jeans and Western boots are a common sight in Fort Worth, but are less frequently seen in Dallas. In deference to the hot weather, dress in both cities becomes more casual during the summer. Note, however, that the omnipresent summer air-conditioning can sometimes be chilly, making a light wrap or jacket advisable, particularly at night.

Weather

The generally mild North Texas climate is one of Dallas' and Fort Worth's principal attractions. Spring and fall are both long and delightful, with mostly sunny days having high temperatures in the 60s or 70s. Winter usually arrives in late December with periodic below-freezing cold fronts. Steadily lengthening stretches of mild weather commence again by February, making January the principal month of winter. Even then snow is rare, and the arctic blasts are moderated by many days with highs in the 40s or 50s. As in most of Texas, summers, lasting here from about mid-June to mid-September, can be very hot. Normal daily highs are in the 90s, but stretches with highs above 100 are not uncommon. Nights are a bit cooler and air-conditioning everywhere—in all buildings, malls, autos, and buses—makes even the hottest days tolerable.

Weather here can also be instantly changeable and the old saying—"If you don't like the weather just wait a minute"—has special relevance. From November to March, "blue northers," blowing in from the Canada, can drop the temperature as much as forty degrees in a few hours. Rain is not frequent, but is similarly capricious. Thunderstorms can appear from nowhere, pour down one or two inches, and be gone within an hour. Such deluges are most likely in the spring and fall. To avoid surprises, it's always a good idea to check a weather forecast when preparing for your day. In addition to the usual newspaper and television forecasts, the *National Weather Service* provides convenient telephone recordings that summarize current and predicted weather. Dallas numbers are 787-1700 (for local weather only) and 787-1701 (for travelers and outdoor recreation). In Fort Worth the numbers are (817) 336-4416 (for local weather) and (817) 787-1701 (for travelers and outdoor recreation).

SiDE AREA KEY

The yellow-bordered pages that follow summarize sixteen of Dallas' and Fort Worth's most appealing districts for shopping, dining, and entertainment. We call these "SiDE Areas," both because they supplement the book's principal focus on sightseeing and also because the capitalized letters in "SiDE" provide an acronym for *Shopping, Dining,* and *Entertainment.* As in the book's sightseeing coverage, these supplementary sections are organized geographically in the belief that travelers prefer to spend their time visiting important *groups of destinations,* rather than trying to locate individual establishments scattered over many miles of urban sprawl.

The SiDE Area discussions include brief ratings (see below) of each Area's relative interest for shopping, dining, entertainment, and ambiance, as well as listings of about two dozen shops, restaurants, or entertainment facilities that are representative of its attractions. With few exceptions, these are locally owned establishments providing goods or services that we believe will be of interest to visitors. The familiar national chains of restaurants and stores have generally been omitted, not because they don't provide quality products or convenient locations, but because visitors generally prefer to experience something unique to Dallas or Fort Worth. This emphasis on locally owned or unusual establishments means that most of the SiDE Areas are *not* traditional shopping malls which, with a few important exceptions, lack the elements of diversity and surprise found in less structured retail districts.

SHOPPING

The shops listed for each SiDE Area are *not* meant to be a complete or exhaustive tabulation of even the best establishments, but rather a representative sample of the shopping available in that Area. When a SiDE Area has numerous shops, these are divided into three general categories:

1) Clothing. This includes wearables for men, women, and children, as well as related accessories.
2) Art, Antiques, and Crafts. This includes all types of "one-of-a-kind," rare, or hand-made objects such as fine arts, antique decorative arts, craft items, etc.
3) Other. All other shops, including those featuring home furnishings, kitchenware, toys, gifts, linens, jewelry, or books.

The listings include a sampling of stores with merchandise in all price ranges. Unlike restaurants, where it can be embarrassing to get up and leave if the prices are an unpleasant shock, shops of all kinds are accustomed to lookers. Furthermore, even the most intimidatingly expensive ones usually have some affordable items to consider. Visits to top-of-the-line shops can be delightful, educational, and free entertainment; don't hesitate to look, even if only in anticipation of some future purchase. Telephone numbers are given for each entry, and an advance call to confirm that the shop hasn't recently moved or closed is a good idea if you have your heart set on visiting a particular establishment.

DINING

The restaurants listed include both modestly priced and expensive establishments that are locally popular and representative of a wide range of culinary specialties. Most either are individually owned or are one of a small local chain; nationally franchised eateries, already abundantly familiar to travelers, are generally omitted.

Drinks

Unless noted as serving "no alcohol," all restaurants can provide at least beer and wine and most have full bar service. Pubs that serve food but that have a clear emphasis on drinking rather than eating are listed under "Entertainment."

Dress

Come-as-you-are places have the notation "casual." In these you'll feel comfortable in jeans, T-shirts, or weather permitting, even shorts. With a cocktail dress or jacket and tie you may feel a bit overdressed, but certainly not unwelcome. At the opposite extreme are a few places noted as "dressy." In these, men will feel uncomfortable *without* a jacket and tie and may not be admitted to a few very haughty establishments. The great bulk of the listed restaurants fall in between, with patrons in both neat sportswear and dressier business or evening attire.

Hours

Unless otherwise noted, all restaurants are open for both lunch and dinner. The handful that are open for breakfast or that accept dinner orders after midnight are noted in the listings. Most serve through the afternoon, but a few close from around 2 or 3 p.m. until 5 or 6 p.m. Some are closed for lunch on weekends, and many close completely one or two days per week, usually Sunday or Monday or both. Precise hours and closing days are not noted, so an advance call may be desirable, particularly on weekends and Mondays.

Reservations

All of the more expensive restaurants and many of the more modest ones will accept advance telephone reservations which can save a long wait, particularly on Friday or Saturday night. Reservations are advised for parties of five or more at any time. A few upscale and very popular restaurants either require or strongly advise reservations; these are noted in the listings.

Cost

At the end of each listing is a notation indicating the cost of a typical *full dinner for one, not including drinks or tip:*

Inexpensive - Under $10
Moderate - $10 to $20
Expensive - $20 to $30
Very Expensive - Over $30

Many restaurants have luncheon prices that are from 10 to 50 percent lower than those indicated for dinner.

ENTERTAINMENT

This section includes listings of the most popular bars, pubs, legitimate theaters, cinemas, and performance halls found in each SiDE Area. We've tried to indicate those nightclubs that have cover charges, live entertainment (which usually changes regularly), and dancing. Note that club formats can alter overnight, so that an advance phone call, or reference to one of the weekly or monthly publications listed in the introduction to "Entertainment" on a preceding page, can avoid a surprise. Note also that most non-continuous entertainment events—concerts, festivals, sporting events, etc.—are discussed in the preceding general introduction to "Entertainment," rather than under individual SiDE Areas.

SiDE Area Ratings

✔✔✔ = **Outstanding, one of the city's finest concentrations**

✔✔ = **Well above average**

✔ = **Present, but not a primary activity**

DEEP ELLUM

This older area of low-rise storefronts and industrial buildings houses much of Dallas' avant-garde creative and artistic talent. The scene is dominated by today's young Bohemians, who are sometimes good-naturedly called PIBs, for "people in black" (although grey or white also seems to be acceptable). All ages and modes of dress are cheerfully tolerated but be forewarned, development is scattered and many establishments are poorly marked or almost invisible from the street.

Shopping: *art and avant-garde*

Dining: ✔

Entertainment: ✔✔

Ambiance: *Bohemian*

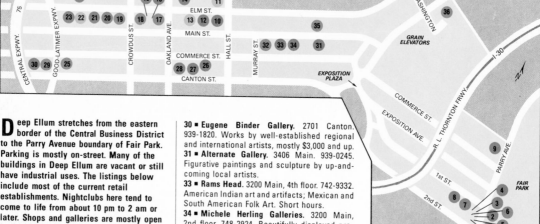

Deep Ellum stretches from the eastern border of the Central Business District to the Parry Avenue boundary of Fair Park. Parking is mostly on-street. Many of the buildings in Deep Ellum are vacant or still have industrial uses. The listings below include most of the current retail establishments. Nightclubs here tend to come to life from about 10 pm to 2 am or later. Shops and galleries are mostly open in the afternoons and closed on Sundays and Mondays. Some shops have late hours. All schedules are a little erratic and subject to last-minute changes. Nightclubs mostly feature local bands, some playing original music, whereas the theater companies tend to stress new and avant-garde plays, the local equivalent of off off-Broadway. Many local artisans and craftsmen have studios here, and several shops and galleries feature their work.

SHOPPING: ART, ANTIQUES, AND CRAFTS

1 ▪ Millennium. 3601 Parry. 824-7325. Mostly 1950s kitsch— furniture, lamps, decorative objects.
2 ▪ Artesania Gallery. 3603 Parry. 827-8430. Ethnic and tribal art from Latin America, Africa, Oceania, and Asia.
7 ▪ La Riviere Gallery. 831 Exposition. 821-1188. Everything from nineteenth-century lithographs to current works by talented high school students. Prices start at $75, with an average of about $250.
8 ▪ Davis Tile Techniques. 827 Exposition. 826-5130. Exquisite custom-designed and hand-painted decorative tiles.
16 ▪ Conduit. 2814 Elm. 939-0064. Gallery representing twelve artists, mostly local.
24 ▪ Deep Ellum Art Group. 2639 Elm. 654-0209. A cooperative gallery effort by fifteen local artists, moderate prices.
26 ▪ Two Women Boxing. 3002 E. Commerce, 2nd floor. 939-1626. Handsome boxes, blank books, and accessories, all hand-covered with imported papers and leathers. Customized portfolios and scrapbooks are a specialty. Irregular hours, call first.
27 ▪ Barry Whistler Gallery. 2909 A Canton. 939-0242. Features works by regional artists, many in the $500-to-$1,000 range, and provides useful art services (packing, photographing, etc.).
28 ▪ D. W. Gallery. 2909 C Canton. 939-0045. Works by thirty artists, mostly Southwestern, many at prices between $300 and $1,000.

30 ▪ Eugene Binder Gallery. 2701 Canton. 939-1820. Works by well-established regional and international artists, mostly $3,000 and up.
31 ▪ Alternate Gallery. 3406 Main. 939-0245. Figurative paintings and sculpture by up-and-coming local artists.
33 ▪ Rams Head. 3200 Main, 4th floor. 742-9332. American Indian art and artifacts; Mexican and South American Folk Art. Short hours.
34 ▪ Michele Herling Galleries. 3200 Main, 2nd floor, 748-2924. Beautifully displayed pre-Columbian, African, Oceanic, and ethnic arts, books, and jewelry.

SHOPPING: CLOTHING

4 ▪ Abraxas. 3613 Parry. 824-7729. Vintage and locally made clothes, crystals, and eclectica.
9 ▪ Howard Wolf Showroom. 3809 Parry. 823-9941. Manufacturer's outlet offers 50% to 70% off retail prices on this label of moderately priced women's clothes.
15 ▪ One. 2818 Elm. 939-3550. Very avant-garde yet wearable clothing in soft fabrics designed and hand-sewn on premises by designer Michael Garrett. Silk-screened scarfs by Lou Kregel and avant-garde jewelry by several talented Dallas designers. Affordable prices.
20 ▪ Ona. 2714 Elm. 748-5636. Very contemporary apparel, accessories, and art. Great hats.
21 ▪ Slix. 2708 Elm. 747-5600. Contemporary sportswear.
23 ▪ Sandra Garratt Designs. 2644 Elm. 939-0649. Carries *Multiples*, Sandra's popular and moderately priced line of modular clothing that appeals to all ages. Her experimental boutique line is also carried here.

SHOPPING: OTHER

3 ▪ Metamorphosis. 3609 Parry. 826-0281. Underground and eclectic music—tapes, albums, videos, and collectibles.
10 ▪ Mozzarella Company. 2944 Elm. 741-4072. Owner Paula Lambert has studied classic Italian cheese-making and produces more than thirty types of fresh cheeses here. Her products won six ribbons at the 1987 annual judging of the American Cheese Society and include mozzarella, mascarpone, crescenza, Texas-style caciottas, and goat cheeses, as well as creme fraiche and fromage blanc. Will ship.
12 ▪ Rudolph's. 2924 Elm. 741-1874. Choice meats since 1895; this small shop prepares its own smoked turkeys, sausages, and deli meats.
14 ▪ Hecho en Mexico. 2903 Elm. 741-4816. Imports new folk art from Mexico.

DINING

11 ▪ La Mansion de Blas. 2935 Elm. 939-0853. Casual Mexican dining. Inexpensive.
13 ▪ Olivia's. 2912 Elm. 741-0522. Casual. Informal country-style homecooking. Breakfast and lunch only, no alcohol. Inexpensive.
22 ▪ Deep Ellum Cafe. 2704 Elm. 741-9012. Sandwiches, salads, and carefully prepared American Nouvelle specials in pleasantly remodeled storefront. Popular with all ages. Inexpensive to moderate.

ENTERTAINMENT

5 ▪ State Bar and Restaurant. 3611 Parry. 821-9246. Popular neighborhood PIB pub.
6 ▪ Bar of Soap. 3615 Parry. 823-6617. Bar, launderette, and entertainment.
17 ▪ Video Bar. 2812 Elm. 939-9113. Features two huge screens with music videos.
18 ▪ Club Clearview. 2806 Elm. 939-0006. Avant-garde club with lots of innovative spaces, large dance floor, and varied entertainment. Very popular with the under-thirty set.
19 ▪ Club Dada. 2720 Elm. 744-DADA. Storefront location lets you preview varied live performances, from classical guitar to new wave bands.
25 ▪ On The Rocks. 2612 E. Commerce. 747-ROCK. Live music with emphasis on Heavy Metal Rock.
29 ▪ Tommy's. 2727 Canton. 747-6336. Large dance floor with varied live music. Open weekends only.
32 ▪ Undermain Theater. 3200 Main. 747-1424. Small, funky basement performance space. Often very experimental.
35 ▪ Deep Ellum Theater Garage. 3411 Main. 744-3832. Alternative theater in former garage.
36 ▪ Pegasus Theater. 3916 Main. 821-6005. This theater tends to present more mainstream productions than the other Deep Ellum companies.

DOWNTOWN DALLAS

Downtown shopping is anchored by the original Neiman-Marcus Department Store, which features a legendary selection of high quality merchandise, and by Foley's, a mid-range department store. Much of downtown's dining and additional shopping is concentrated in small nodes located in large office buildings, or in an underground tunnel system invisible from the street.

Shopping: ✔
(Neiman-Marcus ✔✔✔)

Dining: ✔✔

Entertainment: ✔

Ambiance: ✔✔

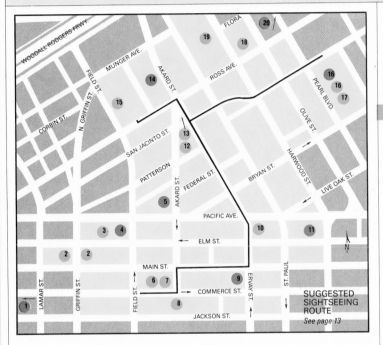

and one of the largest selections of men's Oxxford suits in the country. Beyond these highs, Neiman's superb buyers also excel in finding top-quality merchandise at less-than-lofty prices. The *Zodiac Room Restaurant* and *N-M-To-Go*, featuring light entrees and New York, Texas Cheesecake, are pleasant spots for lunch.

DINING

6 ▪ The French Room. 1321 Commerce (Adolphus Hotel). 742-8200. Dressy. Classic French cuisine in a spectacular setting, dinner only. Reservations required. Very expensive. (See Special Occasion Dining)

7 ▪ The Palm Bar. 1321 Commerce (Adolphus Hotel). 742-8200. Lunch until 3 pm, bar service until 8 pm. Cheerful, sidewalk level setting with picture windows to watch the passing crowd. Inexpensive.

12 ▪ Highland Park Cafeteria. 500 N. Akard (2nd level, Lincoln Plaza). 740-2400. Downtown branch of a long-time local favorite for Southern homecooking. Breakfast and lunch. Inexpensive.

13 ▪ Dakota's. 600 N. Akard. 740-4001. Enter the tiny elevator lobby and go down one floor for American Nouvelle cuisine in a sophisticated setting with pianist and a sunken patio for nice weather. Lunch and dinner. Expensive.

15 ▪ Massimo da Milano. 1445 Ross Avenue (First Interstate Bank Tower). 855-6200. Enjoy the building's spectacular water gardens as you eat tasty Italian salads, entrees, and delicacies from the bakery. Open from 7 am to 7 pm, Mon-Fri. Inexpensive.

17 ▪ Cafe Royal. 650 N. Pearl (atrium, Plaza of the Americas). 979-9000. Dressy. Superior French cuisine and service in elegantly understated surroundings. Lunch and dinner. Reservations advised. Expensive to very expensive. (See Special Occasion Dining)

18 ▪ City Market. 2001 Ross Avenue (2nd level, Trammell Crow Center). 979-2696. Fresh salads, soups, sandwiches, and desserts served cafeteria-style. Breakfast and lunch. Inexpensive.

19 ▪ Gallery Buffet. 1717 N. Harwood at Ross (2nd level, Dallas Museum of Art). 922-0220. Carefully prepared soups, salads, and light entrees. Lunch only. Inexpensive to moderate.

Don't even think about parking in a no-parking or tow-away zone. The police really do send tow trucks, and regularly. There are ample above-ground parking garages, surface parking lots, and underground garages in most newer buildings. Don't forget the handy Hop-A-Bus for getting around while your car is parked. Most downtown restaurants are open for lunch only, Monday through Friday. Evening and weekend openings are noted in the listings. Stores are usually closed at night and on Sundays.

CLUSTERS OF SNACK BARS, RESTAURANTS, AND SHOPS

2 ▪ Underground at First RepublicBank Plaza and One Main Place (between Elm, Main, Lamar, and Field). The most appealing sections of downtown's extensive underground walkway system are the large and airy indoor/outdoor plaza spaces of these two buildings. Several restaurants, as well as snack bars and small service-oriented shops, are located here.

3 ▪ Crystal Court at Renaissance Tower. 1201 Elm. Take the escalator down from the sidewalk level for quick foods in an airy atrium covered by a glass pyramid.

8 ▪ Bell Plaza. Akard at Commerce. A large and inviting ground-level plaza with many tables and chairs for breakfast, lunch, or relaxing snacks. Take-out food is available in several outlets located *inside* Bell One and facing the Plaza in Bell Two.

10 ▪ First City Center. 1700 Pacific. Enter from the Ervay Street plaza or through the building

lobby and down the escalators. A varied group of food vendors and small shops are located in the spacious "Markets" area at basement level.

16 ▪ Plaza of the Americas. 650 N. Pearl. 880-0001. A dramatic and active central atrium houses downtown's largest concentration of activities, including an ice-skating rink, thirty-six restaurants and shops, plus such services as shoe and eyeglass repair. The shops and services are open weekdays, 9 am to 6 pm, and you will always find at least one restaurant open. Shopping includes *Jas. K. Wilson*, men's and women's fine clothing; *Johnston and Murphy*, men's and women's quality shoes; *L'Art de Chine*, Netsuke, porcelain, ivory carvings, and jewelry from the Orient; and *Bag 'n Baggage*, luggage and leather goods.

SHOPPING: DEPARTMENT STORES

4 ▪ Brooks Brothers. 201 N. Field (in Renaissance Tower). 748-4700. Good selection of men's and women's classic clothing, all bearing Brooks Brothers' own label.

5 ▪ Foley's. 303 N. Akard. 749-3990. This is downtown's full-service department store with mostly moderately-priced lines.

9 ▪ Neiman-Marcus. 1618 Main. 741-6911. The original location of a now-famous chain, this store offers an elegant and understated essence of fine shopping. Whether you want a single Godiva chocolate or a fabulous Russian sable coat, by all means visit. The store is really many fine specialty shops combined into one, including boutiques featuring Armani, Chanel, Valentino, Ralph Lauren, and Palmer and Palmer (of Australia) labels; an outstanding perfumery; a Steuben room; a Boehm Porcelain Boutique;

ENTERTAINMENT

1 ▪ At the Top of the Dome Lounge. 300 Reunion (top of Reunion Tower, Hyatt Regency Hotel). 651-1234. Casual. Revolving lounge with spectacular view. Opens at 2 pm weekdays, noon on weekends. Live music nightly.

11 ▪ Majestic Theatre. 1925 Elm. 744-4397 or 880-0137. Classical 1921 vaudeville and movie palace now restored as performance hall with regular schedule of local and touring dance, music, and theatrical performances.

14 ▪ Venetian Room. Ross at Akard (Fairmont Hotel). 720-5227. Nightclub-cabaret with big-name performers and elegant decor.

20 ▪ Dallas Theater Center Arts District Theater. 2401 Flora. 526-8857. Professional resident company performs plays from Oct-May, some productions also in the Kalita Humphreys Theater.

THE GALLERIA

Modeled loosely after the Galleria Vittorio Emanuelle, Milan's historic, glass-roofed shopping arcade, this mall was built to bring national and international "name" shopping to Dallas, including such tenants as Saks Fifth Avenue, Gumps, Tiffany, Macy's, and Charles Jourdan. It also has the usual mall shops with merchandise in all price ranges.

Shopping: ✓✓✓

Dining: ✓

Entertainment: *movies only*

Ambiance: ✓✓

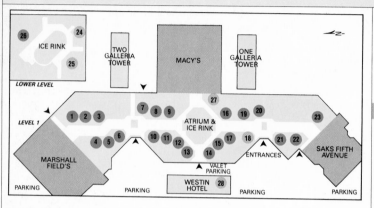

Located in the northeast corner of the busy intersection of the LBJ Freeway (I-35) and the Dallas North Tollway in North Dallas, the Galleria's 185 shops are arranged along a straight, three-level, axis with a large ice-skating rink in the middle. Fast-food outlets are concentrated on a lower level directly around the rink, and several more leisurely restaurants overlook the skaters on this and other levels. In general, the most expensive shops and merchandise are on the first level, with more moderately priced shops above. Parking garages are located at each end of the mall and valet parking is available at the principal entrance near the adjacent Westin Hotel.

SHOPPING: DEPARTMENT STORES

■ **Saks Fifth Avenue.** 458-7000. Wide variety of carefully selected merchandise, but with an emphasis on fine women's clothes and accessories. The loungewear, evening separates, and costume and semiprecious jewelry departments are particularly strong.
■ **Macy's.** 851-3300. A large offspring of New York's largest retailer. This is a family-oriented store with a broad selection to appeal to every age and pocketbook. The Market Place, with its gourmet grocery and snack bar, is especially tempting.
■ **Marshall Field's.** 851-1000. A large and complete department store, patterned after the Chicago original, which carries both moderately priced and top-of-the-line merchandise.

SHOPPING: CLOTHING

1 ■ **The Coach Store.** 392-1772. Classic bags, belts, and other leather accessories made from sturdy, natural-finish leather.
2 ■ **Mark Shale.** 458-2428. Men's clothes are upstairs and women's down in this large store featuring stylish classics, among them Shale's own label of blazers and suits.
4 ■ **Fiori of Italy.** 458-9381. Jazzy Italian leather accessories, including flashy cowgirl boots; wild jewelry.
5 ■ **Jaeger.** 233-0966. Understated knits and soft wool clothing for women.

6 ■ **Laura Ashley.** 980-9858. English chintzes for bed and body.
8 ■ **Bandiera's.** 934-9756. High-quality men's clothing imported from Italy.
9 ■ **Andre Bellini.** 386-7924. Sink into luxurious leather sofas while being fitted with men's and women's luxury shoes such as Bally, Ferragamo, Cole Haan, and Anne Klein.
14 ■ **Charles Jourdan.** 934-2945. Fashionable shoes and dramatic costume jewelry.
16 ■ **Church's English Shoes.** 458-8071. Men's shoes of conservative design imported from England; beautiful bedroom slippers.
19 ■ **Giovanni's For Men.** 387-2332. Fine imported men's clothing.
21 ■ **Gerlo Scherer, Baden Baden.** 233-7411. Small boutique with dressy women's clothing.

SHOPPING: OTHER

3 ■ **Crate and Barrel.** 392-3411. Basic dish-, glass-, cook-, and housewares, all beautifully displayed in a natural wood setting.
7 ■ **F.A.O. Schwarz.** 458-7783. A small branch of the famed Fifth Avenue toy store, with collectable dolls, Brio blocks, and other building systems for children.
10 ■ **Bachendorf's Jewelers.** 392-9900. Precious jewelry, plus a Crystal Room with an assortment of unusual decorative objects, for example, English Caithness paperweights and exotic handmade glass from the Isle of Wight.
11 ■ **Cartier.** 385-7640. Long known for precious jewels, watches, and accessories, Cartier has now introduced the striking *La Maison de Cartier* line of china, crystal, and silver tableware.
12 ■ **Louis Vuitton.** 934-3637. Distinctive, expensive, and virtually indestructible luggage, handbags, and accessories from France.
13 ■ **Fred Joaillier.** 458-9012. Precious jewelry.
15 ■ **William Ernest Brown.** 392-1600. Fine stationery and desk accessories.
17 ■ **Stefan Mann.** 385-8901. Several lines of fine handbags, luggage, and leather goods.
20 ■ **Mark Cross.** 239-4835. Leather goods. Their own brand of luggage is already an experienced traveler. U.S. hides are dyed in Germany, stitched in Italy, and then returned here for sale.
22 ■ **Gump's.** 392-0200. Large store with lovingly displayed decorative objects—over two hundred china patterns; three cases of striking silver, silverplate, and stainless steel; crystal; beautiful picture frames and stunning jewelry

featuring jade, pearls, lapis, coral, and other semiprecious stones.
23 ■ **Tiffany & Co.** 458-2800. Inventive jewelry and watch designs by Elsa Peretti, Paloma Picasso, and Jean Schlumberger. Many small pendants and a full room of silver items to fit every pocketbook.

DINING

18 ■ **Neuhaus Chocolate Shop.** 392-0281. Fine Belgian chocolates and other sweets for a sugary snack.
24 ■ **Polo's Grille & Pub.** Lower Level. 387-0393. Eclectic menu with chicken-burger-salad emphasis. Moderate.
25 ■ **The Artesian Cafe.** Lower Level. 960-0400. Popular sandwich and salad stop with homemade soups. Inexpensive.
27 ■ **Uncle Tai's Hunan Yuan.** Third Level. 934-9998. Dressy home of inventive Chinese dishes. Reservations advised. Expensive. (See Special Occasion Dining)
28 ■ **Blom's Restaurant (Westin Hotel).** 934-9494. Dressy. Highly acclaimed American Nouvelle cuisine, dinner only. Reservations advised. Very expensive.

ENTERTAINMENT:

26 ■ **General Cinema's Galleria.** Lower level. 387-8431. Five-screen movie house with first-run features.

HIGHLAND PARK VILLAGE

An historic landmark of early shopping center design, this beautifully restored 1930s complex of Spanish Eclectic buildings is a visual delight. Its tenants include many upscale boutiques (Chanel, Gucci, Ralph Lauren, etc.), as well as less pricey but equally distinctive shops and neighborhood services for the nearby residents of exclusive Highland Park.

Shopping: ✔✔✔

Dining: ✔

Entertainment: *movies only*

Ambiance: ✔✔✔

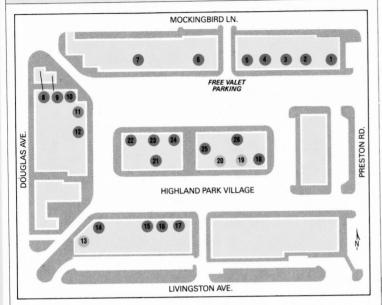

MOCKINGBIRD LN.

FREE VALET PARKING

DOUGLAS AVE.

PRESTON RD.

HIGHLAND PARK VILLAGE

LIVINGSTON AVE.

N

Located at the intersection of Preston Road and Mockingbird Lane in North Dallas, the center has ample surface parking; free valet parking is also available next to the Jas. K. Wilson store (see map). The fifty or so shops are generally open from 10 am to 6 pm, Monday through Saturday.

SHOPPING: CLOTHING

1 ▪ Polo/Ralph Lauren. 58 Highland Park Village. 522-5270. Two stories packed with Lauren's distinctive designs for men, women, boys, and beds.

2 ▪ Torie Steele. 54 Highland Park Village. 559-2119. This sleek boutique features pace-setting Italian designer Gianni Versace's clothing for men and women, expensive.

3 ▪ Florida Adams. 52 Highland Park Village. 520-6611. Features its own *Jessica* label of classically chic designs, affordably priced.

5 ▪ Ann Taylor. 50 Highland Park Village. 522-4700. Taylor's reasonably priced classics with a fashionable flair are showcased in an airy white setting.

6 ▪ Jas. K. Wilson, Ltd. 46 Highland Park Village. 526-7931. Long-time Dallas store with traditional men's clothing, including Hickey-Freeman suits. Small women's boutique.

7 ▪ Foley's. 40 Highland Park Village. 559-1996. If you've always liked department stores, but are now finding them too large and anonymous, you'll love this branch of a regional chain. Its small size and fine merchandise (Fendi, Coach, Villager, Judith Leiber, Cambridge, Liz Claiborne, Christian Dior) make it a shopper's delight.

9 ▪ Lirio's. 34 Highland Park Village. 521-0041. A cheerful store crammed with colorful fine clothing and folk art from Mexico and South America.

10 ▪ Carlos Falchi. 33 Highland Park Village.

528-8521. Features Falchi's striking leather handbags, belts, shoes, calendars, and accessories, as well as silver and semiprecious jewelry by DiAnne Malouf, Ann Cichon, and Stephen Dweck.

12 ▪ Wicker Garden's Children. 31 Highland Park Village. 528-6100. Carousel music and horses set the stage for a large selection of Pamela Scurry's own label of infants' and children's clothing. Also featured are brass and iron baby beds and handpainted children's furniture, as well as "Layettes by Appointment."

14 ▪ Hermes of Paris. 21 Highland Park Village. 528-0197. Absolutely impeccable silk ties, scarves, leather purses, clothing, and accessories for men and women.

15 ▪ Rosemary Byrd. 17 Highland Park Village. 522-1940. Nice mix of party clothes, costume jewelry, dresses, and sportswear.

18 ▪ Leon's. 61 Highland Park Village. 521-0828. Women's designer shoes including Ferragammo and Bruno Magli.

21 ▪ Collections. 71 Highland Park Village. 528-8030. Fashionable women's clothing.

22 ▪ Valentine Furs. 79 Highland Park Village. 528-1172. This fine furrier has been in the same location for forty years.

24 ▪ Chanel. 85 Highland Park Village. 520-1055. Chanel's legendary clothing, exquisite perfumes, and fine cosmetics are presented in a sophisticated beige, black, and mirrored setting.

26 ▪ Harold's. 88 Highland Park Village. 521-4770. Large choice of traditional women's clothing for dyed-in-the-wool preppies.

SHOPPING: OTHER

4 ▪ Williams-Sonoma. 51 Highland Park Village. 696-0348. Copperware, enamelware, utensils, and exotic gadgets to satisfy the most exacting chef.

8 ▪ Boutique Descamps. 35 Highland Park Village. 522-2171. French linens for bed and bath, cozy terry cloth robes, infants' clothes and cuddlers.

16 ▪ William Noble Rare Jewels. 16 Highland Park Village. 526-3890. A meticulous selection of elegant jewelry; carries a large collection of handsome cuff links and Concord watches.

17 ▪ Collectors Covey. 15 Highland Park Village. 521-7880. Hunting prints, decoys, bronzes, paintings, coasters, and mugs—everything to grace the sportsman's den or office.

23 ▪ Pierre Deux. 80 Highland Park Village. 528-5830. Marvelous French fabrics—chintzes, percales, and jacquards. Customized upholstery and adorable baby bassinets. Colorful and affordable fabric-covered frames, purses, and boxes.

25 ▪ John Haynsworth, Photographer. 86½ Highland Park Village. 559-3700. Haynsworth photographed families and celebrities in Palm Beach and the Hamptons for years. Now living in Dallas, he specializes in casual portraits of families and individuals, many taken outdoors. Peek in to see examples of his work.

DINING

13 ▪ Cafe Pacific. 24 Highland Park Village. 526-1170. Dressy mecca for seafood lovers, reservations advised. Expensive. (See Special Occasion Dining)

19 ▪ Village Bakery. 65 Highland Park Village. 528-3100. Casual. Tempting baked goods plus salad and sandwich lunches, opens 7 am. Inexpensive.

20 ▪ Beaujolais Cafe. 69 Highland Park Village. 522-4170. Casual. Country French dishes as well as sandwiches and salads, open for breakfast. Inexpensive to moderate.

ENTERTAINMENT

11 ▪ Village Theater. 32 Highland Park Village. 526-9668. Classic neighborhood movie house converted to smaller four-screen format with first-run features.

KNOX-HENDERSON

Anchored at one end by Henderson Avenue's antique row and at the other by the charming new Travis Walk Building, the strip development in between boasts many interesting shops with antiques, home furnishings, and decorative items, as well as many popular restaurants. The venerable Highland Park Cafeteria (now housed in modern quarters) and the 1920s Highland Park Pharmacy (with an old-fashioned soda fountain) give a feel for the homey neighborhood retail center this once was.

Shopping: ✔✔

Dining: ✔✔✔

Entertainment: ✔

Ambiance: ✔✔

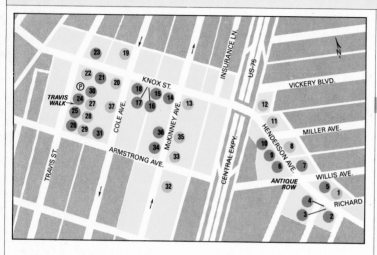

About eighty shops and restaurants are located here off Central Expressway near the Knox-Henderson exit. Knox Street on the west side of Central becomes North Henderson Avenue on the east. A free underground parking garage is located beneath Travis Walk, and many restaurants provide valet parking or private parking lots. Head-in and on-street parking can sometimes be scarce, requiring a short walk from nearby side streets.

SHOPPING: ART, ANTIQUES, AND CRAFTS

2 ▪ Lynn Holley Antiques. 2813 N. Henderson. 824-3774. Includes some very nice American antiques among the more usual English and continental items.
3 ▪ Court Gallery. 2815 N. Henderson. 823-1681. Antiques and "objects of virtue," mostly of the ornate French variety.
4 ▪ Mondays. 2819 N. Henderson. 823-7992. English country furniture. Lamps made from antique porcelain and decorative objects are a specialty as are reproductions of Battersea Boxes.
5 ▪ Jackie's Antique Cottage. 2822 N. Henderson. 824-3242. A long-time favorite, crammed with all kinds of stuff. Open Thurs-Sat only.
6 ▪ Silkz. 2925 N. Henderson. 828-2323. A charming arcade with an eclectic mixture of antiques.
9 ▪ In Good Company. 2933 N. Henderson. 826-0020. Old and new furniture, decorative objects, and tableware—all mixed with a stylish flair.
10 ▪ Les Antiques. 3001 N. Henderson. 824-7322. Three softly lit rooms of antiques and exotic imported decorative objects, all arranged in Victorian style on opulently draped tables.
15 ▪ Peregrinators. 3109 Knox. 521-1950. Lovely Chinese porcelains and furniture, along with many English antiques.
17 ▪ Highland Park Antiques. 3117 Knox. 528-0430. Specializes in sporty nautical pieces

for your favorite sailor.
25 ▪ The Wright Gallery. 4514 Travis (Travis Walk). 526-1839. Represents twenty-two artists from all around the country, all working in the abstract mode.
26 ▪ Tom Hollis Jeweler. 4514 Travis (Travis Walk). 528-4722. Handsome jewelry individually crafted on site by the owner—silver, gold, glass trading beads, and stones with a Southwestern flair.

SHOPPING: CLOTHING

16 ▪ Puttin' on the Ritz. 3113 Knox. 522-8030. Antique fashions, Victorian through 1950s.

SHOPPING: OTHER

7 ▪ The Ice House. 2918 N. Henderson. 823-6663. Contemporary decorative objects—Rosenthal and George Jensen tableware, acrylic furniture, and exotic modern lamps.
14 ▪ Expressions Custom Furniture. 3101 Knox. 522-7820. Numerous sofa and chair frames to be upholstered with your fabric choice and delivered in forty-five days.
18 ▪ Enchanted Lighting. 3121 Knox. 521-9623. A one-stop hospital for sick lamps. Enormous selection of shades, finials, decorative bulbs, and glass globes.
21 ▪ Maggies. 3213 Knox. 520-3031. A warm and homey shop with a tempting array of dried flowers and arrangements, custom bedding, gifts, dolls, and decorative objects.
24 ▪ Inner Space. 4514 Travis (Travis Walk). 521-0777. Innovative gifts and contemporary decorative objects.
31 ▪ Rudy Esquivel Design Gallery. 3210 Armstrong. 522-9196. Imaginative collection of hand-painted furniture, dishes, folk art, and decorative objects, all with a Southwestern accent.
34 ▪ Storkland. 4511 McKinney. 526-7947. This long-time favorite is jam-packed with everything needed for the under-two set, mostly at

slightly discounted prices. Eighty different cribs, from basic to designer, dozens of rockers, strollers, playpens, infant bedding, and clothes.
36 ▪ Shabahang Persian Carpets. 4537 McKinney. 526-8181. Large stock of new and semiantique pieces.

DINING

1 ▪ Bohemia. 2810 N. Henderson. 826-6209. Authentic Czechoslovakian setting and menu, dinner only. Moderate.
8 ▪ Pinot's. 2926 N. Henderson. 826-1949. Neighborhood wine bar with limited menu, dinner only. Inexpensive to moderate.
11 ▪ Chaise Lounge. 3010 N. Henderson. 823-1400. Casual. Tasty Cajun food in roadhouse setting with occasional live entertainment, dinner only. Inexpensive to moderate.
12 ▪ Dickey's. 4610 N. Central Expy. 823-0240. Casual. Popular local barbecue chain with rustic decor and dependable classics, closes at 8 pm. Inexpensive.
13 ▪ Atlantic Cafe. 4546 McKinney. 559-4441. Dressy. Fresh seafood in handsome surroundings. Reservations advised. Expensive.
19 ▪ Highland Park Cafeteria. 4611 Cole. 526-3801. Renowned mother lode of push-your-tray homecooking, no alcohol. Inexpensive.
20 ▪ Hoffbrau. 3205 Knox. 559-2680. Casual. Good-value steaks in informal setting. Inexpensive.
22 ▪ Highland Park Pharmacy. 3229 Knox. 521-2126. Casual. Their old-fashioned soda fountain, which serves sandwiches and breakfasts, has been a neighborhood favorite since the 1920s, closes at 6:30 pm. Inexpensive.
27 ▪ L'Ancestral. 4514 Travis (Travis Walk). 528-1081. Elegant setting with authentic and carefully prepared French menu. Moderate.
28 ▪ Mario's Chiquita. 4514 Travis (Travis Walk). 521-0721. Authentic Tex-Mex dishes as well as many Mexico City-style entrees, cheerful decor. Moderate.
29 ▪ Lombardi's. 4514 Travis (Travis Walk). 521-1480. Local chain with made-from-scratch Italian dishes and elegant surroundings. Moderate.
32 ▪ Chez Gerard. 4444 McKinney. 522-6865. Dressy. Classic country French fare in intimate setting, outdoor tables in good weather. Reservations advised. Moderate to expensive.
33 ▪ Sushi on McKinney. 4502 McKinney. 521-0969. Popular high-tech sushi bar with other Japanese dishes and table service. Inexpensive to moderate.
35 ▪ Crystal Pagoda. 4516 McKinney. 526-3355. Carefully prepared Chinese food and pleasant decor. Moderate.
37 ▪ Three Vikings. 4537 Cole. 559-0987. Authentic Scandinavian fare in cozy surroundings. Moderate.

ENTERTAINMENT

23 ▪ Knox Street Pub. 3230 Knox. 526-9476. Old-fashioned neighborhood bar with limited menu.
30 ▪ Speedy's. 4514 Travis (Travis Walk, level 2). 520-8485. Large pub with lively sing-a-long pianist and youthful patrons.

LOVERS LANE

Shopping: ✔✔

Dining: ✔✔

Entertainment: *movies only*

Ambiance: ✔✔

Dallas' first "Miracle Mile," this automobile-oriented strip is in the process of upgrading from older neighborhood services to upscale shopping. Boutiques with glamorous women's fashions, quality gifts, or elegant home furnishings mix comfortably with old-fashioned shoe repair shops and paint stores. It's a great place to walk even though most locals still drive from store to store—that's what Miracle Miles were all about.

The principal shopping district stretches along both sides of Lovers Lane beginning at Douglas Street on the east and extending for several long blocks to just past Inwood Road on the west. The ample double- or triple-width parking areas located just in front of the stores distinguished the auto-friendly Miracle Miles of the 1940s and 1950s from their streetside counterparts of earlier decades.

SHOPPING: ART, ANTIQUES, AND CRAFTS

2 ■ M. Samuels Antiques. 4346 Lovers Lane. 739-0029. The only American branch of a firm based in Dublin, Ireland. Specializes in fine antique silver and jewelry.

35 ■ Absolutely Necessary. 4421 Lovers Lane. 520-6238. High-quality works by American craftsmen, mostly pottery, wall hangings, and other decorative objects.

SHOPPING: CLOTHING

1 ■ Lou Lattimore. 4320 Lovers Lane. 369-8585. Elegant designer clothing for women. Chanel, Basile, Adrienne Vittadini, and many others are here. Expensive.

16 ■ Jill Handel. 5405 W. Lovers Lane. 351-0037. Moderately priced splashy women's clothes for fun days and evenings. Sequins, rhinestones, costume jewelry.

17 ■ Smyth Bros. Shoe Parlor. 5403 W. Lovers Lane. 350-5599. Upper-end women's shoes (Charles Jourdan, YSL, Anne Klein, Joan and David).

18 ■ Sable. 5301 W. Lovers Lane, Suite 111. 352-9888. Unusually creative made-to-order women's fashions, mostly for evening wear. Some creations have an imaginative, period-costume look.

19 ■ Ann Hartley. 5301 W. Lovers Lane. 956-7761. Women's boutique with fashionable clothes and fun accessories, including one-of-a-kind earrings, bags, and belts by Fort Worth's Z-Designs.

20 ■ Deja Vu a Paris. 5120 W. Lovers Lane. 902-0102. The fun, young, and Bohemian look from France for both men and women.

21 ■ A Pea in the Pod. 7815 Inwood. 352-6665. Terrific clothing for about-to-be mothers.

27 ■ Marie Leavell. 5500 W. Lovers Lane. 357-6441. Everything in this large and exclusive women's wear store is meticulously overseen by the owner, including the striking window displays. Outstanding selection of high-fashion clothing for adults and teens. Exquisite nightwear. Chic accessories. Marrakech Room features Moroccan cotton mix clothes with a soft and romantic ethnic look. Fine linens, silver, china, and gift items as well.

29 ■ Sam Bifano Furs. 5600 W. Lovers Lane, Suite 123. 350-7788. Fine furs.

31 ■ The Children's Collection and Collection II. 5600 W. Lovers Lane, Suite 150. 353-9671. Large and popular selection of clothes, shoes, and accessories for toddlers through teens. Everything from Polo for boys to savvy jewelry, accessories and formal dresses for high school proms.

SHOPPING: OTHER

3 ■ Carla Francis Gems and Jewelry. 4350 Lovers Lane. 361-4350. Sells precious jewelry that shouts rather than whispers. Reflects the personal style of the owner, Dallas socialite and jewelry lover Carla Francis.

4 ■ Room Service. 4354 Lovers Lane. 369-7666. Popular store for country-look linens, fabrics, decorative objects, and furniture for both adults and children.

5 ■ La Paloma. 4442 Lovers Lane. 368-4626. Distinctive Mexican crafts, pottery, and folk art.

7 ■ Happy Tails. 4514 Lovers Lane. 692-1999. Pet boutique offers its own biscuit bakery and designer clothing for finicky hounds and felines.

9 ■ La Creme de Cafe. 5655 W. Lovers Lane, Suite 600. 358-5615. Roasted fresh coffee beans and coffee-making accessories.

11 ■ Benno's Button Store. 5611 W. Lovers Lane. 352-0534. Small shop with enormous selection of buttons and unusual trimmings.

12 ■ Fishin' World. 5601 W. Lovers Lane. 358-4941. Stuffed full of lures, rods, and other tackle for the serious angler.

13 ■ Hillcrest High Fidelity. 5551 W. Lovers Lane. 352-9757. Long-time experts in superior sound systems for the home.

22 ■ Vertu. 7803 Inwood Road. 350-0424. Futuristic crystal, silver, and decorative objects, all dramatically lit in a cave-like setting.

30 ■ Bellini. 5600 W. Lovers Lane, Suite 142. 352-2512. Custom-made bedding, imported children's furniture and accessories, and infants' wear.

32 ■ B. Brocks. 5710 W. Lovers Lane. 350-1743. Furniture and accessories with a country look.

33 ■ Party Bazaar. 4435 Lovers Lane. 528-4795. Invitations, packaged decorations, balloons, favors, wrapping paper, pinatas, and dozens of paper plate "patterns."

34 ■ Scent Shop. 4423 Lovers Lane. 522-3212. Exotic yet affordable oils, spices, herbs, flavors, and essences for you to create your own perfume, potpourri, or pomanders. Pre-mixed selections and "scent-a-likes" also available.

36 ■ Plate & Platter. 4401 Lovers Lane. 521-9980. Large selection of casual and everyday china, glassware, and stainless steel, plus cookware and gifts.

37 ■ Pier 1 Imports. 4325 Lovers Lane. 521-0970. Wind chimes and wicker, pillows and pallets, baskets and brass from all around the world. Perfect for creating pleasing interiors at minimum cost.

DINING

6 ■ The Everyday Gourmet. 4446 Lovers Lane. 373-0325. Casual. Particularly tempting array of gourmet dishes to take home. A few small tables for eat-ins, no alcohol. Inexpensive.

8 ■ City Cafe. 5757 W. Lovers Lane. 351-2233. Inventive American Nouvelle dishes carefully prepared in open kitchen. Moderate to expensive.

10 ■ Mr. Peppe. 5617 W. Lovers Lane. 352-5976. Long-time neighborhood favorite for traditional French fare, dinner only. Expensive.

14 ■ Massimo da Milano. 5519 W. Lovers Lane. 351-1426. Casual. Popular Italian bakery-cafe with fresh pizza, pastas, and salads. Inexpensive.

15 ■ Dunston's. 5423 W. Lovers Lane. 352-8320. Casual. Local chain with bargain steaks in rustic, mesquite-grilled atmosphere. Inexpensive.

23 ■ La Tosca. 7713 Inwood Road. 352-8373. Dressy. Italian classics in minimalist setting, dinner only. Expensive.

24 ■ The Riviera. 7709 Inwood. 351-0094. Dressy and stylish mecca for French/American Nouvelle devotees, dinner only. Reservations required. Very expensive. (See Special Occasion Dining)

28 ■ Casa Rosa. 165 Inwood Village. 350-5227. Traditional Tex-Mex classics in a colorful setting. Moderate.

ENTERTAINMENT

25 ■ The Lounge. 5458 W. Lovers Lane (Inwood Theatre). 350-7834. Small but lively bar-bistro with limited menu and high-tech decor.

26 ■ Inwood Theatre. 5458 W. Lovers Lane. 352-6040. Excellent foreign and offbeat American films shown on three screens in converted 1940s movie house.

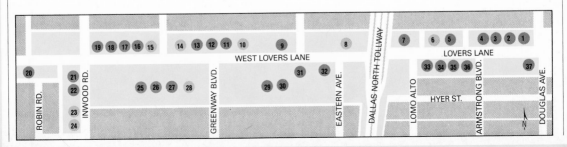

LOWER GREENVILLE

Funky old neighborhood shopping strip that today houses many popular restaurants and nightclubs in a homey atmosphere. Shopping is secondary and emphasizes offbeat merchandise. Patrons are of all ages, most of them casually dressed.

Shopping: ✔

Dining: ✔✔

Entertainment: ✔✔✔

Ambiance: ✔✔

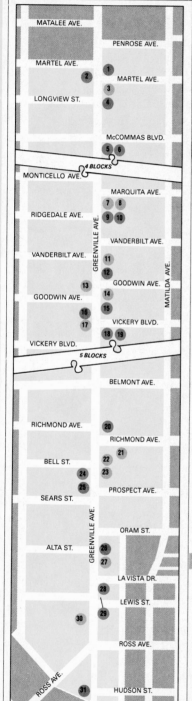

The district has three distinct nodes, all located on Greenville Avenue between Ross Avenue on the south and Mockingbird Lane on the north. The accompanying map abbreviates the several block intervals that separate the nodes. There are a few parking lots, mostly located *behind* the buildings they serve. Much of the parking is on-street, and spaces can sometimes be hard to find at night.

SHOPPING

5 ▪ Waterbird Traders. 3420 Greenville. 821-4606. American Indian, Spanish Colonial, and primitive art and antiques.
6 ▪ Country Classics. 3418 Greenville. 824-1285. Handwoven, braided, and rag rugs from Ohio and Pennsylvania; gifts, handcrafts, and decorative objects.
9 ▪ H. D.'s Clothing Company. Women's shop at 3014 Greenville. 821-8900. Men's shop at 3018 Greenville. 821-5255. Great avant-garde clothes for youthful PIBs (people in black).
10 ▪ The Ole Moon & Other Tales. 3016 Greenville. 827-9921. Beautiful craftsmen's pieces— raku, stoneware, ceramics, blown glass, jewelry, and wood. Also masks and vintage Japanese clothing.
15 ▪ Cabbage Patch Country Store. 2802 Greenville. 826-5436. The country look in furniture, decorative objects, toys, and linens.
18 ▪ Avant. 2716 Greenville. 824-0260. Trendy, youthful clothing for men and women; interesting costume jewelry and accessories.
19 ▪ The Roxy. 2714 Greenville. 827-8593. Both antique and reproduction Art Deco and Art Nouveau furniture and accessories.
20 ▪ Whole Foods Market. 2218 Greenville. 824-1744. Large natural foods supermarket with small cafe.
24 ▪ Assassins. 1927 Greenville. 821-2458. Leather belts, boots, skirts, etc., for the Heavy Metal, biker look.
28 ▪ Decorators Anonymous. 1806 Greenville. 821-6026. Two floors plus a warehouse filled with furniture for sale on consignment.
29 ▪ Antique Warehouse. 1802 Greenville. 821-4843. Mostly 1910s-1920s vintage home furnishings.

DINING

3 ▪ Snuffer's. 3526 Greenville. 826-6850. Casual. Renowned burgers and munchies, open till 2 am. Inexpensive.
7 ▪ San Francisco Rose. 3024 Greenville. 826-2020. Popular sandwich-and-salad fern bar with some outdoor tables, open till 2 am. Inexpensive.
8 ▪ St. Martin's. 3020 Greenville. 826-0940. Wine bar with cheese-pâté-salad menu and daily specials. Moderate to expensive.
11 ▪ Zanzibar. 2912 Greenville. 828-2250. Casual. Limited but very tasty natural-food menu, dinner only, open till 2 am. Inexpensive.
13 ▪ Blue Goose Cantina. 2905 Greenville. 823-6786. Casual. Large portions of Tex-Mex favorites and fresh tortillas made while-you-watch on a rotating machine. Inexpensive to moderate.

14 ▪ The Grape. 2808 Greenville. 823-0133. Intimate and unpretentious wine bistro with cheese boards and daily entrees. Moderate.
17 ▪ Terilli's. 2815 Greenville. 827-3993. Popular, upscale restaurant-pub featuring Italian food. Live jazz after 9 pm, open till 2 am. Moderate.
21 ▪ Pietro's. 5722 Richmond. 824-9403. Hearty Italian homecooking in informal setting, dinner only. Moderate.
22 ▪ Arcadia Bar. 2114 Greenville. 821-1300. Casual. Neighborhood pub with limited but carefully prepared Cajun menu, dinner only, till 2 am. Live entertainment.
23 ▪ Nero's. 2104 Greenville. 826-6376. Intimate Italian cafe with the usual standards plus blackboard specials, dinner only. Moderate.
27 ▪ Little Gus'. 1916 Greenville. 826-4910. Casual. Small sandwich diner by day, cozy Greek restaurant at night, open for breakfast. Inexpensive to moderate.
30 ▪ Saigon. 1731 Greenville. 828-9795. Casual. Tasty Vietnamese dishes in cheerful cafe setting. Inexpensive.
32 ▪ Banno Bros Seafood. 1516 Greenville. 821-1321. Casual. Fried seafood classics in funky surroundings. Inexpensive to moderate.

ENTERTAINMENT

1 ▪ Fast & Cool. 3606 Greenville. 827-5544. Lower Greenville's *in* place for 60s, 70s, and just-released music and dancing. Open till 4 am on Friday and Saturday. Cover charge.
2 ▪ Greenville Avenue Country Club. 3619 Greenville. 826-5650. Popular neighborhood pub with outdoor tables and limited menu.
4 ▪ Granada Cinema and Draft House. 3524 Greenville. 823-9610. Serves beer, wine, and food at your seat during movies. Shows always at 7:30 and 9:45 with midnight classics on weekends.
12 ▪ Stan's Blue Note. 2908 Greenville. 824-9653. Old-fashioned neighborhood bar emphasizing pool, shuffleboard, and beer.
16 ▪ Greenville Avenue Bar and Grill. 2821 Greenville. 823-6691. Austere but lively neighborhood pub with limited menu and live entertainment, open till 2 am.
17 ▪ Terilli's. See under "Dining" above.
25 ▪ Arcadia Theater. 2005 Greenville. 826-7554. Neighborhood movie theater now booked with concerts for the teen-age set.
26 ▪ Poor David's Pub. 1924 Greenville. 821-9891. High-quality live music with performers, some nationally known, changing nightly. Includes rock, blues, folk, and country.
31 ▪ Greenville Avenue Pocket Sandwich Theatre. 1611 Greenville. 821-1860. Fun neighborhood theater with both melodramas and more challenging plays. Enjoy drinks and munchies while you watch. Open Thurs-Sun.

MARKET DISTRICT

Shopping: *home furnishings*

Dining: ✔

Entertainment: ✔

Ambiance: *warehouses*

This light industrial area has some retail stores and discount factory outlets as well as one of the country's largest concentrations of wholesale showrooms featuring home furnishings and antiques. The latter, informally known as the "Design District," has a variety of policies for would-be purchasers.

Here's how the Design District works. There are four official wholesale complexes: the original *Decorative Center*, the *Dallas Design Center*, the *Oak Lawn Design Plaza*, and the new *Contract Design Center*. Most of these have large and attractive show windows, and this incredible window shopping is accessible to everyone. Surrounding these complexes are numerous *independent* warehouse-showrooms with similar tenants. Showrooms in the four wholesale centers, and some in the surrounding stores, are open "to the trade" only. This means they can only *sell* to someone with a tax resale number and are not set up to deal with drop-in purchasers. Although the policy varies, many showrooms are gracious about allowing serious shoppers to *look around*, particularly if you have a letter or business card from an interior designer that you are working with. Other shops are very curt in telling you that you are not welcome to browse. Stores that deal primarily in small samples that are difficult for a nonprofessional to evaluate (fabrics, wallpapers, carpets, etc.) seldom allow browsers except when accompanied by a professional designer. Some shops outside of the four official wholesale complexes will sell direct to the public; these have been indicated in the listings. All establishments listed are happy to have browsers. A few shops can recommend an interior designer that works closely with them.

SHOPPING: DESIGN DISTRICT

1 ■ **John Henry Sterry.** 1401 Oak Lawn. 744-3316. Outstanding collection of English antiques and classic Oriental rugs.
2 ■ **The Plant Plant.** 1645 Dragon. 747-2415. Large stock of silk house plants and flowering plants. Open to the public.
3 ■ **Ming Ching Antiques and Arts, Inc.** 1615 Dragon. 741-6906. Small group of old and reproduction Oriental imports. Open to the public.
4 ■ **Gregor's Studios.** 1611 Dragon. 744-3385. Handsome hand-carved mantels, custom furni-

ture, some with faux finishes; selected antiques, mostly French. Open to the public.
5 ■ **Cele Johnson Custom Lamps.** 1410 Dragon. 651-1645. Open to the public.
6 ■ **Benfontes Custom Furniture.** 302 Cole. 744-5187. Manufactures furniture to order, from photo or sketch. Open to the public.
7 ■ **Leather Center.** 1319 Dragon. 742-1300. Over one hundred furniture frames available in your choice of soft or traditional leathers. Open to the public.
8 ■ **Dathon.** 1302 Dragon. 748-1393. Manufacturer and importer of fine carpets and custom rugs.
9 ■ **The Sporting Scene.** 1203 Dragon. 748-7831. A gallery of art, antiques, and memorabilia for the sports lovers. Open to the public.
10 ■ **Feizy Oriental Rugs.** 961 Slocum. 521-4600. Rug importer.
11 ■ **Patterson Edwards.** 1313 Slocum, Suite 101. 651-0833. Direct importers of lovely Oriental decorative objects, mostly new, some old. Many would make perfect lamp bases.
12 ■ **Oriental Treasures.** 1322 Slocum. 760-8888. Large showroom of antique and new Asian furniture and fine arts.
13 ■ **San Miguel Allende.** 1418 Slocum. 760-9118. Furniture, stone, and brasswork done by the renowned craftsman of the Mexican village with the same name. Will do custom work.
14 ■ **Country French Interiors.** 1428 Slocum. 747-4700. Imported country French furniture and accessories.
15 ■ **Yang's Double Happiness.** 1436 Slocum. 747-8606. This custom lamp shop will produce a lamp out of any base you bring in, make special shades and bases, etc.
16 ■ **Orion Antique Importers.** 1435 Slocum. 748-1177. A large selection of quality French antiques. Chandeliers and mirrors are a specialty, as are huge armoires converted into home entertainment centers.
17 ■ **Louis Rosenbach Antiques.** 1518 Slocum. 748-0906. English and French antiques.
19 ■ **Pflaster's Zimports.** 1532 Hi-Line. 741-1332. A huge showroom filled with imported decorative objects, furniture, and antiques.
20 ■ **Rudi South.** 1519 Hi-Line, Suite C. 742-6921. Dramatic and high-quality decorative objects from Asia, South America, and Africa.
21 ■ **Antique Showcase.** 1323 North Stemmons Frwy. 651-7579. Twenty-five dealers have small stalls in this building. Open to the public.

SHOPPING: FACTORY OUTLETS AND DISCOUNT STORES

For the latest update on discount shopping in Dallas see the ads in *Hidden Values Magazine.* This is available at many of the outlets below or from the publisher at 5307 E. Mockingbird Lane (at Central Expressway), Suite 401. 828-5053.

26 ■ **Vantage Shoe Warehouse.** 2222 Vantage. 631-4812. Over 50,000 pairs of shoes on display at 40 to 90% off retail. Many top brands scattered among more modest lines.
27 ■ **Just Justin.** 1505 Wycliff. 630-2858. Discount prices on Justin boots; other Western wear as well.
28 ■ **Willoughby & Taylor, Ltd.** 8908 Ambassador Row. 630-6677. This outlet store for the mail-order catalogue features jewelry, clothing, and decorative objects at 40% to 70% off retail.
29 ■ **Terry Costa, Designer.** 3211 Irving, Suite 103. 634-8089. Mostly discounted party dresses, many from Victor Costa. Favorite pre-prom destination.

DINING

18 ■ **Trieste.** 1444 Oak Lawn (Oak Lawn Design Plaza, Suite 600). 742-4434. French menu in charming setting. Moderate.
22 ■ **Nana Grill.** 2201 Stemmons Frwy. (Anatole Hotel, 27th floor). 748-1200. Eclectic menu in elegant tower location with spectacular view of downtown. Bar has live entertainment nightly. Expensive.
23 ■ **L'Entrecote.** 2201 Stemmons Frwy. (Anatole Hotel). 748-1200. Dressy. Innovative French cuisine. Dinner only. Reservations required. Expensive to very expensive. (See Special Occasion Dining)
24 ■ **Plum Blossom.** 2201 Stemmons Frwy. (Anatole Hotel). 748-1200. Dressy. Superior Chinese dining. Reservations required. Expensive. (See Special Occasion Dining)

ENTERTAINMENT

25 ■ **Crocodile.** 2201 Stemmons Frwy. (Anatole Hotel). 748-1200. Dressy. Comfortable cocktail lounge with DJ playing music for grown-ups.

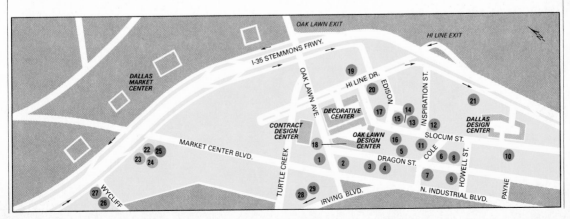

NORTHPARK

This is Dallas' first enclosed mall, built by developer and art collector Raymond Nasher. Attention to design and detail, understated human scale, a handy location, and careful tenant selection have combined to make NorthPark a perennial shoppers' favorite.

Shopping: ✔✔✔

Dining: ✔

Entertainment: ✔

Ambiance: ✔✔✔

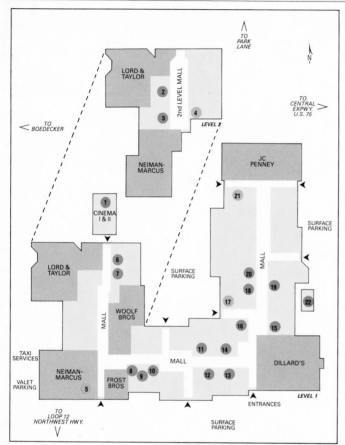

Rite and an adorable "Baby Box" selection.

16 ■ The Shoe Box. 369-7544. This was the first location of what has become a popular Southwestern chain featuring a large selection of fashionable women's footwear in a slightly chaotic atmosphere.

18 ■ Banana Republic. 739-8577. The premier purveyor of the safari look for those addicted to cotton and khaki comfort.

19 ■ Victoria's Secret. 373-8238. If it was a secret before, it probably won't be once you've donned the revealing lingerie offered here.

SHOPPING: OTHER

7 ■ Dunhill. 691-0191. A branch of the English store famous for luxury smoking goods—lighters, pipes, tobacco, and cigars, the latter items housed in the Humidor Room to the rear.

8 ■ Linz. 363-5577. The Linz family opened their original downtown store in 1877, shortly after the first railroad arrived. Their namesake store is still a favorite source for high-quality jewelry, china, and silver.

10 ■ Rizzoli International Bookstore. 739-6633. This handsome branch of the New York bookstore and publishing house emphasizes nonfiction, with the arts, architecture, and photography as particular strengths.

11 ■ James Avery Craftsman. 750-7324. Affordable sterling silver jewelry from a Central Texas workshop. The charms, tie tacks, and dangle rings, many in the $10-$20 range, are favorites of area teenagers.

15 ■ The Enchanted Village. 361-6883. Large selection of intelligent toys, science kits, children's computers, blocks, crafts, trains, and books. Not a cartoon monster doll in sight.

20 ■ Noah's Ark. 692-9206. Be careful or you'll end up flooding your favorite stuffed animal collector with the cuddly specimens sold here.

DINING

4 ■ Fresh Market (Neiman-Marcus, 2nd level mall entrance). 363-8311. Salads, soups, and sandwiches in sidewalk-like setting, lunch only. Inexpensive.

5 ■ Zodiac Room (Neiman-Marcus, 3rd level). 363-8311. Stylish decor and creative menu emphasizing salads and soups, lunch only. Inexpensive to moderate.

17 ■ L & N Seafood Grill. 363-4722. Seafood standards in pub-like setting. Moderate.

21 ■ Fletcher's Corny Dogs. 987-3780. Casual. A local chain serving frankfurters deep-fried with cornbread coating, a popular area favorite first served at the State Fair of Texas in the 1940s. Inexpensive.

ENTERTAINMENT

1 ■ General Cinema NorthPark 1-2. 363-7541. First-run features in two large-screen theaters adjacent to the main mall.

22 ■ Dallas Repertory Theater. 369-8966. A well-designed 215-seat theater features familiar musicals and theatrical classics. Located on the Central Expressway side of the mall.

NorthPark is located at the intersection of Central Expressway and Northwest Highway in North Dallas. Its 130 tenants are arranged so that, with a few exceptions, stores with less expensive merchandise are concentrated in the eastern section, between Penney's and Dillard's, whereas those with progressively more expensive items are found westward, toward Neiman-Marcus and Lord & Taylor. There is ample surface parking, and valet parking is available at the Neiman-Marcus entrance.

SHOPPING: DEPARTMENT STORES

■ **Neiman-Marcus.** 363-8311. This legendary retailer was founded in downtown Dallas, and NorthPark was the first mall location. You'll feel a part of retailing history as you explore the store's superb selection of clothing and gift items, which range from mid-priced to very expensive.

■ **Frost Bros.** 369-7300. This small branch of a much larger San Antonio store has upscale men's clothing, fine cosmetics, a huge Gucci boutique, and Richard Eisemen's jewelry.

■ **Lord & Taylor.** 691-6600. Moderate to expensive merchandise.

■ **Woolf Bros.** 369-8811. Conservative, well-tailored classic men's and women's clothing and furnishings. Features a Burberry shop, a business women's shop, and a broad selection of men's suits and sports coats.

SHOPPING: CLOTHING

2 ■ The Carriage Shop Terrace. 368-6411. The most upscale branch of a popular local chain which features timeless women's fashions.

3 ■ Lester Melnick. 363-0606. A Dallas-based chain with moderate to expensive women's clothes. A penchant for beautiful colors, affordable coats, and elegant evening clothes (many of the latter by Dallas-based designer Victor Costa), sets this store apart.

6 ■ Cuzzens. 363-6488. Imported men's suits, jackets, and accessories of the highest quality.

9 ■ The Carriage Shop. 368-6411. Another branch of the local chain renowned for its moderately priced yet classic women's clothes and omnipresent sale racks.

12 ■ Laura Ashley: Mother and Child. 373-9381. Storybook-proper clothes for children.

13 ■ Gap Kids. 692.5134. National chain with a variety of kids' clothes, mostly in denims or bright colors.

14 ■ The Shoe Box Jr. 750-0008. Great selection of children's shoes and boots, including Stride

WEST END HISTORIC DISTRICT

This is a compact and lively area of picturesque early warehouses renovated to house a concentration of nightclubs, restaurants, and a festival market. Lots of street life, including surrey rides. You'll find something here for all ages and tastes.

Shopping: *festival market*

Dining: ✔✔

Entertainment: ✔✔✔

Ambiance: ✔✔✔

16 ■ 311 Lombardi's. 311 Market. 747-0322. Popular, prepared-from-scratch Italian fare. Reservations advised. Moderate.
19 ■ The Palm. 701 Ross. 698-0470. Dressy crowd but informal setting, excellent steaks and people watching. Reservations advised. Very expensive.
21 ■ Grumbles. 302 Market. 651-1226. Casual. Burgers and munchies in pub-like atmosphere. Inexpensive.
23 ■ Pacific Pearl. 601 Pacific. 745-1688. Chinese dining in attractive setting. Moderate to expensive.
25 ■ Morton's of Chicago. 501 Elm. 741-2277. Features hearty steaks in comfortable basement quarters. Expensive.

ENTERTAINMENT

3 ■ Starck Club. 703 McKinney (Brewery Bldg.). 720-0130. Dressy. High-tech disco dancing and people watching. Open Thurs-Sun nights only, late evening crowd. Cover charge.
4 ■ Prohibition Room. 703 McKinney (Brewery Bldg.). 954-4407. Casual. Billiards, live music, and dancing. Cover charge weekends.
5 ■ Alley Cats. 603 Munger (Dallas Alley). 988-WEST. Popular sing-along, bounce-along format. One cover charge admits to all Dallas Alley clubs.
6 ■ Back Stage. 603 Munger (Dallas Alley). 988-WEST. Quiet piano bar. No cover charge.
7 ■ Froggy Bottoms. 603 Munger (Dallas Alley). 988-WEST. Live Rhythm and Blues listening in intimate surroundings with limited menu. One cover charge admits to all Dallas Alley clubs.
8 ■ The Boiler Room. 603 Munger (Dallas Alley). 988-WEST. Disco dancing in multi-level setting. One cover charge admits to all Dallas Alley clubs.
17 ■ Dick's Last Resort. 1701 Market. 747-0001. Casual. Live jazz in crowded, rustic atmosphere with limited menu.
18 ■ Outback Pub. 1701 Market. 761-9355. Limited menu stressing Australian style items. Occasional live music.
20 ■ West End Cabaret. 702 Ross. 742-4800. Theater with drinks and changing programs, including the Dallas Lyric Opera.
22 ■ Voodoo Room. 1482 Pacific. 655-2627. Exotic bar with steel band reggae music on weekends.
24 ■ West End Pub. 211 Record. 748-5711. Friendly old-fashioned bar with limited but carefully prepared menu items.

Located on the western edge of the Dallas Central Business District, the area has more than thirty restaurants and nightclubs. Hundreds of surface parking spaces surround the district, and there is a convenient self-park garage at Lamar and Woodall Rodgers Freeway (entrance on Munger; see map).

SHOPPING

■ West End Marketplace. 603 Munger. 954-4350. Opens 11 am (noon Sunday); closes 10 pm (8 pm Sunday, midnight Friday and Saturday).

Most of the West End's shopping is concentrated in this early warehouse complex that has been converted into a four-level festival market designed around an airy central atrium. About one hundred small shops and vendors emphasize casual clothing, fun gift items, T-shirts, mementos, and snack food, the latter clustered on the upper (4th) level. Adjacent Dallas Alley houses a half-dozen popular nightclubs (see "Entertainment"), each with a different mood and theme. One cover charge provides admission to all.

10 ■ Frillz. 2nd level, Marketplace. 747-5800. Hand-painted clothing, mostly shirts with soft floral designs.
11 ■ Satin & Lace & Funny Face. 2nd level, Marketplace. 720-2206. Hand-painted porcelain-and-fabric dolls by Lindell of Denver.
12 ■ Cajun Connection. 2nd level, Marketplace. 954-1772. Books and spices to bring out the bayou in you.
13 ■ Dallas Western Wear. 3rd level, Marketplace. 954-1050. Large shop with jeans, boots, hats, and all the trimmings.
14 ■ D.B. McCalls. 3rd level, Marketplace. 954-0719. Mock country store with new Americana gifts and local-interest books.

DINING

1 ■ Newport's. 703 McKinney (Brewery Bldg.). 954-0220. Fresh seafood in renovated brewery. Reservations advised. Expensive.
2 ■ Kuby's. 703 McKinney (Brewery Bldg.). 954-0004. Authentic German fare with live entertainment nightly. Full-meal spinoff of the noted Sausage House in the Snider Plaza SiDE Area. Inexpensive to moderate.
9 ■ Bubble's Beach Diner. 603 Munger (1st level, Marketplace). 720-0313. Casual. Classic roadside diner with Art Deco decor, open for breakfast. Inexpensive.
15 ■ Spaghetti Warehouse. 1815 Market. 651-8475. Casual. Standard Italian food amongst an intriguing hodge-podge of nostalgic antiques. Inexpensive.

UPTOWN

Uptown, the location of many of the city's finest shops, galleries, and restaurants, offers old storefronts along brick-paved McKinney Avenue; the elegant new Crescent development; funky Victorian houses crammed with art and antiques; and the sophisticated, post-Modern Quadrangle retail center.

Shopping: ✔✔✔

Dining: ✔✔✔

Entertainment: ✔✔

Ambiance: ✔✔✔

Loosely bounded by McKinney Avenue on the south and Cedar Springs Road on the north, this lively area is located just a few blocks north of the Central Business District. There is free underground parking at the Crescent (entrance at corner of Cedar Springs and Maple), surface parking at the Quadrangle, valet parking at many restaurants in the evening, and on-street parking everywhere.

SHOPPING: ART, ANTIQUES, AND CRAFTS

1 ▪ Peregrine Gallery. The Crescent. 871-3770. Lithographs of forty contemporary artists, mostly from the Southwest, whose works are carefully produced at the nearby Peregrine Press in Deep Ellum. Many inexpensive works.
2 ▪ Shopping English Countryside. The Crescent. 871-8333. Handsome antique furniture, paintings, and accessories—gathered while "shopping the English Countryside"—are displayed in thematic rooms. Wonderful, affordable stuffed animals with an old-fashioned look.
3 ▪ Hall Galleries. The Crescent. 871-3400. Nineteenth- and twentieth-century French and American Impressionists, including many highly sought after artists.
4 ▪ Gerald Peters Gallery. The Crescent. 871-3535. A branch of a Santa Fe establishment, this features primarily Southwestern art and contemporary American realists.
5 ▪ Ken Riney Jewelry. The Crescent. 871-3640. Antique watches, pins, jewelry, and silver.
8 ▪ Boehm. The Crescent. 855-7999. Exquisite porcelains, best known for limited editions of birds and flowers.

14 ▪ Phillips Galleries. 2517 Fairmount. 871-2334. Specializes in contemporary French artists painting in the Impressionist mode. Most in the $2000-$5000 range.
15 ▪ Heirloom House. 2521 Fairmount. 871-0012. Good selection of eighteenth-century European and Continental antiques.
16 ▪ P.S. (Johnson-Kraynick) Galleries. 2525 Fairmount. 871-1197. Moderately priced older oil paintings.
17 ▪ Victory Antiques. 2604 Fairmount. 871-9034. British and Continental antiques.
18 ▪ Militaria. 2615 Fairmount. 871-1565. Everything military—swords, hats, medals, books, and miniature soldiers.
19 ▪ Uncommon Market. 2701 Fairmount. 871-2775. Antique light fixtures, hardware, leaded glass, and unusual scientific instruments.
20 ▪ Victorian Gallery. 2722 Fairmount. 871-2474. Large and varied selection of British Victorian paintings, most have had restoration work in England. Prices range upward from $1000.
25 ▪ Adams-Middleton Gallery. 3000 Maple. 871-7080. Three floors of an old house converted to a handsome contemporary gallery carrying both abstract and realistic works.
36 ▪ Afterimage. 2800 Routh. (The Quadrangle). 871-9140. One of the oldest photography galleries in the country with works by many well-known photographers, both old and new. Many available in the $100-$500 range.
37 ▪ Dorrace Pearle Antiques. 2736 Routh. 827-1116. Mostly small English antiques—jewelry, figurines, plates, and bric-a-brac.
39 ▪ Walter-Delipsey. 2615 Routh. 871-8856. A turreted Queen Anne house packed with all manner of antiques and old things.

45 ▪ Beverly Gordon Gallery. 2702 McKinney. 741-9600. Contemporary American art.
46 ▪ McKinney Avenue Market. 2710 McKinney. 824-1696. Forty individually managed stalls offer a large and tasteful selection of antiques, with some handmade craft and clothing items.

SHOPPING: CLOTHING

6 ▪ Jean Claude Jitrois. The Crescent. 871-3590. Luxurious and dramatic leatherwear designed by Jitrois.
13 ▪ Esprit Superstore. 2425 McKinney. 871-8989. A dramatic hi-tech setting showcases Esprit's complete collection of reasonably priced clothes for women and children.
21 ▪ Bifano Fur Co. 2909 Fairmount. 871-1111. Old-line Dallas furrier.
35 ▪ Hippolyte. 2800 Routh (The Quadrangle). 855-5081. Elegant imported men's clothing.
36A ▪ Handel's. 2800 Routh (The Quadrangle). 748-6401. Small but well-selected offering of understated women's clothing.

SHOPPING: OTHER

7 ▪ The Altomar Collection. The Crescent. 871-3128. Stunning hand-crafted Brazilian jewelry designed by Haroldo Burke Mark.
24 ▪ Aldredge Book Store. 2909 Maple. 871-3333. Excellent stock of used and rare books.
29 ▪ La Mariposa. 2817 Routh. 871-9103. Charming, colorful Mexican folk art and clothing.
30 ▪ Sample House and Candle Shop. 2811 Routh. 871-1501. Every nook and cranny of this

SNIDER PLAZA

This upgraded neighborhood center still has the feel of a small town Main Street from the 1920s. Many locally owned shops serve Park Cities residents, as well as students from nearby Southern Methodist University.

Shopping: ✔✔

Dining: ✔

Entertainment: *theater only*

Ambiance ✔✔

The Plaza includes about eighty small shops and is located one block west of Hillcrest Avenue, between Lovers Lane and Rosedale Avenue. Ample surface parking is available, and it's easy to walk the entire center. Except for a restaurant or two and the Plaza Theatre, everything is closed by 6 pm.

SHOPPING: ART, ANTIQUES, AND CRAFTS

3 ▪ David L. Gibson Rare Prints and Maps. 6606 Snider Plaza. 739-2391. Large and varied selection of fine contemporary and classic prints.
4 ▪ Clifford Gallery. 6610 Snider Plaza. 363-8223. Represents fifteen established but lesser-known artists from throughout the Southwest. Many works in the $100-to-$1,000 range.
6 ▪ Two Moons Trading Co. 3411 Rosedale.

373-8822. Cowboy and Indian art and artifacts. Western saddles, belts, buckles, and jewelry.
11 ▪ Eldred Wheeler. 6906 Snider Plaza. 369-1276. Just one of a half-dozen Plaza shops offering country-cottage gifts, antiques, accessories, and quilts. Among the others are **The Rosedale House** (3409 Rosedale), **The Sampler** (6817 Snider Plaza), **Notable Accents** (6701 Snider Plaza), and **The Muse** (6727 Snider Plaza).
13 ▪ Goblets, Etc. Antiques. 6920 Snider Plaza. 368-0313. Emphasis on English bric-a-brac.
22 ▪ The Veranda. 6715 Snider Plaza. 739-0021. Asian art and antiques directly imported by the owner.

SHOPPING: CLOTHING

1 ▪ Cotton Island. 6601 Hillcrest, Suite D. 373-1085. Relaxed and trendy cotton and denim

clothing, including Bis and other imports.
5 ▪ Susan Brannian. 6634 Snider Plaza. 739-2602. Careful selection of women's clothing, some with a Western flair; handsome costume and silver jewelry, both antique and new, mostly with a Santa Fe or ethnic look; Mexican folk art.
8 ▪ Mary Ellen's. 6730 Snider Plaza. 750-8121. Tempting display of women's clothing, colorful accessories, and costume jewelry.
9 ▪ Silhouettes. 3415 Milton. 363-8727. Distinctive pre-teen and children's wear.
12 ▪ Momma Please. 6910 Snider Plaza. 692-9432. Designer clothing for infants and for girls to age six. Antique christening gowns, enchanting English Emily Jane coats, and French Babybotte children's shoes are specialties.
17 ▪ Haltom's. 6833 Snider Plaza. 692-6338. Women's clothing for the traditional but fashionable look. **Top Secret** (6722 Snider Plaza) and **Sabrina's Clothiers** (6829 Snider Plaza) offer other selections in the same vein.

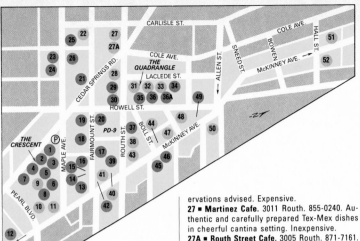

much expanded old house is filled with interesting household accessories, candles, baskets, gift wraps, etc.
49 ■ AIA/Dallas Bookstore. 2811 McKinney Ave. 871-9511. Large selection of books on architecture and design.

DINING

9 ■ La Cucina Italiana. The Crescent. 871-5155. Classic Italian food in modern, elegant setting. Moderate.
10 ■ Beau Nash Restaurant and Bar. 400 Crescent Court (Hotel Crescent Court). 871-3240. Creative American Nouvelle menu, trendy patrons, and handsome setting, open for breakfast. Expensive. The bar is an after-work favorite.
11 ■ Sam's Cafe. 100 Crescent Court (The Crescent). 855-2233. Southwestern Nouvelle menu, see-and-be-seen bar, delicious desserts.
22 ■ Lawry's, The Prime Rib. 3008 Maple. 521-7777. Dressy mecca for prime rib lovers (the only main dish for dinner), baronial setting. Res-

ervations advised. Expensive.
27 ■ Martinez Cafe. 3011 Routh. 855-0240. Authentic and carefully prepared Tex-Mex dishes in cheerful cantina setting. Inexpensive.
27A ■ Routh Street Cafe. 3005 Routh. 871-7161. Dressy and widely acclaimed temple of "Southwestern Nouvelle" cuisine, soft-tech setting, dinner only. Reservations required. Very expensive. (See Special Occasion Dining)
28 ■ Ruggeri's. 2911 Routh. 871-7377. Well-prepared Italian classics in attractive surroundings. Reservations advised. Moderate to expensive.
31 ■ Actuelle. 2800 Routh (The Quadrangle). 855-0440. Dressy crowd and inventive French/ Southwestern menu, elegant patio for good weather. Reservations advised. Expensive. (See Special Occasion Dining)
32 ■ Dream Cafe. 2800 Routh (The Quadrangle). 954-0486. Casual. Inventive natural foods and omelettes, cheerful setting, no alcohol. Open for breakfast. Inexpensive to moderate.
33 ■ J. Pepes. 2800 Routh (The Quadrangle). 871-0366. Popular Tex-Mex cafe with many outdoor tables. Inexpensive to moderate.
38 ■ Baby Routh. 2708 Routh. 871-2345. Less-expensive offspring of nearby Routh Street Cafe (see above), with Southwestern Nouvelle menu available till 1 am. Moderate to expensive.
40 ■ Petuluma. 2515 McKinney. 871-2253. Popular bakery-deli open for breakfast and lunch, weekdays only. Inexpensive.

41 ■ San Simeon. 2515 McKinney. 871-7373. Dressy and elegant American Nouvelle dining. Reservations advised. Expensive to very expensive. (See Special Occasion Dining)
43 ■ Hard Rock Cafe. 2601 McKinney. 827-8282. Burgers and munchies while admiring rock-and-roll memorabilia and T-shirt purchasers.
44 ■ S&D Oyster Company. 2701 McKinney. 823-6350. Casual. Popular and crowded New Orleans-style seafood cafe. Inexpensive to moderate.
47 ■ Josef's. 2719 McKinney. 826-5560. Fresh seafood in one of the street's few surviving houses. Moderate to expensive.
48 ■ Le Boul' Mich. 2704 Worthington. 826-0660. French country fare in a small Victorian house. Moderate to expensive.
50 ■ Dixie House. 2822 McKinney. 824-0891. Casual. Local chain providing dependable and hearty Southern homecooking. Inexpensive.
51 ■ Primo's. 3309 McKinney. 520-3303. Casual. Storefront cafe-bar with hearty Mexican fare, open till 2 am. Inexpensive.
52 ■ La Trattoria Lombardi. 2916 N. Hall. 528-7506. Classic, freshly prepared Italian food in bistro setting. Moderate to expensive.

ENTERTAINMENT

12 ■ Jazba. 1901 McKinney. 871-2900. Popular jazz club in basement of seafood restaurant, open Thurs-Sat only.
23 ■ The Lion's Den. 2927 Maple (Stoneleigh Terrace Hotel). 871-7111. Intimate hotel bar for quiet conversation.
26 ■ Stoneleigh P. 2926 Maple. 871-2346. Casual. Favorite neighborhood pub with limited menu.
34 ■ Theatre Three. 2800 Routh (The Quadrangle). 871-3300. Jac Alder and Norma Young have presided over this 240-seat theater-in-the-round for over twenty-five years. They offer an eclectic variety of well-produced plays, including occasional performances for children.
42 ■ San Simeon - The Club. 2525 McKinney. 871-7373. Posh club for late evening dancing. Thurs-Sat only. Cover charge.

SHOPPING: OTHER

7 ■ The Perfect Setting. 6726 Snider Plaza. 373-6302. High-quality gifts, Saint Louis crystal, place settings and charming hand-painted figurines from Herand, a Hungarian porcelain firm.
10 ■ M.E. Moses. 6828 Snider Plaza. 363-2361. One-third of a block filled with classic dime-store merchandise, including an entire half-aisle of nothing but hard-to-find cloth ribbons (while you're at it, the **Craft Studio** at 6627 Snider Plaza has over one thousand varieties of the same).
14 ■ Adele Hunt. 7015 Snider Plaza. 363-2528. High-quality new furniture in traditional styles, including Kindel's fine reproductions of pieces in the collections of Winterthur and the National Trust for Historic Preservation.
16 ■ Needlework Patio. 6925 Snider Plaza. 363-0351. A multitude of yarns, painted canvases, needlework kits, and pattern books.
18 ■ Pierce Hardware. 6823 Snider Plaza. 368-2851. Large selection of decorative hardware. Everything from simple drawer pulls to opulent brass fittings.
21 ■ Rootabaga Bookery. 6717 Snider Plaza. 361-8581. A superb children's bookstore arranged by level and subject in an appealing, colorful setting. Also records, tapes, and some toys.
23 ■ For Heaven's Sake. 6705 Snider Plaza. 696-8899. Crafty jewelry and gifts.

24 ■ V. Y. Rejebian & Son. 6619 Snider Plaza. 363-3110. Oriental rugs from a long-established Dallas dealer.

DINING

2 ■ Peggy's Beef Bar. 6600 Snider Plaza. 692-5999. Casual. Old-fashioned barbecue and renowned fried onion rings. Inexpensive.
15 ■ Amore. 6931 Snider Plaza. 739-0502. Classic Italian fare. Inexpensive.
19 ■ Steve's Ice Cream. 6731 Snider Plaza. 361-5051. Casual. Famed for its mixed-on-the-spot flavors.
25 ■ Le Brussels. 6615 Snider Plaza. 739-1927. Authentic French-Belgian cuisine in cheerful setting. Expensive.

26 ■ Kuby's Sausage House. 6601 Snider Plaza. 363-2231. Casual. Popular German grocery store-cafe, with hearty sandwiches and wurst plates, lunch only, no alcohol. Inexpensive.
27 ■ Bubba's Cooks Country. 6617 Hillcrest. 373-6527. Casual. The name says it all, open for breakfast, no alcohol. Inexpensive.

ENTERTAINMENT

20 ■ Plaza Theatre. 6719 Snider Plaza. 363-7000. Former neighborhood movie house converted for plays and variety acts.

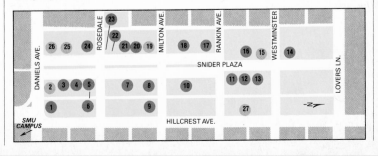

STOCKYARDS

The older commercial buildings along Exchange Avenue adjacent to the Stockyards were "rusticated" in the 1950s to imitate the Old West. Today these house mostly souvenir shops and saloons, along with some fine stores with truly authentic Western wear. At night it's a fun place to join the lively crown that strolls from saloon to saloon listening and dancing to Country-and-Western music. Dress is mostly casual, with an emphasis on carefully pressed jeans and cowboy boots.

Shopping: *Western wear*

Dining: ✔✔

Entertainment: ✔✔✔

Ambiance: ✔✔✔

The area's fifty saloons, cafes, and small shops are located two miles north of downtown near the intersection of North Main Street and Exchange Avenue. Parking is mostly on-street or in large parking lots near the intersection of North Main and Stockyards Boulevard.

SHOPPING

2 ▪ Mule Alley Emporium. 131 E. Exchange (Livestock Exchange Building). (817) 625-4021. Several rooms filled with framed reproductions of Western art and some hand-crafted jewelry.
5 ▪ Ryon's Saddle and Ranch Supply. 2601 N. Main. (817) 625-2391. This long-time Fort Worth establishment has an entire room full of saddles and lots of Western apparel as well.
8 ▪ Stockyards Souvenirs and Western Gifts. 104 E. Exchange. (817) 624-1626. Stock includes books on Fort Worth and the West.
9 ▪ Fincher's Western Stores. 115 E. Exchange. (817) 624-7302. Large store with Western wear, souvenir items, and large selection of children's boots and apparel.
12 ▪ The Willow Branch. 2402-B N. Main. (817) 625-7473. A small store with wall hangings, rugs, and gifts with a Santa Fe accent.
15 ▪ M. L. Leddy's Boot and Saddlery. 2455 N. Main. (817) 624-3149. This store has been outfitting area stockmen and cowboys since 1922. Handmade custom and off-the-shelf boots; full range of Western clothing plus such specialized items as chaps, saddles, spurs, and bridles.

DINING

1 ▪ Old Spaghetti Warehouse. 600 E. Exchange. (817) 625-4171. Hearty Italian food in the historic Swift and Company headquarters building. Inexpensive.
4 ▪ Brown Derby. 2525 Rodeo Plaza. (817) 624-6834. Popular for steaks and its well-stocked bar. Inexpensive to moderate.
10 ▪ Booger Red's Restaurant and Saloon. 109 E. Exchange (Stockyards Hotel). (817) 625-6427. Old West decor and a menu with such Texas favorites as barbecue and chicken-fried steak. Inexpensive to moderate.
11 ▪ Cattlemen's Steak House. 2458 N. Main. (817) 624-3945. This funky restaurant has served the best steaks in Fort Worth since 1947. Moderate to expensive. (See Special Occasion Dining)

ENTERTAINMENT

3 ▪ Billy Bob's Texas. 2520 Rodeo Plaza. (817) 625-9897. This long-time favorite, the largest saloon in Texas, is closed and looking for a new life as this book goes to press. It may have found it by the time you read this.
6 ▪ Upstairs at the White Elephant. 106 E. Exchange. (817) 624-9712. Fort Worth's popular Hip Pocket Theatre performs plays in this intimate space during the winter months.
7 ▪ White Elephant Saloon. 106 E. Exchange. (817) 624-1887. Live Country music seven nights a week. Fun outdoor space for good weather. Cover charge.
13 ▪ Fort Worth City Limits. 2409 N. Main. (817) 626-4242. Dancing to rock music with the younger set. Cover charge.
14 ▪ P.R.'s. 2411 N. Main. (817) 624-1477. Club with youthful patrons and contemporary music for dancing. Cover charge.
16 ▪ Filthy McNasty's. 114 W. Exchange. (817) 624-1401. Popular despite its name, this saloon has a small dance floor, pool tables, and video games.
17 ▪ The Cadillac. 124 W. Exchange. (817) 625-6622. Dancing to recorded Country or rock music in Western setting.
18 ▪ Big River Cattle Company Cafe and Saloon. 2413 Ellis. (817) 626-2666. Rustic club with food, dancing, and billiards.
19 ▪ Rodeo Exchange. 221 W. Exchange. (817) 626-0181. Large dance floor with Country-and-Western bands. Cover charge.

CULTURAL DISTRICT

Several art galleries and fine restaurants are located in this small district of old storefronts and converted houses near the Kimbell Museum. Many of these are quite inconspicuous and understated on the outside, depending on their strong local reputations, rather than flashy quarters, to attract customers.

Shopping: *art*

Dining: ✔✔✔

Entertainment: ✔✔

Ambiance: ✔✔

This district includes only about two dozen shops and restaurants. Plenty of parking is available both on-street and in small parking lots.

SHOPPING: ART, ANTIQUES, CRAFTS

6 ▪ Eclections. 3408-B Camp Bowie. (817) 332-4407. Handsome hand weaving, jewelry, and ceramics from regional craftsmen. Moderate prices.
8 ▪ Scott and Stuart Gentling. 902 Boland. (817) 332-7059. These talented Fort Worth twins paint extraordinary watercolors in the realistic tradition of the Wyeths and Audubon. Birds, nature, and the Southwest are frequent subjects. There is no sign and you might call before visiting to be sure someone is in.
9 ▪ Fort Worth Gallery. 901 Boland. (817) 332-5603. Knowledgeable proprietor represents top local artists and sponsors high-quality shows featuring works of differing styles and periods.
11 ▪ Norma Baker Antiques. 3311 W. 7th. (817) 335-1152. Emphasis on glass, porcelain, silver, and Victoriana.
15 ▪ Evelyn Siegel Gallery. 3612 W. 7th. (817) 731-6412. Twentieth-century and American Indian art. Moderate prices.

DINING

4 ▪ The Buffet at the Kimbell. 3333 Camp Bowie (Kimbell Art Museum). (817) 332-8451. On nice days one can sit in the small adjacent sculpture garden. Lunch only, snacks until 4 pm. Inexpensive.
5 ▪ Sardines. 3410 Camp Bowie. (817) 332-9937. Italian fare in bistro-like converted house. Live jazz nightly. Inexpensive to moderate.
7 ▪ Back Porch. 3400-B Camp Bowie. (817) 332-1422. Casual. Homemade soups and ice cream, salad bar, and sandwiches. Inexpensive.
12 ▪ Weldon's Tea Room. 3405 W. 7th. (817) 336-1100. A popular and delightfully old-fashioned tea room. Lunch only. Inexpensive.
13 ▪ Tours. 3429-B W. 7th. (817) 870-1672. Small and understated French restaurant receiving high marks for quality menu. Moderate to expensive.
14 ▪ La Maree. 3416 W. 7th. (817) 877-0838. Tiny French market, with gourmet takeout, French

SUNDANCE SQUARE

Several blocks of early retail buildings in the heart of downtown have been renovated and restored to re-create the spirit of turn-of-the-century Fort Worth. This is a delightful area for browsing, eating, or taking an evening surrey ride.

Shopping: ✔✔

Dining: ✔✔

Entertainment: *Caravan of Dreams*

Ambiance: ✔✔✔

Centered on Main and Houston streets at the north end of downtown, this area has about two dozen street-oriented shops and restaurants plus a similar number within nearby Tandy Center. There is plenty of parking, both on-street and in nearby surface lots.

SHOPPING

1 ▪ Luskey's Western Stores. 101 N. Houston. (817) 335-5833. A family-run local chain that specializes in authentic Western apparel.

4 ▪ Tandy Center. 200 Throckmorton. (817) 390-3720. This modern, mixed-use complex includes an ice skating rink surrounded by about two dozen small shops and restaurants. Not surprisingly, there are two large *Radio Shack* stores, since the Center was built by that chain's parent, the Fort Worth based Tandy Corporation. *Dillard's*, on the south end, is the center's anchor department store.

5 ▪ Stanley Eisenman's Fine Shoes. 406 Houston. (817) 332-1950; 654-1950 (metro). A small shop with lots of fashionable shoes.

8 ▪ Pier 1 Imports. 410 Houston. (817) 332-7762. Affordable dishes, home furnishings, and decorative objects from around the world.

10 ▪ Fort Worth Books and Video. 400 Main. (817) 877-1573. Browse two levels of titles until 9 pm each night except Sun.

12 ▪ McCluer's Luggage and Gifts. 310 Main. (817) 332-4981. Fine leather goods and small gifts pleasingly displayed.

13 ▪ Metro Cards and Gifts. 302 Main. (817) 877-5550. Hi-tech setting with offbeat cards and novelty gifts.

16 ▪ Victoria's Women's Accessories. 101 W. 2nd. (817) 877-3741. After perusing the accessories, climb the corner stair to the Attic Gallery which features works by young Fort Worth artists, many in the $100-to-$500 range.

DINING

2 ▪ The Bridge at the Worthington Hotel. 200 Main. (817) 870-1000. This light and airy space, with a view down Houston Street, has pasta and salads at lunch, tea in the afternoon, and a bar at night. Calm place to watch the evening crowd.

3 ▪ Reflections. 200 Main (Worthington Hotel). (817) 870-9894. Flawless American Nouvelle cuisine and decor. Reservations advised. Expensive. (See Special Occasion Dining)

6 ▪ Houston Street Bakery. 300 Houston. (817) 870-2895. Casual. Has a few tables for sampling the tasty baked goods.

11 ▪ Main Street Grill and Creamery. 316 Main. (817) 870-9165. Casual. Salads, sandwiches, and charbroiled entrees in cheerful setting. Lunch daily, dinner Fri and Sat only. Inexpensive.

14 ▪ Winfield's 08. 301 Main. 870-1908. Eclectic menu, comfortable surroundings. Inexpensive to moderate.

15 ▪ Tutti Pazzi. 300 Main. (817) 737-2781. Classic Italian fare. Inexpensive to moderate.

17 ▪ Juanita's. 115 W. 2nd. (817) 335-1777. Casual. Tex-Mex dishes in cantina-like setting. Inexpensive to moderate.

ENTERTAINMENT

7 ▪ Caravan of Dreams. 312 Houston. (817) 877-3000. First-floor nightclub books top jazz and blues performers. A theater and outdoor roof garden are upstairs.

9 ▪ Billy Miner's Saloon. 150 W. 3rd. (817) 877-3301. Casual. Pub with burgers, chili, and grilled items in rustic surroundings. Inexpensive.

---

cakes, and a few tables for lunch and snacks. Inexpensive.

16 ▪ Saint-Emilion. 3617 W. 7th. (817) 737-2781. Dressy. Upscale cuisine in country inn setting with fixed-price menu. Reservations advised. Moderate to expensive. (See Special Occasion Dining)

17 ▪ Bessie's on the Boulevard. 3716 Camp Bowie. (817) 735-1580. A local favorite for Cajun homecooking. Frequent live entertainment. Moderate.

ENTERTAINMENT

1 ▪ Johnnie High's Country Music Revue. 3301 W. Lancaster (Will Rogers Auditorium). (817) 481-4518. One of the longest running Country-and-Western shows in the country. Performances every Saturday night at 7 pm.

2 ▪ Fort Worth Theatre. 3505 W. Lancaster (Modern Art Museum). (817) 738-6509. Formerly the Fort Worth Community Theatre, volunteer actors perform theatrical classics.

3 ▪ Casa Manana. 3101 W. Lancaster. (817) 332-6221. Summer musicals in this theater-in-the-round are a Fort Worth tradition. Children's plays are presented during the non-summer months by the Casa Playhouse. (817) 332-9319.

10 ▪ J & J's Hideaway. 3305 W. 7th. (817) 877-3363. Old-fashioned neighborhood bar.

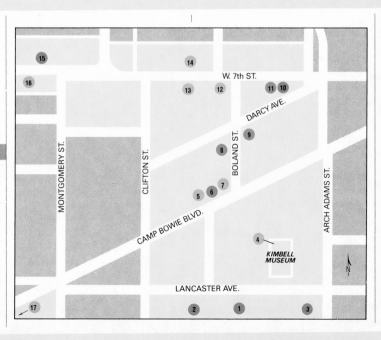

CAMP BOWIE BOULEVARD

Shopping: ✔✔✔

Dining: ✔✔

Entertainment: ✔

Ambiance: ✔

Camp Bowie Boulevard, once the heart of a World War I army training center, has developed into Fort Worth's principal shopping street in the decades since the 1920s. Modern renovation of the older buildings and a number of new retail centers continue the area's long tradition as the city's foremost concentration of shops and restaurants.

About two miles southwest of the Cultural District are well over a hundred shops and restaurants scattered along Camp Bowie Boulevard and the side streets that angle into it. Originally a roadside strip development, this area of older storefronts and newer buildings has ample adjacent parking.

SHOPPING: ART, ANTIQUES, AND CRAFTS

5 ▪ William Campbell Contemporary Art and Gallery One Frames. 4935 Byers. (817) 737-9571. Fine contemporary art, mostly by Texas artists; excellent custom framing.

7 ▪ Collections. 5001 El Campo. (817) 737-8991. A beautifully arranged shop with antiques, old linens, and interesting decorative objects.

SHOPPING: CLOTHING

2 ▪ Gingersnaps. 4806 Camp Bowie. (817) 732-7709. Roomy displays of boys' and girls' clothing and accessories for infants to size 14, fine christening gowns.

6 ▪ Bunny Hutch. 5001 El Campo Ave. (817) 738-7891. A wonderful selection of women's sleepwear, ranging from demure white cottons to seductive black laces and from comfy terry cloth robes to sophisticated loungewear.

9 ▪ Pitterpat. 5110 Camp Bowie. (817) 763-9611. Children's clothing.

14 ▪ Henry's. 5800-G Camp Bowie. (817) 731-2951. Comfortable, casual clothes for men and women, including the Izod and Polo labels.

15 ▪ Seville Shop. 5836 Camp Bowie. (817) 731-6331. Fashionable women's dresses and separates.

22 ▪ The Wardrobe. 6330 Camp Bowie. (817) 732-5411. Women's clothing with a flair, including the Jeanne Marc label.

24 ▪ Cambridge Clothier. 6333 Camp Bowie. (817) 738-7692. Large, traditional men's clothing store.

26 ▪ Clothes Horse. 6333 Camp Bowie. (817) 732-6677. Roomy quarters house an excellent selection of women's wear, including Anne Klein, Carolina Herrera, and Diane Fres; handsome costume jewelry.

27 ▪ Stanley Eisenman's Fine Shoes. 6333 Camp Bowie. (817) 731-2555. Women's shoes with a fashionable flair.

SHOPPING: OTHER

1 ▪ Designs for Children. 4800 Camp Bowie. (817) 732-6711. Carefully chosen toys, including particularly winsome dolls.

3 ▪ Plate and Platter. 4808 Camp Bowie. (817) 732-2577. Spacious shop filled with everyday china, glass, and cookware.

4 ▪ Holding Company. 4828 Camp Bowie. (817) 738-0978. Containers for just about everything.

10 ▪ The Letter. 5124 Camp Bowie. (817) 731-2032. Handsome gifts including Herand, Ceralene, and Cartier china, as well as cards and stationery.

17 ▪ Chad's Rainbow. 6100 Camp Bowie. (817) 737-8697. Toys that teach, including many fascinating science kits.

20 ▪ Haltom's Jewelry. 6102 Camp Bowie. (817) 738-6511. A Fort Worth institution since 1896.

21 ▪ Mary Haltom's. 6326 Camp Bowie. (817) 763-0677. Run by a fourth-generation member of the distinguished family of Fort Worth jewelers, this shop features handsome and wearable pieces, including necklaces of tigers eye, lapis, etc.

23 ▪ Taylor's Books. 6346 Camp Bowie. (817) 763-0011. Local chain with unusually large stock of new books.

25 ▪ The Legacy. 6333 Camp Bowie. (817) 735-4698. Sizeable selection of silver, fine china, crystal, and gifts.

28 ▪ The Strawberry Patch. 6333 Camp Bowie. (817) 731-4227. A Fort Worth favorite for needlepoint yarns and canvases.

DINING

8 ▪ Heights Corner Cafe. 5036-B Pershing Ave. (817) 731-9910. Casual. Sandwiches and daily specials, lunch and early dinner. Inexpensive.

11 ▪ The Carriage House. 5136 Camp Bowie. (817) 732-2873. A local favorite for steak and seafood. The setting and service are quietly elegant but, like Fort Worth itself, not oppressively formal. Reservations advised. Moderate to expensive.

12 ▪ Szechuan Chinese Restaurant. 5712 Locke. (817) 738-7300. Popular neighborhood favorite. Inexpensive to moderate.

13 ▪ Tejano Cafe. 5716 Camp Bowie. (817) 737-7201. Casual. Standard Tex-Mex menu. Inexpensive.

18 ▪ Mike's Ice Cream. 6100 Camp Bowie. (817) 731-9838. Casual. Delicious, custom-mixed ice cream flavors.

19 ▪ The Balcony of Ridglea. 6100 Camp Bowie, 2nd floor. (817) 731-3719. Classic upscale menu served in intimate setting, dinner only. Reservations advised. Moderate.

29 ▪ Hedary's Lebanese Restaurant. 3308 Fairfield. (817) 731-6961. Popular Mecca for tasty Middle Eastern food. Inexpensive.

ENTERTAINMENT

16 ▪ Ridglea Theatre. 6025 Camp Bowie. (817) 738-7101. Old neighborhood theater newly renovated to multi-screen format with first-run features.

30 ▪ West Side Stories. 3900 Highway 377 S. (several blocks south of Camp Bowie). (817) 560-SODA. Two-level space with comedy club, pool tables, pizza, live music, and dancing for the younger set. Cover charge.

INDEX

ACKNOWLEDGMENTS

All photographs were specially commissioned for the book and taken by Joe Mullan, Mullan Photography Co., except those listed below which were provided through the courtesy of the individuals and institutions noted:

Anatole Hotel, 30 (top); Jeannette Brantley, 73 (top); R. O. Bumpass, cover, 5; Burson & Cox Architects, 8; Cadillac Fairview, 14 (bottom right); *The Cattleman* Magazine, 51 (bottom two); Dallas Museum of Art, 21—(top) gift of Mrs. Eugene McDermott, The Roberta Coke Camp Fund, and The Art Museum League Fund, (middle) anonymous gift, (bottom left) commissioned to honor John Dabney Murchison, Sr. for his arts and civic leadership, and presented by his Family, (bottom right) The Faith P. and Charles L. Bybee Collection of American Furniture; Dallas Museum of Natural History and Aquarium, 29 (right top and bottom); Dallas Public Library, Texas/Dallas History and Archives Division, 6, 10 (bottom), 30 (bottom); DeGolyer Library, Southern Methodist University, 51 (second from top); General Dynamics, 41; Infomart, 31; Kimbell Art Museum, 56 (all); Las Colinas, 38 (top); M. L. Leddy's Boot & Saddlery, 65 (bottom); North Fort Worth Historical Society, 51 (top); Science Place, 29 (center); Six Flags Over Texas, 38 (bottom); Southern Methodist University, 34; Southwestern Exposition, 74 (middle), 75 (top); Ben Stewart, 26 (bottom), 27, 72; Texas Department of Commerce, Tourism Division, 16, 18, 32 (bottom), 37, 40, 45 (bottom), 47, 48 (bottom), 50, 57 (bottom), 70 (top), 71, 73 (middle), 74 (bottom), 75 (bottom), 76 (bottom); Texas Department of Highways, 55, 70 (bottom); Theatre Three, 73 (bottom); Downing Thomas, 29 (left top); Doug Tomlinson, title page, 10 (top), 12, 13, 14 (top), 15 (top two and bottom right), 17, 19, 22, 26 (top), 28 (top, bottom), 36 (top), 39, 43, 48 (top); Trammell Crow Co., 14 (bottom left), 20.

The editors express their thanks to the following people and organizations for their help in the preparation of this book:

Charlotte St. Martin and the Dallas Convention and Visitors Bureau for acting as an invaluable resource for the project; Edward Fjordbak of the Communities Foundation of Texas; Jerry Allen; Teddy Diggs; Ron Emrich; Jane Garrett; the Greenmans: Elise, Judie, Judie, and Suzi; Paula Peters; Deborah Phelan; John Scovell; Texas and Southwestern Cattle Raisers Foundation (Carol Williams); Tourism Division, Texas Department of Commerce (Larry Todd, Mari Schnell); Liz Wally; Michael Young and Partners for generously allowing the use of their isometric drawings of many downtown Dallas buildings.

Administrative Assistant: Millyanne Tumlinson
Designer: Lisa Govan
Cover Design: Janet Odgis & Co.
Printer & Binder: Kingsport Press

Library of Congress Cataloging-in-Publication Data
McAlester, Virginia, 1943– • Discover Dallas-Fort Worth.
Bibliography: p. • Includes index • 1. Dallas Region (Tex.)—Description and travel—Guide books. 2. Fort Worth Region (Tex.)—Description and travel—Guide-books. I. McAlester, A. Lee (Arcie Lee), 1933– II. Title.
F394.D23M37 1988 917.64'28120463 87-46192 • ISBN 0-394-75705

The sixteen SiDE Areas were chosen for interest to visitors and to reflect a range of what is available in each city. Space limitations made it impossible to include every shopping or entertainment center and the fact that any one is not included does not necessarily imply that it is inferior to those discussed. The individual listings within each SiDE Area are intended to be a *sampling* of its restaurants, shops, and entertainment. In many instances, establishments of equal quality have been omitted because of space constraints.

FORT WORTH SIGHTSEEING DISTRICTS AND SiDE AREAS

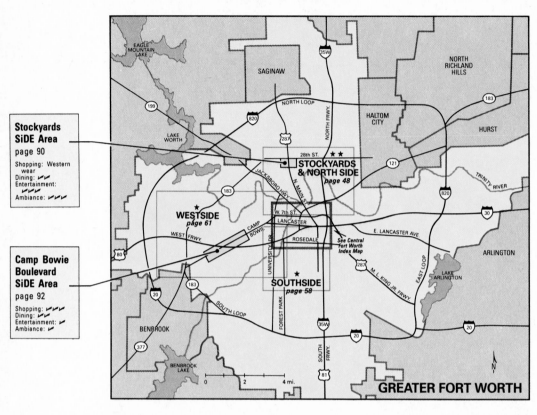

Stockyards SiDE Area
page 90
Shopping: Western wear
Dining: ✔✔
Entertainment: ✔✔✔
Ambiance: ✔✔✔

Camp Bowie Boulevard SiDE Area
page 92
Shopping: ✔✔✔
Dining: ✔✔
Entertainment: ✔
Ambiance: ✔

EAGLE MOUNTAIN LAKE

SAGINAW

NORTH RICHLAND HILLS

199

820

287

NORTH LOOP

NORTH FRWY.

HALTOM CITY

183

HURST

LAKE WORTH

28th ST. ★★
STOCKYARDS & NORTH SIDE
page 48

121

TRINITY RIVER

JACKSBORO HWY.

183

★ **WESTSIDE**
page 61

W. 7th ST.
LANCASTER
ROSEDALE

N. MAIN ST.

E. LANCASTER AVE.

820

30

WEST FRWY.

CAMP BOWIE

UNIVERSITY DR.

See Central Fort Worth Index Map

ARLINGTON

80

183

287

M. L. KING JR. FRWY.

EAST LOOP

LAKE ARLINGTON

20

★ **SOUTHSIDE**
page 58

FOREST PARK

35W

20

BENBROOK

SOUTH LOOP

SOUTH FRWY.

20

377

BENBROOK LAKE

0   2   4 mi.

81

N

GREATER FORT WORTH

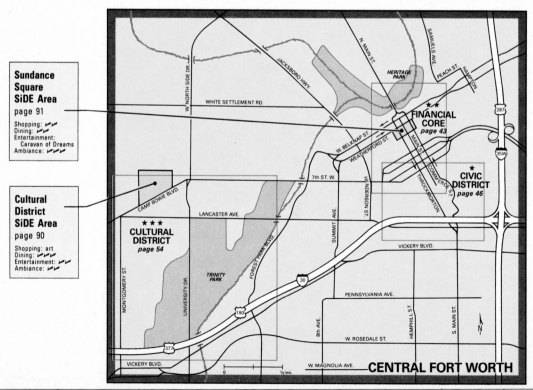

Sundance Square SiDE Area
page 91
Shopping: ✔✔
Dining: ✔✔
Entertainment: Caravan of Dreams
Ambiance: ✔✔✔

Cultural District SiDE Area
page 90
Shopping: art
Dining: ✔✔✔
Entertainment: ✔✔
Ambiance: ✔✔

W. NORTH SIDE DR.

WHITE SETTLEMENT RD.

JACKSBORO HWY.

N. MAIN ST.

HERITAGE PARK

SAMUELS AVE.

PEACH ST.

HAMPTON

287

★★ **FINANCIAL CORE**
page 43

W. BELKNAP ST.

WEATHERFORD ST.

HENDERSON ST.

MAIN ST.

COMMERCE ST.

THROCKMORTON

35W

7TH ST. W.

★ **CIVIC DISTRICT**
page 46

CAMP BOWIE BLVD.

LANCASTER AVE.

SUMMIT AVE.

VICKERY BLVD.

★★★ **CULTURAL DISTRICT**
page 54

FOREST PARK BLVD.

TRINITY PARK

MONTGOMERY ST.

UNIVERSITY DR.

30

PENNSYLVANIA AVE.

8TH AVE.

HEMPHILL ST.

S. MAIN ST.

180

W. ROSEDALE ST.

377

VICKERY BLVD.

W. MAGNOLIA AVE.

0   ½ mi.

N

CENTRAL FORT WORTH